Rowan's Greatest Knits

Rowan's Greatest Knits

Edited by Kate Buller

The Taunton Press

The Taunton Press
Inspiration for hands-on living®

The Taunton Press, Inc.,
63 South Main Street, PO Box 5506,
Newtown, CT 06470-5506
email: tp@taunton.com

First published in Great Britain in 2009 by
Rowan Yarns, Green Lane Mill,
Holmfirth, West Yorkshire HD9 2DX

Text Editor Sally Harding
Technical Editor Sue Whiting
Designer Nicky Downes
Pattern checker Lisa Richardson

Library of Congress Cataloguing-in-
Publication Data

Rowan's greatest knits.
      p. cm.
   ISBN 978-1-60085-250-3
   1. Knitting--Patterns. 2. Rowan Yarns.
   TT820.R748 2009
   746.43'2--dc22
                              2009016364

Reproduced and printed in Singapore

**Page 1: Electra by Louisa Harding
(Magazine 38)**
The pattern with an updated colorway for this
design is given on pages 117–119.

**Page 2: Long Leaf Coat by Kaffe Fassett
(Magazine 12)**
The front of this elegant coat is shown on
page 16.

**Right: Raphael by Marie Wallin
(Magazine 44)**
An embroidered knit in Kid Classic.

**Opposite page: Florentine by Sarah Dallas
(Magazine 36)**
This colorwork sweater worked in Rowan
4-Ply Soft and Lurex Shimmer. See page 38
for the cardigan version of the design.

Contents

Introduction

Over the last 30 years, the Rowan brand has become synonymous with innovative design and high-quality yarns. During this time it has attracted some of the best names in fashion knitting to its magazine, from which all the images of the designs in this retrospective book are drawn.

The pattern pages of the book offer 30 great patterns from Rowan's archive, profiling a cross-section of the designers who helped to build its reputation—including Kaffe Fassett, Kim Hargreaves, Erika Knight, Annabel Fox, Sarah Dallas, Louisa Harding, Marion Foale, Sharon Miller, Brandon Mably, Jean Moss, Sasha Kagan, Martin Storey, Marie Wallin, and Sarah Hatton. We have tried to include a wide selection of garment styles: cardigans, jackets, sweaters, coats, capes, boleros, scarves, and shawls. And a great range of yarns and yarn weights. In addition to the 30 patterns in the book, there are more than 20 other stunning archive designs featured in the Rowan history section (see pages 8–51).

One of the early magazines, issue 10, featured the then very young Kate Moss in a truly brilliant "Swallows and Amazons" themed shoot, echoing the famous children's series of that name by Arthur Ransome (see pages 22 and 23). Issue 10, unsurprisingly, is now a collector's item and two designs from this issue, Jester and Fisherman, are included in the pattern section (see pages 62–67).

Since many of the patterns in this book are now nearly 30 years old, a lot of the original yarns and colors used for them have long gone. They have been replaced with new ones from the current Rowan range—and, as anyone who knits knows, choosing replacement yarns and colors is an art in itself. Some yarns in the current range knit to the gauge of the old ones, but have a different "loft" or feel to them. And while some of the new ranges have an unrivaled number of colors, they are not necessarily in the same tonal range as some of the older ones.

Where substitute yarns have been selected to replace the originals, Sue Whiting, the technical editor, has reswatched them, made minor alterations to the instructions where necessary, and written helpful notes for the knitter. Where yarns and colors have been replaced, the new swatch is shown at the beginning of the pattern instructions, alongside the original image. In some places, a yarn is used double to achieve the right gauge. In others, the needle sizes have changed slightly to achieve the required gauge. If you want to attempt substitutions of your own, a guide for this is given on pages 54 and 55.

We hope that as our yarns develop, we meet the needs of the increasingly wide range of knitters, across the generations, who look to Rowan for a lead. That being said, some of our long-standing yarns are still some of our most popular today. The Rowan Kidsilk yarns seem to be enduringly popular, in part perhaps because the yarn structure takes the dye beautifully and has a really lustrous depth of color to it.

I hope you enjoy revisiting the archive and knitting some of the designs as much as we enjoyed both creating the designs and bringing them back to life.

Kate Buller
Senior Brand Manager, Rowan Yarns

Left: The Mill at Holmfirth, the home of Rowan in the Yorkshire Dales for the last 30 years.

The Rowan Story

Above: Rowan founders Stephen Sheard (center), a weaver by training, and Simon Cockin (left) began their business selling weaving kits. Their interest in yarn led them on to establishing a knitting business and founding the Rowan yarn company.

Left: The young Kaffe Fassett in the 1970s—one of the first designers to be spotted by Rowan, whose career had been launched through his designs for fashion designer Bill Gibb and Italian house, Missoni, famed for their exquisite textiles and wonderful color harmonies.

Thirty years have elapsed since the Rowan label was born, but its aims and values have remained the same over three decades. That may, in part, be because its roots lie in the exquisite Yorkshire Dales, the center in England for the woolen and weaving industry for over a hundred years.

Rowan was founded by Stephen Sheard, a Yorkshireman who had studied woven textiles, and his former school friend, Simon Cockin. Their first ventures were with weaving yarns, weaving kits, and hand-woven rugs. A year into their partnership they bought the current headquarters of Rowan, an old gaberdine weaving mill on the edge of Holmfirth. In a deep narrow valley typical of the region, and with the River Ribble running past (it drove the original mill wheel), it is an idyllic setting. But at the time the Mill was idle and in disrepair. Crouched in the top part of the Mill with wood-burning stoves to keep them warm and some wonderful views to look out upon, Stephen dreamed up the unique soft color range that was to provide the core of Rowan's success.

They worked with the mills to adapt tapestry wools for knitters, and to create a unique Rowan paintbox of colors. This approach attracted some key knitwear designers to their label, none more so than Kaffe Fassett, who met Stephen at a craft fair in the '80s. Kaffe became a major influence in the development of the unique Rowan color palette. He has worked with them to create yarns and patterns, host workshops, and has occasionally appeared as a model. As Stephen himself points out, it was a symbiotic relationship. Rowan helped to promote Kaffe's name, and Kaffe's huge gift for communication helped to promote Rowan. His book *Glorious Knitting* was a huge success, and Rowan did all the kits for the sweaters in the book.

But home-grown talent was also instrumental in promoting the reputation of Rowan. The Hargreaves family, based in Holmfirth, have been involved with Rowan from its earliest days. Kathleen Hargreaves was Stephen's right-hand woman in the design department; and her daughter Kim started out with them, working there as a teenager during vacations. Kim Hargreaves had knitted throughout her childhood, but had no formal design training. Her undeniable artistic gifts were spotted by Stephen and she gradually took over the creative look of Rowan. Although she left the company in 2003, she still designs with Rowan yarns under her own label. Sister Lindsay continues to work for Rowan to this day.

Rowan's photo shoots are legendary and they have assiduously sought to bring the best names in fashion photography to their shoots, raising the profile of knitting from being a simple craft to fashion icon status.

By the late '80s Rowan had extended its sphere of influence, and the Rowan Club had an international membership which has grown since then to its current ranks of over 6,900 members, under the stewardship of Claire Armitage.

It was not until the 1990s that Rowan's current brand manager, Kate Buller, a knitwear designer herself, joined the company, as a demonstrator in the John Lewis stores. Under her aegis, the principle of having design consultants in-store was established and helped hugely to connect the company with its knitting customer base, with their team of design consultants both in-store and peripatetic, who run workshops as well, teaching people every aspect of the craft.

Rowan's ability to harness the creative talents of sought-after knitwear designers over the years has been part of their success in managing to keep hand knitting at the forefront of fashion, and also to ensure that, while keeping hand knitting traditions alive, they also succeed in attracting a new generation of knitters to join their ranks.

In recent years, knitting has experienced a similar boom to the one that started it all in the early 1980s. Film stars, like Julia Roberts and Russell Crowe, have been photographed knitting on film sets, with the result that knitting became cool again, helped along by young textile students like Freddie Robbins in the UK and *Stitch 'n Bitch* author, Debbie Stoller, in the US. Knitting clubs have mushroomed in towns and cities both in the UK and the US, as young women choose to socialize while they knit. And, perhaps, as an antidote to the increasing reliance on computers, many young people have a growing interest in creating something of their own. Increasingly, too, people are interested in the "green" aspects of life, a fact recognized by Rowan in its search for ethically resourced yarns and dyes in some of its most recent yarn ranges.

Above: A sepia image from the now sought-after Magazine 4, which was photographed by Eamonn J. McCabe and styled by Karen Harrison.

Below: Models and designers Annabel Fox and Kaffe Fassett strike a pose in Rowan's magazine.

Designs in the '80s

The very first Rowan magazine appeared in 1986. Although aspects of the design have been modified, the earliest magazine was the same format then as it is now. It included 25 designs by trendsetters like Annabel Fox, Kaffe Fassett, and Sandy Black.

The prevailing fashion mood was for high color and vibrant pattern. Knitting was riding high, with an explosion of interest in the craft and in the hand-knitted look in ready-to-wear. The first books of hand knits by knitwear designer Patricia Roberts had created a wave of interest in knitting and encouraged the young Kaffe Fassett to start knitting and designing knitwear himself.

Prior to Rowan's first magazine, knitting patterns from yarn manufacturers were primarily homely and old fashioned, practical rather than alluring. The first magazine blew a breath of fresh air into the craft. This was the time, too, when Nova magazine was making a huge impact on the fashion world. Stephen spotted the work of Caroline Baker, then its fashion editor, and realized hers was the look he wanted for Rowan. He commissioned her to art direct and she in turn chose to use photographer Eamonn J. McCabe, whose meteoric rise to fame had barely begun.

Other photographers who joined the Rowan roll call for the magazine include Tony Boase, Tim Brett-Day, and Joey Toller, all of whom contributed to the brilliantly eclectic look of the early magazines, with soft-focus photography of quirkily dressed and very natural-looking models.

By the late 1980s, Rowan had begun to establish itself in a wider context, appealing to knitters in other parts of the world.

Right: A section of the Rowan 30-year retrospective exhibition, featuring designs by, among others, Kaffe Fassett and Sandy Black (now Professor at the London College of Fashion). The image on the top right is of the young Kaffe Fassett modeling with Annabel Fox, both of whom had hand-knit designs in the first Rowan magazine in 1986.

SANDY BLACK

1987 - 1988
Magazines 1, 2, 3 & 4

Right: **Brioche by Annabel Fox
(Magazine 1)**
From the very first issue of the Rowan
magazine, this classic ribbed sweater
was originally knitted in Rowan Fleck DK
in a warm soft oatmeal. Big casual
sweaters like this one were popular in
the early 1980s, part of a relaxed style of
dressing. For the pattern on pages
56–57, the design has been reworked in
Rowan's Scottish Tweed DK.

Big and beautiful

During this era, knitwear designers were making a splash with big knits, often in chunky yarns. The look was casual and easy going but eye-catching. Individualistic knits were also in vogue, as these two highly patterned designs demonstrate. Designers of the period vied with each other to create beautiful intricate designs, turning each knitted piece into an heirloom knit.

Above left: **Peacock by Kim Hargreaves (Magazine 6)**
A generously sized garment, this jacket was knitted in Rowan Designer DK, and Wool Cotton. The wonderful crewelwork-inspired design was typical of the period, when designers created extravagantly patterned knits, which were challenging to make.

Above right: **Turkish Leaves by J & J Seaton (Magazine 4)**
Another splendidly baroque-style pattern, also from one of the earliest magazines. The husband and wife design team J & J Seaton went on to establish the highly successful clothing and homeware company Toast. Their creation here was knitted in Rowan Designer DK.

Red alert

Although Rowan are now renowned for their soft art shades, their designers know how to use strong color to great effect, too. Each design in this collection employs traffic-stopping red in various degrees of intensity—in the intricacy of Kaffe Fassett's fascinating Foolish Virgins design, as a strong color statement in Kim Hargreaves's glittering eye-catching beaded cardigan, and in two highly patterned Mediterranean inspired designs, the deep Tuscany by Kim Hargreaves and the more delicate Amorgos by Sarah Dallas.

Left: **Foolish Virgins by Kaffe Fassett (Magazine 7)**
Knitted in Cotton Glace, one of Rowan's most durable yarns with a great range of colors, this design is one of Kaffe's own favorites. He recolored and remodeled the Foolish Virgins design as a scarf in Scottish Tweed 4-Ply in his recent book *Kaffe Knits Again*.

Above: **Beaded cardigan by Kim Hargreaves (Magazine 9)**
The beaded cardigan is an ever-popular design with knitters, and this one by Kim was no exception, so the pattern has been included on pages 58–61. It was originally knitted in a fine cotton, which has been replaced in the new instructions with Rowan Classic Cashsoft 4-Ply.

Top right: **Tuscany by Kim Hargreaves (Magazine 9)**
With its mixture of flowers and geometrics, reminiscent of an antique tile, this cardigan has a strong Renaissance feel. It was knitted in a range of Rowan yarns: Wool Cotton, Mercerized Cotton, Sea Breeze, and Cotton Glace.

Above: **Amorgos by Sarah Dallas (Magazine 7)**
Knitted in a mixture of Rowan Cotton Glace and Chenille, Sarah Dallas's design bears her usual delicate touch. Although she likes bright colors, she tends to use them in quite subtle ways, so that the overall effect is one of delicacy rather than strong contrasts.

Designer profile

Long Leaf Coat (Magazine 12)
Right: A veritable tour de force, this
exquisitely shaded multicolored coat
was originally knitted in Rowan's
Lambswool Donegal. The design
employed more than 40 colors. Each
leaf includes a wonderful blend of
shades, so the effect is vibrant but at
the same time extremely subtle.

Kaffe Fassett

Born in San Francisco, Kaffe studied painting at the Museum of Fine Art in Boston, Massachusetts. After just three months at art school, Kaffe left the United States and traveled to London in order to paint. London has been his home ever since.

Kaffe became interested in the world of fashion and worked closely with fashion designer Bill Gibb, creator of intricate and iconic kaftans and dresses of the period. It was during a trip to a Scottish wool mill that Kaffe began to use yarn as an art medium. Inspired by the colors in the surrounding landscape, he was thrilled to find the same colors in yarns so he bought 20 shades of the Shetland wool and some knitting needles. And—as the legend goes—was taught to knit by a fellow passenger on the train home to London.

Kaffe embarked on his first pieces of knitting, and his very first design appeared as a full-page spread in Vogue magazine. While continuing to work with Bill Gibb, Kaffe found himself in demand and was commissioned to produce designs for Missoni. The roll call of celebrities who have bought his one-off designs is to be envied; they include film stars Lauren Bacall, Barbara Streisand, and Shirley Maclaine.

As Kaffe's reputation grew he began to give lectures and inspirational talks and it was after one such event that he was approached by Stephen Sheard, who asked him to produce some kits for Rowan Yarns. At the time Kaffe was producing chenille knitting kits of his own, but he was so inspired by the beautiful yarns and vibrant colors being produced by Rowan Weavers (as Rowan Yarns was then known) that he agreed to get involved. In 1983 the first Kaffe Fassett knit kit range—packaged in luxury boxes—was launched and sold through yarn shops and department stores. At first the trade considered these kits too costly and believed they were too complicated for the home knitter; however, they were thankfully proved wrong as Rowan knitting kits became a staple income for Rowan over the years. Kaffe's first book *Glorious Knitting* was published by Ebury Press in 1985. The book contained 30 designs and became a compulsory addition to every knitter's collection. To inspire knitters yet further, Kaffe presented his own six-part television series entitled "Glorious Colour" for Channel 4. The series was aired in 1986 and proved so popular that it has been repeated three times.

By the mid 1980s Kaffe had also become heavily involved in designing needlepoints inspired by surface decoration on

Right: **Moss Stone Jacket Magazine 2**
Another of Kaffe's signature pieces, this jacket is another clever exercise in shading and toning, this time in quite neutral colors.

Above: **Carpet (Magazine 18)**
Knitted in Rowan Lambswool Donegal, Kidsilk Haze and Magpie Aran, this jacket has been designed with striking zigzags of sophisticated color, inspired by the patterns often seen in antique kilims.

Left: **Shaded Diamonds (Magazine 35)**
Diamond patterns are a favorite of Kaffe's, as witnessed here in a long, elegant coat, a couple of decades after his first diamond patterns appeared (see opposite page, bottom). Knitted in Rowan Summer Tweed, these large diamonds are each subtly shaded in a cool blue/gray/brown palette.

china and artifacts, as well as vegetation and natural landscapes. In 1987 Kaffe launched his needlepoint book *Glorious Needlepoint*, and his interest in needlepoint is yet another branch of his wide-ranging career.

Kaffe's love of textiles led him to travel extensively. The international charity Oxfam asked him to work with poverty-stricken weaving villages in India and Guatemala, to advise on designs that would be more marketable in the West. As a result, he created a range of colorful hand-woven cloth for use as shirt fabric, bed throws, and patchwork fabric. This formed the basis of his Kaffe Fassett range of fabrics for Rowan (working with Westminster Fibers in the US). The success of the fabrics, and the books that showcase them, is attested to by the fact that he is about to embark on his thirteenth book in the series for Rowan.

In 1988 Kaffe became the first living textile artist to have a one-man show at the Victoria & Albert Museum in London. The exhibition attracted such crowds that the museum doubled attendance figures during the run and the show proved so popular that it was subsequently converted into an international traveling show which visited nine countries.

Kaffe continues to lecture and tutor workshops. His passion for all his chosen and closely related crafts is infectious, and his lectures are often sell-outs. According to Kaffe, "being the dinosaur of patchwork and knitting guarantees that people will come and listen to me," but the truth is his genius for color is such that his appeal is evergreen.

Top right: **Jeweled Polo (Magazine 16)**
This striped design was knitted in Rowan Magpie Tweed. Kaffe's stripes have always been a great treat, with their brilliantly orchestrated, graduated color choices, and this is one of his easier patterns to knit.

Right: **Red Diamonds (Magazine 4)**
Kaffe has recreated this diamond pattern more than once, in different colorways. This version is knitted in a mixture of Silkstones and Designer DK. It shows one of Kaffe's trademark design features: repeating the colors of the main pattern in the striped ribbing.

The designs in the '90s

By the 1990s, the Rowan magazine was starting to get established, and a more grown-up and cohesive approach began to be adopted for the styling, photography, and layout.

The photo shoots started to develop a strong "theme," in part influenced by the fashion of the period and in part by the individual style of Rowan's own art direction and photography.

The first of these was the "Swallows and Amazons" shoot in Magazine 10 (see pages 22 and 23), and by the mid-1990s the strongly themed shoots became a key feature of the magazine, helping to underline the response to changing fashions and styles. Magazine 18, midway through the decade, had two themes. One, "Free Spirit," echoed the then current desire for colorwork, but used in a more low-key and subtle manner than in the designs of the '80s. The other key theme, "Brief Encounter," looked to bringing more sophisticated garment shapes to knitting, which ushered in a new direction and approach for Rowan.

By the last issue of the decade, the growing fashion for minimalism, started in chain stores like Habitat, had begun to take hold in the knitwear industry, too. Magazine 25 is all about cotton yarns, simple shapes and clear colors, photographed in bright light against plainer grounds. The patterned designs are more pastel and more softly toning, and there is a stronger emphasis on texture, with crochet making its mark as an alternative to knitting.

Right: This part of the 30-year Rowan retrospective exhibition features designs from the early part of the 1990s, which still show the strong pattern influence of the '80s. By the latter part of the decade, a more minimalist style had been adopted.

1991

Magazine 10

KAFFE FASSETT

ROWAN

Retro country

A nostalgic return to the past was a key theme in early part of the '90s. In Magazine 10, the theme of "Swallows and Amazons"—taken from Arthur Ransome's classic children's series set in England's Lake District—created one of the most memorable stories in the Rowan magazine's history. With Kaffe Fassett's exquisitely subtle color harmonies and Kim Hargreaves's eye for line and form, modeled with great aplomb by the then unknown young model Kate Moss, the knitwear designs caught the public's imagination. Such has been the success of this issue that it is now a collector's item, exchanging hands at unprecedented prices.

Right: **Kilim by Kaffe Fassett (Magazine 10)**
A typically complex and subtle Kaffe Fassett design, this carpet-pattern-inspired sweater was modeled by the young Kate Moss. In order to have as many colors as possible available for this creation, Kaffe used several Rowan yarns for it, including Rowanspun, Lightweight Tweed, Kid Silk, Silkstones, Fox Tweed, Donegal Tweed, Chenille, and Botany.

Above: **Jester by Kim Hargreaves (Magazine 10)**
Kate Moss models this lovely design by the young Kim Hargreaves, with its witty scalloped edging and simple shape. Its appeal is timeless and could just as easily be worn today. Knitted in Rowan Wool Cotton, it comes in two lengths: this one and a cropped version. The patterns for both versions are on pages 62–64.

Right: **Fisherman by Kim Hargreaves (Magazine 10)**
A Rowan classic, inspired by the beautiful traditional Aran sweaters of Britain's fishing community. The soft cream color shows up the texture to perfection. The reworked pattern for this design uses Rowan's Pure Wool Aran as a replacement for the original yarn (see pages 65–67).

Bold stripes

During the '90s, Rowan's designers produced some show-stopping color knitting, using wonderfully vibrant mixes of colors. Indian Summer (right) by Kim Hargreaves focuses on broad stripes of deep art shades, and is detailed with intricate brocade-like borders along the hem and cuffs.

By contrast, Louisa Harding's for Sugar Plum (opposite page) is more pared down, using texture as well as color for its impact.

Right: **Indian Summer by Kim Hargreaves (Magazine 8)**
The deep, rich colors of the Rowan Paintbox range were used by Kim for this boxy, short cardigan with wide stripes.

Opposite page: **Sugar Plum by Louisa Harding (Magazine 12)**
Beautifully textured cables and bobbles run in panels up the body and sleeves of this sweater. Originally knitted in the now discontinued Rowan Designer DK, the design has been adapted for the current Rowan Pure Wool DK on pages 68–70.

Pattern details

In the early part of the decade, big knits and thick, soft yarns were still popular. But for many designers, colorwork pattern was not always the all-singing, all-dancing event it had been in the '80s. Both Louisa Harding and Kim Hargreaves began to use pattern in more discreet ways, to enliven otherwise plainer garments, and the patterns became more tonal and subtle, often using a mix of yarns to create the effects. In order to prevent the garment from becoming too heavy or lumpy, finer yarns were sometimes used for colorwork borders.

Left: Russian Jacket by Louisa Harding (Magazine 14)
This boxy, short-length jacket has a pretty crewelwork-inspired pattern on the shawl collar and turned back cuffs. Although the main body of the cardigan was in Fox Tweed DK, the patterned areas were created in much finer Kid Silk. A revised version of the instructions, using Rowan's Scottish Tweed DK and Kid Classic, are given on pages 71–74.

Right: Fringed Cardigan by Kim Hargreaves (Magazine 8)
This duffle-coat design by Kim Hargreaves employs a more traditional Fair Isle style border around the hem and above the sleeve cuffs, in gently toning colors. The body of the cardigan was knitted in thick, soft Rowan Magpie Aran, and the colorwork pattern in a mix of finer cotton yarns.

**Left: Millais by Sharon Peake
(Magazine 20)**
This very neat, fitted peplum jacket,
knitted in Rowan 4-Ply Botany, has a
wonderful organic curling abstract pattern
in dark blue and cream on a rich wine-
colored background. The collar and
sleeves both feature a lacy inset. The
design has a classic style.

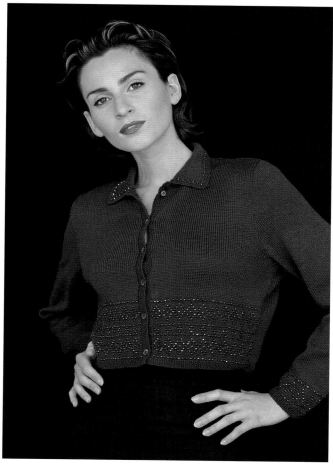

Rich sophistication

By the latter part of the 1990s a new mood was taking hold in knitwear design, with more body-hugging shapes and more sophisticated patterns. These three designs by Sharon Peake, Erika Knight, and Louisa Harding all have a grown-up style about them. Deeper, richer colors bring a touch of glamour to knitting, moving it away from the more homespun traditions of the past.

Above left: **Clara by Erika Knight (Magazine 24)**
Knitted in Magpie Aran, this jacket with its long lean line is an elegant updating of thick knits of the previous decade.

Above right: **René by Louisa Harding (Magazine 18)**
A cool, cropped take on the classic beaded cardigan, Louisa's design was knitted in deep purple Rowan 4-Ply Botany, which had a naturally crisp finish that held its shape really well. There is a reworked pattern for René in Rowan Pure Wool 4-Ply (an identical substitute) on pages 75–78.

Designer profile

Right: Able (Magazine 33)
Knitted in Summer Tweed, a softly
flecked silk and cotton mix yarn,
this pretty summery cover-up with
its cabled detail at the front captures
Kim's relaxed, elegant yet timeless
style. For the pattern, which uses the
original yarn, turn to pages 101–103.

Kim Hargreaves

Although born in New Zealand, Kim Hargreaves has lived most of her life in Holmfirth. Brought up surrounded by knitting, sewing, crochet, and needlepoint, she has always had a particular passion for clothes and how they are put together. Although she has had little formal training, Kim's natural instinct for color and design has led to her worldwide reputation for producing amazing designs.

Kim arrived at the Rowan Mill as a local teenager keen to help her mother Kathleen with any jobs that needed doing during her holidays. Although Kim had knitted throughout her childhood, she had no formal design training. Nevertheless, her potential soon became clear to Stephen Sheard who encouraged her to produce her first design for Rowan's *The Cotton Collection* in 1987.

Kim built on her early design success and soon became Rowan's head in-house designer, creating hundreds of designs and selecting new yarn colors, as well as overseeing the photography, styling, and production of all the fashion stories within the magazines. Kim has been responsible for creating the image and philosophy of Rowan, which she achieved through her designs, her influence on photographic style, and through commissioning some of the best talent in design knitwear to contribute to the Rowan magazines.

Kim's own designs are just as popular today as they were when they were originally published. Her design style has always been feminine and pretty, with special attention paid to fit and simple styling.

In 2003 Kim left Rowan to set up her own label "Kim," producing beautiful Kim Hargreaves designs using Rowan yarns, in kits which are sold through her internet business. In 2008 Kim launched her first two independently published books *Heartfelt* and *Nectar*. These books were instantly bestsellers around the globe. More recently Kim has worked with Rowan to produce a palette of her own shades in some of her favorite Rowan yarns, which are used in her two most recent books *Amber* and *Thrown Together*.

Above: **Elfin (Magazine 34)**
Another of Kim's very popular hand knits, Elfin is knitted in Rowan Felted Tweed, with a ruffle detail on the front and sleeve cuffs in Kidsilk Haze. Classic with a feminine touch, this design is guaranteed to flatter most women.

Texture and simplicity

By the latter part of the '90s many of the Rowan designs had started to echo the minimalism that was holding sway in fashion. Simpler shapes were the order of the day, often in a single color or with very subdued toning colors. Texture became an important feature of many of the designs, with soft rolled collars or fluted hems. Two of the designs featured here are part of the "Winter's Chill" feature on Kim Hargreaves's designs for Magazine 26.

Above left: **Flighty by Kim Hargreaves (Magazine 23)**
This neatly tailored little camisole with its distinctive seaming was originally knitted in Rowan 4-Ply Cotton with both a plain and a striped colorway. A revised version in both plain and striped colorways in Rowan Classic Siena is included in this book on pages 79–80.

Above right: **Chilli Sweet and Dew by Kim Hargreaves (Magazine 26)**
Knitted in Rowan DK Soft, this little scarf, called Dew, has a very attractive stitch pattern which would also look great knitted larger in Kidsilk Haze on bigger needles, for an evening-style scarf. But if you prefer the original, knit it in Rowan Classic Baby Alpaca DK following the pattern on page 81.

Right: **Dove by Kim Hargreaves
(Magazine 26)**
Knitted originally in Rowan DK Tweed, this
poncho is really easy to knit and just as easy to
wear. It was part of a collection of simple but
very wearable designs by Kim in this issue. It is
worked in one long piece and has a broad seed
stitch border and a soft cowl-style turtleneck.
Like all large pieces of knitting, it benefits from
being knitted in a springy pure wool yarn that
holds its shape well. The updated pattern for
it on pages 82–83 uses Rowan Felted Tweed,
a yarn with a touch of supersoft alpaca in its
wool mix.

Designs of the '00s

By the start of the twenty-first century, Rowan's design ideas had started to move into a more urban, contemporary scenario. Many of the early issues of this decade featured quicker to knit, thicker yarns, like Rowan Polar. Another strong popular yarn of that period was Rowan Denim, which gave a particular good crisp finish to textured patterns such as cables. On a different note, Rowan also introduced another classic, Kidsilk Haze, which has proved incredibly popular with knitters, particularly for ethereal shawls and scarves, and for little accessories. It also provides a great range of accent colors that can be inserted into designs with colorwork.

In the latter part of the decade, Rowan has returned to some of its own inspiration, recreating subtle but strong color combinations in stripes and brocade, but in a deeper and richer color palette, with an autumnal twist in collections orchestrated by the current Rowan designer, Marie Wallin.

Designers like Erika Knight, with her strong sense of pared-down elegance, and Martin Storey, with his subtle and contemporary twist on traditional knit designs, continue to ensure that people look to Rowan for a range of inspiration, rather than one single look.

The art shades so beloved of Rowan over three decades continue to be the mainstay of their color palette, accented here and there with stronger brights.

As is always the case, the yarns inspire the designers, who find new ways to present them.

Right: These highlights of the '00s in the Rowan 30-year retrospective exhibition Illustrate the range of knitwear design innovation that Rowan continues to promote and their ongoing production of sophisticated yarn colors.

2008
Magazines 43 & 44

MARIE WALLIN

ERIKA KNIGHT

Traditional cables

Proving that cables never go out of fashion, even in the present day, here are designs from the early 1990s and two others from 1980s Rowan magazines.

Left: **Surf by Martin Storey (Magazine 31)**
This classic cable design, knitted in the perennially popular Rowan Denim, is modeled here by Martin himself as part of a feature about him and his work. Martin's beautifully crafted designs, traditional with a modern twist, have been the mainstay of Rowan's Classic label for several years. The pattern for Surf, written in men's and women's sizes, is on pages 97–100.

Above: **Queenie by Louisa Harding (Magazine 15)**

Right: **Dales Aran by Martin Storey (Magazine 16)**

'00s

Fair Isle and intarsia

These hand–knit designs use pretty repeating small colorwork patterns that never go out of fashion in knitting. Three of them are created using the Fair Isle technique, in which the colors are stranded across the back of the work. And the fourth, the Buena Vista bolero, uses intarsia, in which each color is introduced only in its individual area of the design. With any small repeating pattern, the way the colors work against each other is very important for the overall effect. Some patterns are deliberately soft and toning, while others rely more on contrast for the impact. When recoloring Fair Isle designs, you have to pay attention to the tones as much as the hues of each color.

Opposite page, left: **Emmeline by Sarah Dallas (Magazine 28)**
This cropped but generously sized cardigan is flattering for almost any figure shape. The design was very popular, and a pattern with substitute yarns and colors is given on pages 93–96.

Opposite page, right: **Florentine by Sarah Dallas (Magazine 36)**
Knitted in Rowan Felted Tweed and DK Soft, only the fronts of this very feminine cardigan are worked in Fair Isle, and the rest in a single color.

Above: **Fairisle by Kim Hargreaves (Magazine 28)**
This classic Fair Isle colorwork pattern is soft and timeless. It is knitted in Rowan 4 ply Soft and Kidsilk Haze.

Right: **Buena Vista by Jean Moss (Magazine 33)**
Dotted with a pretty flower pattern in intarsia, this little bolero was originally knitted in Rowan Calmer and Summer Tweed. As the shades are no longer available, the pattern was updated with Rowan Wool Cotton (see pages 104–107).

Muted pattern

By the beginning of the twenty-first century, knitted colorwork pattern returned to popularity, but with softer hues and gentle harmonies. The garments became more fitted and figure hugging, often with a just-below-the-hip length. Classic and timeless, some of these elegantly patterned designs have great appeal.

Left: **Laurel Leaf by Kim Hargreaves (Magazine 27)**
Knitted in Rowan Cotton Glace, this pretty all-over leaf pattern is worked in harmonizing, cool tones. It makes a versatile short-length cardigan that can be dressed up or down. The pattern with a revised palette is on pages 84–87.

Right: **Champagne Please by Brandon Mably (Magazine 27)**
Brandon's aptly named design has a definite touch of quiet class, with its traditional diamond pattern in delicate pastel colors on a neutral ground. Knitted in Rowan Cotton Glace, a yarn still available in the Rowan range, the cardigan has been given a new color scheme in the updated pattern on pages 88–92. The reworked colorway reflects the mood of the original.

Sweet and pretty

These great softly colored designs in neat, fitted shapes have a very feminine appeal. The neutral backgrounds provide a good foil for the prettily colored patterns on each design, so that the pattern is visible without being overwhelming. On Rosebud, Sasha Kagan has also added lacy panels for an extra feminine touch.

Above right and left: **Hydrangea Camisole and Cardigan by Kaffe Fassett (Magazine 41)**
Originally knitted in Rowan 4 ply Cotton, this attractive little camisole and cardigan combo has a contemporary edge, with its bright border stripes picking up the colors of the little cloud-like all-over pattern on the cardigan. Updated in Rowan Classic Sienna, both patterns are given on pages 120–124.

Right: **Rosebud by Sasha Kagan (Magazine 34)**
Unashamedly girlie, this cardigan with its alternating trailing rosebuds and lace panels is a '40s inspired design—a great treat for avid knitters. It is knitted in Rowan Wool Cotton, one of Rowan's ever-popular classic yarns, and the pattern is on pages 109–112.

Mohair/silk extravaganza

The designs here are all knitted with Rowan Kidsilk Haze and show just how versatile this yarn is. It has proved one of Rowan's most popular yarns, and deservedly so. Once knitters have mastered its cobwebby structure, they find it is definitely a yarn for all seasons, as it is both amazingly warm but also wonderfully light.

Left and above: Earth Stripe Wrap and Tunic by Kaffe Fassett (Magazine 42)
Kaffe has used the many colors in the Kidsilk Haze range to make a shawl and tunic with exquisitely soft gradations of colors. He created even more colors by using two strands of yarn together and mixing the shades. Turn to pages 130–133 for the patterns.

Right: Anice by Sharon Miller (Magazine 41)
Like all good shawls, Sharon Miller's delicate, gossamer wrap is not only superbly textured but light and soft. The chart and pattern for it are on pages 125–126.

Right: Doon Coat by Erika Knight (Magazine 42)
There is a hint of the Victorian novel about this romantic coat, worked with warm and soft Rowan Kid Classic in an exquisitely deep plum/maroon shade. With a revered collar and a fitted waist and belt, it has a great retro feel to it. For the pattern, see pages 127–129.

Sophisticated glamour

Cool, elegant, and chic, these three designs focus on how knitting can be as refined as you want it to be! Erika Knight is a master of the understated, with her focus on texture, shape, and tone, and Sarah Hatton is a versatile young designer who can play the "chic" card with aplomb.

Above left: **Geneva Cardigan by Erika Knight (Magazine 42)**
A delicate, very light cardigan cum wrap to wear over the Geneva Camisole. It is knitted in Kidsilk Haze, and the pattern for it is on pages 137–139.

Above right: **Geneva Camisole by Sarah Hatton (Magazine 42)**
This design recalls the days of '30s glamour with its deep V-neck and long slim line. Originally knitted in Rowan 4 ply Soft, it has been translated into Rowan Classic Pure Silk DK in the pattern on pages 134–136.

Designer profile

Right: Veronica (Magazine 36)
One of Marion Foale's fashionably shaped timeless cardigans. It was originally knitted with two strands of wool yarn for the Rowan magazine, and the pattern has been reworked for a single strand of Rowan Classic Cashsoft Aran, a yarn containing a mix of wool and cashmere. See pages 113–116 for the pattern.

Marion Foale

Marion Foale is one of the accomplished designers that Rowan has been lucky to have as a contributor to their magazine. She is an innovative knitwear designer and is the founder and designer of "Marion Foale"—a unique hand-knitting label that is coveted (and sold) all over the world.

Back in the swinging '60s, just after graduating from the London's Royal College of Art, she and fellow student Sally Tuffin had a fashion boutique in Carnaby Street. Their clothes were about as cool as you could get at the time, and even Hollywood choose to use Foale & Tuffin to dress Audrey Hepburn in "Two for the Road." But marriage and children changed all that for the best part of a decade. However, in the quieter moments, Marion taught herself to knit until she began to relaunch herself as a knitwear designer. Her designs were elegant, classic and simple—much removed from the patterned colorwork popular at the time. When she showed her designs to Paul Smith, an old friend, his comment was, "too simple! I shouldn't bother." She says now that they have a good laugh about it!

In 1981 the *Sunday Times* put two of her children's patterns on the fashion page, inviting readers to apply for the pattern. They were inundated with over 5,000 requests. That was the kick-start for her wholesale fashion knitwear business. Designers like Margaret Howell and fashion stores like Whistles added Marion's designs to their collections, and she wrote a book, *Marion Foale's Classic Knitwear*, which is still regarded as the best book for anyone who wants wonderfully tailored knits.

Marion began to design the shaped, tailored garments that have become her trademark. She has transformed her early skills with fabric to cut the basic shape of her knitwear on a dummy, using a jersey fabric which performs the function of a calico toile. Once the shape is determined, the technicality of turning it into a knitting pattern takes over, working out when and where to increase or decrease the stitches to mold the form. A commission from Marks & Spencer in the '90s gave her the challenge of transposing her tailored knitwear technique for a range for them. "It was tricky, but it worked and those sweaters and cardigans were bestsellers." In 1987 Marion opened another shop, this time in Hinde Street, near Marylebone High Street in London.

For some years, though, Marion has lived and worked in Atherstone, Derbyshire, with a dedicated and loyal team of colleagues, including Karen Jackson, originally her part-time secretary and now a co-director. The designs are shown twice yearly at London Fashion Week and the Paris Collections. She loves the fact that the business is comparatively small. As she says, she enjoys making very special hand-made things, something which would be lost if the company grew too big.

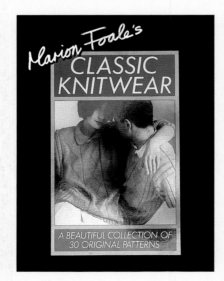

Right: Marion's book *Marion Foale's Classic Knitwear* which was a great success when it first came out and is still in demand today.

'00s

Vintage charm

Two quite different takes on a vintage look bring Rowan's three decades of design to a fitting point. In Marion Foale's smart little jacket, there is a hint of the tailored look of the '40s, with the classic basketweave pattern, fitted waist, and neat collar. As always with Marion's designs there is great concentration on precise detail. Marie Wallin goes further back for her inspiration, with an almost Renaissance feel to the warm autumnal colors of this delicate crochet tunic with its square neck and clever paneling.

Right: **Fontaine by Marion Foale (Magazine 44)**
Originally knitted in Rowan 4 ply Soft, the yarn for this cardigan has been updated to Rowan Classic Cashsoft 4 ply in the pattern on pages 140–143.

Opposite page: **Donatello by Marie Wallin (Magazine 44)**
Crocheted in a mix of Rowan Wool Cotton and Kidsilk Aura, Marie Wallin's creation is full of vintage charm. The pattern is given on pages 144–146.

The Patterns

The following updated patterns are a selection taken from the Rowan magazine during its long history. They include designs from a cross-section of Rowan's designers, with particular emphasis on those designers who have been closely associated with Rowan over the years. Where the yarns or colors are no longer in stock, substitutions are suggested. There is also advice at the beginning of this section for readers who want to try their hand at their own substitutions.

For more information about working from knitting patterns, turn to pages 147–148, where you will find a full list of knitting abbreviations. Detailed yarn information and yarn supplier addresses are given on pages 149–151.

Designs included in the book but not in this pattern section will be available on the Rowan website (knitrowan.com) as facsimiles of the original patterns, not updated ones.

Substituting yarns

Rowan Yarns has always been a fashion-led brand, and over the years their yarns and colors have changed to reflect trends. So when choosing patterns from the Rowan magazines for *Rowan's Greatest Knits*, we found that some of the older designs used yarns that were no longer in production, or the yarn was still available but the colors weren't. For these designs, substitute yarns and/or new colors were selected. The replacement yarns and colors echo as closely as possible the originals.

Substituting yarns is not always straightforward and much testing and re-testing went into our new yarn choices. Each substitution we chose is shown as a swatch with the relevant pattern. If you want to try to substitute yarns yourself, read the guidelines that follow and be aware that some patterns may prove difficult to find substitutes for, either because the original colors are hard to match or because a particular yarn or stitch pattern make the task harder than usual.

Substituting a standard-weight yarn

The easiest yarns to find substitutes for are ordinary smooth yarns in one of the standard weights—for example, UK 4-ply, double-knitting and Aran weights, and US sport and worsted weights. But even a standard-weight wool yarn won't necessarily have the exact same thickness (or diameter) as another yarn in the same category. This is because yarns have different loft—air between the fibers—and springiness. So a standard yarn weight is not determined by its diameter but by ideal gauge measured over stockinette stitch using a specific needle size.

Even though yarn manufacturers attempt to match the recognized standard gauges for their standard-weight yarns, these are not always precisely the same from brand to brand. Before purchasing a substitute for a standard-weight yarn, check the yarn label and see if it matches the recommended gauge and needle size of the original yarn. The specifications for the yarns used in this book are listed on pages 149–150 for this purpose.

If gauge and needle size match exactly, you have probably found a good substitute. If the stitch gauge is the same but the row gauge is slightly different, you may still be able to use it as your substitute as long as your garment has a simple shape without shaped sleeve caps and the pattern tells you to knit to a certain measurement rather than a certain number of rows.

Choosing a matching yarn texture

Finding substitutes for non-standard-weight yarns or yarns in anything other than ordinary smooth wool yarns is a little more difficult, but it follows the same principle: look for a yarn with the same recommended gauge and needle size.

Aside from yarn weight, you must also try to match the original yarn's fiber content and texture. Using a yarn with a totally different fiber content is unlikely to give you a garment that looks like the original. It won't have either the same drape or the same firmness. So, for example, if the original yarn is a cotton, look for a cotton replacement. Choosing a substitute for a mohair yarn illustrates this point very clearly. If you choose anything other than another mohair yarn, the result will be vastly different from the original design (see opposite page).

Testing a your substitute yarn

Once you've found what you think will be a good substitute yarn, it is essential to knit a gauge swatch to test its suitability, even if you are substituting a smooth, standard-weight yarn. Buy just one ball for this purpose and only buy all the balls you need once you have tested your substitute.

Left: Four swatches all knitted in Rowan Classic Extra Fine Merino DK, using the same size needle, and with the same number of stitches and rows. The stitch patterns give them all different gauges. This shows why manufacturers use stockinette stitch gauge to illustrate a yarn's weight.

Knit as many swatches as you need to until you achieve the correct gauge with your replacement yarn, following the instructions on page 147. (If you can't achieve the correct gauge, you'll need to look for another substitute.)

Having achieved a gauge that matches the one specified in the pattern, study your swatch carefully. Does it feel nice? Does it look like the fabric in the photograph? If your swatch is floppy but the garment looks structured, try another, firmer yarn or one that it very slightly thicker. You may need to try a few substitutes before you find one that gives you just the right feel and look.

Choosing substitute colors

A substitute yarn may not come in the same shade as the one-color original design, but most yarns have a good selection of colors for you to choose from. Multicolored designs are more difficult to find good matches for, so keep this in mind when choosing a replacement yarn. If the shade range is too limited, you may need to look for an alternative or create a new colorway.

When creating a colorway (or trying to find colors that match the originals), bear in mind the depth and tone of each of the original shades. Check the original photograph. Does one color "jump out" at you? If so, then choose your new colors so that this shade will still "jump out". Or do all the colors subtly harmonize with each other? In which case, your substitute colors must harmonize as well.

Take into account the lightness and darkness of the various shades in the design as much as the actual hue of the color. The less contrast there is between the various tones, the more subtle and soft the colorway, and the higher the contrast the bolder the effect.

The best way to choose your replacement colors is to arrange the different colored balls of yarn roughly in the order they appear in the chart. Holding single strands together isn't as helpful and won't give you a feel for the type of effect the shades will create. Then test your choices with a swatch. Press your swatch, and pin it up on a board so you can check it from a distance, as well as close up, before deciding on your final colors.

Purchasing the right amount of yarn

Once you are ready to purchase all the yarn needed for your garment, calculate how many yards/meters you need. Don't try to determine yarn amounts by ball weight, as yarns, even of those in the same weight category, vary in weight per yard/meter.

Successful yarn substitutions

Armed with the basics for yarn substitution, you're ready to go out and "play" with different yarns and colors. Whatever you do, just remember you must match the gauge in the pattern instructions and, ideally, you should aim for a knitted fabric of a similar weight and firmness or drape. Beyond that, the only limitation is your imagination and creativity.

Below: Two swatches both knitted in the same lace stitch pattern (the one used for the Anice shawl on pages 125–126), with the same size needle and the same number of stitches and rows, but different yarns. The two yarn types produce the same gauge but very different looks and textures; one is knitted in Rowan Kidsilk Haze (top) and the other in Rowan Pure Wool Aran (bottom). The Anice shawl (right) was knitted in cream Rowan Kidsilk Haze and the red swatch shows a good color alternative for it.

Brioche

ANNABEL FOX

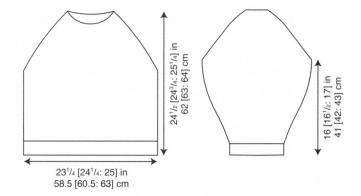

Measurements diagram:
24½ [24¾: 25¼] in
62 [63: 64] cm

23¼ [24¼: 25] in
58.5 [60.5: 63] cm

16 [16½: 17] in
41 [42: 43] cm

SIZES AND YARN

	S	M	L	
To fit bust	34	36	38	in
	86	91	97	cm

Rowan Scottish Tweed DK

| Oatmeal 025 | 15 | 16 | 17 | x 50 g |

Originally knitted and photographed (above) in Rowan Fleck DK

NEEDLES

1 pair size 3 (3mm) needles
1 pair size 5 (3.75mm) needles

NEW YARN SUBSTITUTION

The yarn used for this sweater featured in the first ever Rowan magazine is, not surprisingly, no longer available. But we found the perfect substitute in the current Rowan range—Scottish Tweed DK. Using this yarn we've been able to match the gauge, the tweedy texture, and the color. The perfect example of a successful substitute yarn—all features match exactly.

GAUGE

18 sts and 44 rows to 4 in (10 cm) measured over patt using size 5 (3.75mm) needles.

BACK

Using size 3 (3mm) needles, cast on 105 [109: 113] sts.
Row 1 (RS): K1, *P1, K1, rep from * to end.
Row 2: P1, *K1, P1, rep from * to end.
These 2 rows frm rib.
Cont in rib until work measures 2½ in (6 cm), ending with RS facing for next row.
Change to size 5 (3.75mm) needles.
Next row (RS): K1, *yarn from back to front between two needles, sl 1 purlwise, take yarn over right needle to complete yo and K next st on left needle, rep from * to end.
Now work in patt as foll:
Row 1 (WS): Sl 1, K tog next (slipped) st and the yo, *yarn from back to front between two needles, sl 1 purlwise, take yarn over right needle to complete yo and K tog next (slipped) st on left needle and the yo of previous row, rep from * to last st, K1.
Row 2: Sl 1, *yarn from back to front between two needles, sl 1 purlwise, take yarn over right needle to complete yo and K tog next (slipped) st on left needle and the yo of previous row, rep from * to last 2 sts, yarn from back to front between two needles, sl 1 purlwise, take yarn over right needle to complete yo and K tog next (slipped) st on left needle and the yo of previous row, K1.
These 2 rows form patt.
(**Note:** When working patt, the yo and the slipped st below it count as **ONE** st **throughout** and are always knitted together on foll row. When working shaping, do **NOT** work the "sl 1 purlwise, yo" on end sts of rows, but work edge sts as "sl 1" at beg or "K1" at end.)
Cont in patt until back measures 14½ in (37 cm), ending with RS facing for next row.
Shape raglan armholes
Place a marker at each end of last row to mark base of raglan armholes.
Keeping patt correct, dec 1 st at each end of next and 19 foll 4th rows, then on foll 14 [16: 18] alt rows. 37 sts.
Work 1 row, ending with RS facing for next row.

Shape back neck

Next row (RS): Work 2 tog, patt 10 sts and turn, leaving rem sts on a holder.

Work each side of neck separately.

Keeping patt correct, bind off 4 sts at beg of next row.

Dec 1 st at beg (raglan armhole edge) of next row.

Bind off 4 sts at beg of next row, ending with RS facing for next row.

Next row (RS): K2tog and fasten off.

With RS facing, rejoin yarn to rem sts, bind off center 13 sts, patt to last 2 sts, work 2 tog.

Complete to match first side, reversing shapings.

FRONT

Work as given for back until 41 sts rem in raglan armhole shaping.

Work 1 row, ending with RS facing for next row.

Shape neck

Next row (RS): Work 2 tog, patt 14 sts and turn, leaving rem sts on a holder.

Work each side of neck separately.

Keeping patt correct, bind off 4 sts at beg of next row.

Dec 1 st at beg (raglan armhole edge) of next row.

Bind off 4 sts at beg of next row. 6 sts.

Dec 1 st at raglan armhole edge of next and foll alt row **and at same time** dec 1 st at neck edge of next 2 rows. 2 sts.

Work 1 row, ending with RS facing for next row.

Next row (RS): K2tog and fasten off.

With RS facing, rejoin yarn to rem sts, bind off center 9 sts, patt to last 2 sts, work 2 tog.

Complete to match first side, reversing shapings.

SLEEVES

Using size 3 (3mm) needles, cast on 43 sts.

Work in rib as given for back for 2 in (5 cm), ending with RS facing for next row.

Change to size 5 (3.75mm) needles.

Next row (RS): K1, *yarn from back to front between two needles, sl 1 purlwise, take yarn over right needle to complete yo and K next st on left needle, rep from * to end.

Beg with row 1, now work in patt as given for back, shaping sides by inc 1 st at each end of 4th and every foll 6th row to 59 [71: 81] sts, then on every foll 8th row until there are 81 [85: 89] sts, taking inc sts into patt.

Work even until sleeve measures 16 [16½: 17] in (41 [42: 43] cm), ending with RS facing for next row.

Shape raglan

Place a marker at each end of last row to mark base of raglan armhole.

Keeping patt correct, dec 1 st at each end of next and 24 foll 4th rows, then on foll 6 [8: 10] alt rows. 19 sts.

Work 1 row, ending with RS facing for next row.

Bind off.

FINISHING

Press as described on page 148.

Sew both front and right back raglan seams using backstitch, or mattress stitch if preferred.

Neckband

With RS facing and using size 3 (3mm) needles, pick up and knit 20 sts from top of left sleeve, 13 sts down left side of neck, 13 sts from front, 13 sts up right side of neck, 20 sts from top of right sleeve, then 34 sts from back. 113 sts.

Beg with row 2, work in rib as given for back for 2½ in (6 cm), ending with RS facing for next row.

Bind off in rib.

See page 148 for finishing instructions. Fold neckband in half to inside and loosely stitch in place.

About Annabel Fox

Annabel was born in England in 1958, but growing up in an army family meant she traveled the world when she was young. This experience led to an early interest in the arts. Her mother, an experienced needlewoman, also encouraged her to try crochet, weaving, embroidery, and patchwork, which sparked a love of textiles. Despite her early introduction to needlecraft, Annabel only learned to knit in art college because she changed the direction of her degree course. When a fellow student taught her to knit, it changed her life!

After studying art and then fashion and textiles, Annabel went on to setting up business in England with her first small collection of hand-knitted sweaters. Her distinctive hand knits were supplied to prestigious stores in Britain, the United States, and Japan. She twice won the Courtelle Handknit Award.

Although we have chosen her classic ribbed sweater Brioche for this book, Annabel is reknowned for her distinctive, eye-catching colorwork designs.

Beaded Cardigan

KIM HARGREAVES

SIZES AND YARN

	S	M	L	
To fit bust	34	36	38	in
	86	91	97	cm

Rowan Classic Cashsoft 4-Ply

| Redwood 429 | 11 | 12 | 12 | x 50 g |

Originally knitted and photographed (above) in Rowan Cabled Mercerised Cotton in Firethorn 337

NEEDLES

1 pair size 1 (2.25mm) needles
1 pair size 3 (3mm) needles

BUTTONS—8

BEADS—approx 3,700 small bronze glass beads

NEW YARN SUBSTITUTION

This cardigan was originally knitted in a very fine, firm cotton yarn that's not available now. The gauge is fairly tight, so we chose a "squishy" 4-ply yarn (below) as the substitute. Although our substitute yarn is usually knitted on larger needles than used here, we were able to match the gauge perfectly while still creating a fabric that feels good and has a luxury evening look.

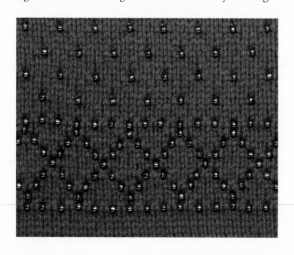

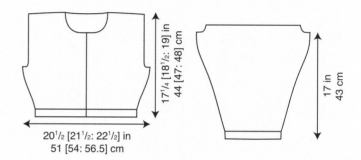

20¹⁄₂ [21¹⁄₂: 22¹⁄₂] in
51 [54: 56.5] cm

17¹⁄₄ [18¹⁄₂: 19] in
44 [47: 48] cm

17 in
43 cm

GAUGE

31 sts and 41 rows to 4 in (10 cm) measured over St st and 31 sts and 46 rows to 4 in (10 cm) measured over beaded patt, both using size 3 (3mm) needles.

SPECIAL ABBREVIATIONS

bead 1 = place a bead by taking yarn to RS of work and slipping bead up next to st just worked, slip next st purlwise from left needle to right needle and take yarn back to WS of work, leaving bead sitting in front of slipped st on RS.

Beading note: Before starting to knit, thread beads onto yarn. To do this, thread a fine sewing needle that will easily pass through the beads with sewing thread. Knot ends of thread and pass end of yarn through this loop. Thread a bead onto sewing thread, then gently slide it along and onto knitting yarn. Continue in this way until required number of beads are on yarn. Do not place beads on edge sts of rows as this will interfere with seams.

BACK

Using size 1 (2.25mm) needles, cast on 135 [143: 151] sts.
Row 1 (RS): K1, ★P1, K1, rep from ★ to end.

Row 2: Rep row 1.

These 2 rows form seed st.

Work in seed st for 10 rows more, ending with RS facing for next row.

Change to size 3 (3mm) needles.

Beg and ending rows as indicated, work in beaded patt from chart A (see page 60) as foll:

Work 10 [12: 14] rows.

Keeping patt correct, inc 1 st at each end of next and 1 [1: 0] foll 4th row. 139 [147: 153] sts.

Work 3 [1: 3] rows, thereby completing all 18 rows of chart A and ending with RS facing for next row.

Beg with a K row, cont in St st, inc 1 st at each end of next [3rd: 3rd] and 5 [1: 0] foll 4th rows, then on 4 [8: 10] foll 6th rows. 159 [167: 175] sts.

Work even until back measures 7¾ [9: 9½] in (20 [23: 24] cm), ending with RS facing for next row.

Shape armholes

Bind off 4 sts at beg of next 2 rows. 151 [159: 167] sts.

Work 2 rows.

Next row (RS): K3, K3tog tbl, K to last 6 sts, K3tog, K3.

Work 3 rows.

Rep last 4 rows once more. 143 [151: 159] sts.

Work 2 rows more, ending with RS facing for next row.

Beg and ending rows as indicated, working chart rows 1–18 **once only** and then repeating chart rows 19–26 **throughout**, cont in beaded patt from chart B as foll:

Work even until armhole measures 9½ in (24 cm), ending with RS facing for next row.

Shape shoulders and back neck

Bind off 17 [18: 19] sts at beg of next 2 rows. 109 [115: 121] sts.

Next row (RS): Bind off 17 [18: 19] sts, patt until there are 20 [22: 24] sts on right needle and turn, leaving rem sts on a holder.

KNITTER'S TIP

When working a beaded design like this one, you will be sliding the beads along the yarn all the time once they've been threaded onto the yarn. This can tend to "rough up" the yarn a little, so it's best not to thread them onto the yarn until you are ready to start knitting with them. Work up to the point where you need to start using beads and then break the yarn. Thread on the beads, rejoin the yarn, and continue knitting. Because repeatedly sliding lots of beads along the yarn can be tiresome as well as cause damage, it's often a good idea to only thread a few hundred beads onto the yarn each time. Use up these beads first and then break the yarn. Thread on more beads, rejoin the yarn, and carry on knitting. But remember—to keep your work neat, do NOT break and rejoin the yarn in the middle of a row.

Work each side of neck separately.

Bind off 4 sts at beg of row.

Bind off rem 16 [18: 20] sts.

With RS facing, rejoin yarn to rem sts, bind off center 35 sts, patt to end.

Complete to match first side, reversing shapings.

LEFT FRONT

Using size 1 (2.25mm) needles, cast on 67 [71: 75] sts.

Work in seed st as given for back for 12 rows, ending with RS facing for next row.

Change to size 3 (3mm) needles.

Beg and ending rows as indicated, work in beaded patt from chart A as foll:

Work 10 [12: 14] rows.

Keeping patt correct, inc 1 st at beg of next and 1 [1: 0] foll 4th row. 69 [73: 76] sts.

Work 3 [1: 3] rows, thereby completing all 18 rows of chart A and ending with RS facing for next row.

Beg with a K row, cont in St st, inc 1 st at beg of next [3rd: 3rd] and 5 [1: 0] foll 4th rows, then on 4 [8: 10] foll 6th rows. 79 [83: 87] sts.

Work even until left front matches back to beg of armhole shaping, ending with RS facing for next row.

Shape armhole

Bind off 4 sts at beg of next row. 75 [79: 83] sts.

Work 3 rows.

Next row (RS): K3, K3tog tbl, K to end.

Work 3 rows.

Rep last 4 rows once more. 71 [75: 79] sts.

Work 2 rows more, ending with RS facing for next row.

Beg and ending rows as indicated, working chart rows 1–18 **once only** and then repeating chart rows 19–26 **throughout**, cont in beaded patt from chart B as foll:

Work even until 27 rows less have been worked than on back to beg of shoulder shaping, ending with **WS** facing for next row.

Shape neck

Keeping patt correct, bind off 4 sts at beg of next and foll 2 alt rows. 59 [63: 67] sts.

Dec 1 st at neck edge of next 4 rows, then on foll 2 alt rows, then on 3 foll 4th rows. 50 [54: 58] sts.

Work 2 rows, ending with RS facing for next row.

Shape shoulder

Bind off 17 [18: 19] sts at beg of next and foll alt row.

Work 1 row.

Bind off rem 16 [18: 20] sts.

RIGHT FRONT

Using size 1 (2.25mm) needles, cast on 67 [71: 75] sts.

Work in seed st as given for back for 12 rows, ending with RS facing for next row.

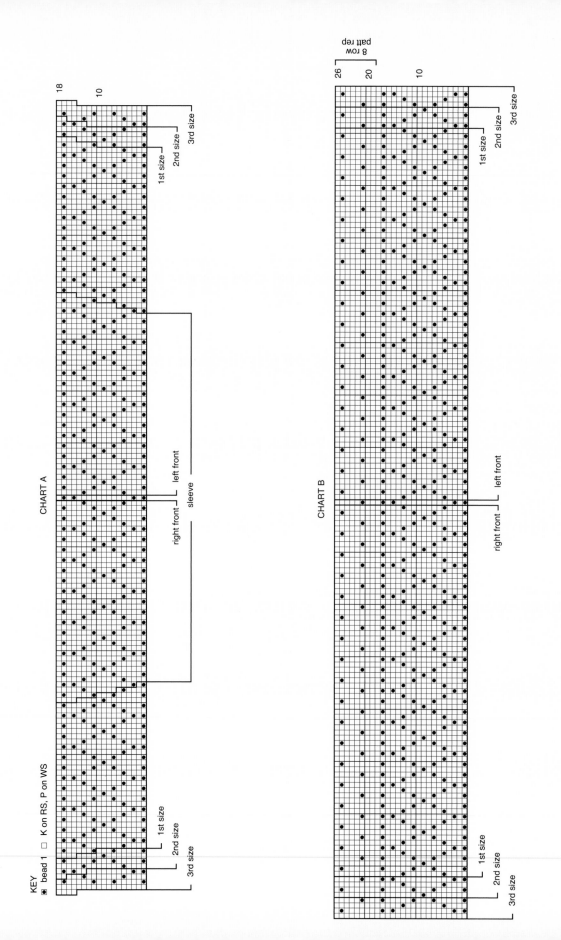

KEY
◉ bead 1   □ K on RS, P on WS

CHART A

CHART B

Change to size 3 (3mm) needles.

Beg and ending rows as indicated, work in beaded patt from chart A as foll:

Work 10 [12: 14] rows.

Keeping patt correct, inc 1 st at end of next and 1 [1: 0] foll 4th row. 69 [73: 76] sts.

Complete to match left front, reversing shapings.

SLEEVES

Using size 1 (2.25mm) needles, cast on 71 sts.

Work in seed st as given for back for 12 rows, ending with RS facing for next row.

Change to size 3 (3mm) needles.

Beg and ending rows as indicated, work in beaded patt from chart A as foll:

Inc 1 st at each end of 3rd and 3 foll 4th rows. 79 sts.

Work 3 rows, thereby completing all 18 rows of chart A and ending with RS facing for next row.

Beg with a K row, cont in St st, shaping sides by inc 1 st at each end of next and every foll 4th row to 137 sts, then on every foll alt row until there are 147 sts.

Work even until sleeve measures 17 in (43 cm), ending with RS facing for next row.

Shape sleeve cap

Bind off 4 sts at beg of next 2 rows. 139 sts.

Work 2 rows.

Next row (RS): K3, K3tog tbl, K to last 6 sts, K3tog, K3.

Work 3 rows.

Rep last 4 rows once more, ending with RS facing for next row.

Bind off rem 131 sts.

FINISHING

Press as described on page 148.

Sew both shoulder seams using backstitch, or mattress stitch if preferred.

Button band

Using size 1 (2.25mm) needles, cast on 8 sts.

Row 1 (RS): (K1, P1) 4 times.

Row 2: (P1, K1) 4 times.

These 2 rows form seed st.

Cont in seed st until button band, when slightly stretched, fits up entire left front opening edge from cast-on edge to neck shaping, ending with RS facing for next row.

Bind off in seed st.

Slip stitch button band in place.

Mark positions for 8 buttons on button band—first to come ⅜ in (1 cm) up from cast-on edge, last to come ⅜ in (1 cm) below neck shaping, and rem 6 buttons evenly spaced between.

Buttonhole band

Work as given for button band with the addition of 8 buttonholes worked to correspond with positions marked for buttons as foll:

Buttonhole row (RS): Seed st 3 sts, bind off 2 sts (to make a buttonhole—cast on 2 sts over these bound-off sts on next row), seed st to end.

When band is complete, ending with RS facing for next row, bind off in seed st.

Slip stitch buttonhole band in place.

Collar

Using size 1 (2.25mm) needles, cast on 111 sts.

Row 1 (RS): K2, *P1, K1, rep from * to last 3 sts, P1, K2.

Row 2: Rep row 1.

These 2 rows set the sts—first and last 2 sts of every row in garter st with all other sts in seed st.

Keeping sts correct as now set and taking inc sts into seed st, cont as foll:

Row 3: K2, M1, seed st to last 2 sts, M1, K2.

Row 4: K2, seed st to last 2 sts, K2.

Rep last 2 rows until collar measures 2½ in (6.5 cm), ending with **WS** facing for next row.

Bind off in patt.

Positioning ends of cast-on edge of collar halfway across top of bands, sew cast-on edge of collar to neck edge.

See page 148 for finishing instructions, setting in sleeves using the shallow set-in method.

Jester

KIM HARGREAVES

SIZES AND YARN

	S	M	L	
To fit bust	34	36	38	in
	86	91	97	cm

Rowan Wool Cotton

Longer version

| Dream 929 | 13 | 14 | 14 | x 50 g |

Cropped version

| Verdigris 972 | 11 | 12 | 12 | x 50 g |

Originally knitted and photographed (above) in the original Rowan Wool/Cotton (this yarn is slightly thicker now) in Rosemary 922, and Edina Ronay Silk and Wool in Camel 851

NEEDLES

1 pair size 1 (2.25mm) needles
1 pair size 2 (2.75mm) needles

BUTTONS—3

NEW YARN SUBSTITUTION

Although the new Rowan Wool Cotton (below) we chose for this design would normally be knitted on much bigger needles than used here, the combination of a loose stitch pattern and a thicker yarn that "squashes" down well allowed us to create the perfect fabric while achieving the correct gauge.

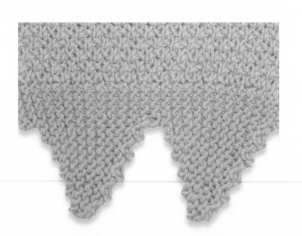

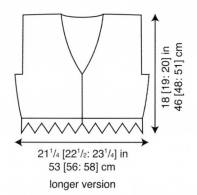

18 [19: 20] in
46 [48: 51] cm

21¼ [22½: 23¼] in
53 [56: 58] cm

longer version

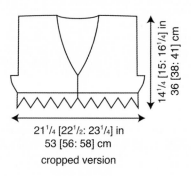

14¼ [15: 16¼] in
36 [38: 41] cm

21¼ [22½: 23¼] in
53 [56: 58] cm

cropped version

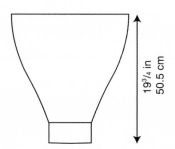

19¾ in
50.5 cm

GAUGE

28 sts and 44 rows to 4 in (10 cm) measured over patt using size 2 (2.75mm) needles.

Longer version

BACK

Using size 2 (2.75mm) needles, cast on 133 [141: 147] sts.

Row 1 (RS): Knit.

Row 2: K1, *P1, K1, rep from * to end.

Row 3: Knit.

Row 4: P1, *K1, P1, rep from * to end.

These 4 rows form patt.

Cont in patt, shaping side seams by inc 1 st at each end of 5th [5th: 7th] and every foll 8th [8th: 10th] row until there are 149 [157: 163] sts, taking inc sts into patt.

Work even until back measures 6½ [7½: 8½] in (17 [19: 22] cm), ending with RS facing for next row.

Shape armholes

Keeping patt correct, bind off 8 sts at beg of next 2 rows. 133 [141: 147] sts.

Work even until armhole measures 9 in (23 cm), ending with RS facing for next row.

Shape shoulders and back neck

Bind off 11 [12: 12] sts at beg of next 2 rows, then 11 [12: 13] sts at beg of foll 2 rows. 89 [93: 97] sts.

Next row (RS): Bind off 12 [12: 13] sts, patt until there are 16 [17: 17] sts on right needle and turn, leaving rem sts on a holder.

Work each side of neck separately.

Keeping patt correct, bind off 4 sts at beg of row.

Bind off rem 12 [13: 13] sts.

With RS facing, rejoin yarn to rem sts, bind off center 33 [35: 37] sts, patt to end.

Complete to match first side, reversing shapings.

LEFT FRONT

Using size 2 (2.75mm) needles, cast on 66 [70: 73] sts.

Row 1 (RS): Knit.

Row 2: K0 [0: 1], *P1, K1, rep from * to end.

Row 3: Knit.

Row 4: P0 [0: 1], *K1, P1, rep from * to end.

These 4 rows form patt.

Cont in patt, shaping side seam by inc 1 st at beg of 5th [5th: 7th] and every foll 8th [8th: 10th] row until there are 74 [78: 81] sts, taking inc sts into patt.

Work even until left front matches back to beg of armhole shaping, ending with RS facing for next row.

Shape armhole and front slope

Keeping patt correct, bind off 8 sts at beg and dec 1 st at end of next row. 65 [69: 72] sts.

Work 3 rows, ending with RS facing for next row.

Dec 1 st at end of next and 11 [13: 15] foll 4th rows, then on 7 [6: 5] foll 6th rows. 46 [49: 51] sts.

Work even until left front matches back to beg of shoulder shaping, ending with RS facing for next row.

Shape shoulder

Bind off 11 [12: 12] sts at beg of next row, 11 [12: 13] sts at beg of foll alt row, then 12 [12: 13] sts at beg of foll alt row.

Work 1 row.

Bind off rem 12 [13: 13] sts.

RIGHT FRONT

Using size 2 (2.75mm) needles, cast on 66 [70: 73] sts.

Row 1 (RS): Knit.

Row 2: *K1, P1, rep from * to last 0 [0: 1] st, K0 [0: 1].

Row 3: Knit.

Row 4: *P1, K1, rep from * to last 0 [0: 1] st, P0 [0: 1].

These 4 rows form patt.

Cont in patt, shaping side seam by inc 1 st at end of 5th [5th: 7th] and every foll 8th [8th: 10th] row until there are 74 [78: 81] sts, taking inc sts into patt.

Complete to match left front, reversing shapings.

SLEEVES

Using size 1 (2.25mm) needles, cast on 55 sts.

Row 1 (RS): K1, *P1, K1, rep from * to end.

Row 2: P1, *K1, P1, rep from * to end.

These 2 rows form rib.

Cont in rib until sleeve measures 3 in (7.5 cm), ending with **WS** facing for next row.

Next row (WS): (Rib 5, M1) 10 times, rib 5. 65 sts.

Change to size 2 (2.75mm) needles.

Beg with row 1, now work in patt as given for back, shaping sides by inc 1 st at each end of 3rd and every foll 4th row to 89 sts, then on every foll 6th row until there are 129 sts, taking inc sts into patt.

Work even until sleeve measures 19¾ in (50.5 cm), ending with RS facing for next row.

Bind off.

FINISHING

Press as described on page 148.

Sew both shoulder seams using backstitch, or mattress stitch if preferred.

Set sleeves into armholes using the square set-in method as explained on page 148.

Sew side and sleeve seams.

Hem border

Using size 2 (2.75mm) needles, cast on 6 sts.

Row 1 (WS): Knit.

Row 2 and every foll alt row: Knit.

Rows 3, 5, 7, 9, and 11: Cast on 2 sts at beg on row, K to end.

Row 13: Knit.

Rows 15, 17, 19, 21, and 23: Bind off 2 sts, K to end.

Row 24: Knit.

These 24 rows form patt.

Cont in patt until straight edge of hem border fits neatly along entire cast-on edges of back and fronts, ending with patt row 24. Bind off.

Slip stitch straight edge of hem border in place.

Front band

Using size 1 (2.25mm) needles, cast on 5 sts.

Beg with row 1, work in rib as given for sleeves until front band, when slightly stretched, fits up entire left front opening edge, up left front slope, across back neck, and down right front slope to beg of front slope shaping, sewing band in place as you go along.

Mark positions for 3 buttons along left front opening edge—first to come ⅜ in (1 cm) up from lower edge, last to come just below beg of front slope shaping, and rem button evenly spaced between.

Cont in rib until front band fits down left front opening edge, with the addition of 3 buttonholes worked to correspond with positions marked for buttons as foll:

Buttonhole row (RS): K1, P1, yo (to make a buttonhole), P2tog, K1.

When band is complete, ending with RS facing for next row, bind off in rib.

Slip stitch rem section of band in place.

See page 148 for finishing instructions.

Cropped version

BACK

Using size 2 (2.75mm) needles, cast on 129 [137: 143] sts.

Row 1 (RS): Knit.

Row 2: K1, *P1, K1, rep from * to end.

Row 3: Knit.

Row 4: P1, *K1, P1, rep from * to end.

These 4 rows form patt.

Cont in patt, shaping side seams by inc 1 st at each end of next [3rd: next] and every foll alt [alt: 4th] row until there are 149 [157: 163] sts, taking inc sts into patt.

Work even until back measures 2¾ [3½: 4¾] in (7 [9: 12] cm), ending with RS facing for next row.

Complete as given for back of longer version from beg of armhole shaping.

LEFT FRONT

Using size 2 (2.75mm) needles, cast on 64 [68: 71] sts.

Row 1 (RS): Knit.

Row 2: K0 [0: 1], *P1, K1, rep from * to end.

Row 3: Knit.

Row 4: P0 [0: 1], *K1, P1, rep from * to end.

These 4 rows form patt.

Cont in patt, shaping side seams by inc 1 st at beg of next [3rd: next] and every foll alt [alt: 4th] row until there are 74 [78: 81] sts, taking inc sts into patt.

Work even until left front matches back to beg of armhole shaping, ending with RS facing for next row.

Complete as given for left front of longer version from beg of armhole and front slope shaping.

RIGHT FRONT

Using size 2 (2.75mm) needles, cast on 64 [68: 71] sts.

Row 1 (RS): Knit.

Row 2: *K1, P1, rep from * to last 0 [0: 1] st, K0 [0: 1].

Row 3: Knit.

Row 4: *P1, K1, rep from * to last 0 [0: 1] st, P0 [0: 1].

These 4 rows form patt.

Cont in patt, shaping side seam by inc 1 st at end of next [3rd: next] and every foll alt [alt: 4th] row until there are 74 [78: 81] sts, taking inc sts into patt.

Complete to match left front, reversing shapings.

SLEEVES

Work as given for sleeves of longer version.

FINISHING

Work as given for longer version.

KNITTER'S TIP

The shaped edge of the hem border of this cardigan forms the actual finished lower edge. So, to help keep this edge neat and tidy, make sure you join in any new balls of yarn along the straight edge—the one that's sewn onto the garment.

Fisherman

KIM HARGREAVES

SIZES AND YARN

	S	M	L	
To fit bust	34	36	38	in
	86	91	97	cm

Rowan Pure Wool Aran

| Ivory 670 | 9 | 9 | 10 | x 100 g |

Originally knitted and photographed (above) in Rowan Magpie Aran in Natural 002

NEEDLES

1 pair size 6 (4mm) needles
1 pair size 8 (5mm) needles
Size 6 (4mm) circular needle

NEW YARN SUBSTITUTION

The original yarn for this cozy sweater is no longer available, but it was really easy to find the perfect substitute. Although the gauge is halfway between that of an aran and chunky weight yarn, Rowan Pure Wool Aran was the perfect choice. It's a nice "full" yarn that gave a good soft but stable fabric when we matched the gauge, and, of course, classic cream was available.

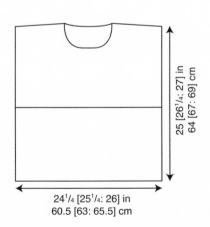

25 [26¼: 27] in
64 [67: 69] cm

24¼ [25¼: 26] in
60.5 [63: 65.5] cm

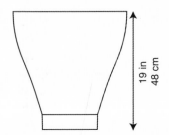

19 in
48 cm

KNITTER'S TIP

We chose a classic aran yarn as the substitute here—but you could change the look of your garment by using a yarn with a different texture. Try using Rowan Felted Tweed Aran to create a really outdoor rugged look, or sleek Rowan Classic Cashsoft Aran for a much softer smoother feel. But make sure you check your gauge.

GAUGE

17 sts and 24 rows to 4 in (10 cm) measured over St st and 17 sts and 32 rows measured over patt, both using size 8 (5mm) needles.

BACK

Using size 8 (5mm) needles, cast on 103 [107: 111] sts.
Work in garter st for 8 rows, ending with RS facing for next row.
Row 9 (RS): Knit.
Row 10: K4, P to last 4 sts, K4.
Row 11: K7 [5: 7], *K4, P1, K3, rep from * to last 8 [6: 8] sts, K8 [6: 8].
Row 12: K5 [4: 5], P3 [2: 3], *P2, K1, P1, K1, P3, rep from * to last 7 [5: 7] sts, P2 [1: 2], K5 [4: 5].
Row 13: K5, (P1, K1) 1 [0: 1] times, *K2, P1, K3, P1, K1, rep from * to last 8 [6: 8] sts, (K2, P1) 1 [0: 1] times, K5 [6: 5].
Row 14: K4, P2 [0: 2], K1, P1, *K1, P5, K1, P1, rep from * to last 7 [5: 7] sts, K1, P2 [0: 2], K4.
Row 15: K7 [5: 7], *P1, K7, rep from * to last 8 [6: 8] sts, P1, K7 [5: 7].
Row 16: Rep row 14.
Row 17: Rep row 13.
Row 18: Rep row 12.
Row 19: Rep row 11.
Row 20: Rep row 10.
Rows 21 and 22: Knit.
Row 23: Rep row 10.
Beg with a P row, now work in St st until back measures 11¾ [13: 13¾] in (30 [33: 35] cm), ending with RS facing for next row.
Now work in yoke patt as foll:
Row 1 (RS): Purl.
Rows 2 and 3: Knit.
Row 4: Purl.
Row 5: K3 [1: 3], *P1, K7, rep from * to last 4 [2: 4] sts, P1, K3 [1: 3].
Row 6: P2 [0: 2], K1, P1, *K1, P5, K1, P1, rep from * to last 3 [1: 3] sts, K1, P2 [0: 2].
Row 7: K1, (P1, K1) 1 [0: 1] times, *K2, P1, K3, P1, K1, rep from * to last 4 [2: 4] sts, K2, (P1, K1) 1 [0: 1] times.
Row 8: K1 [0: 1], P3 [2: 3], *P2, K1, P1, K1, P3, rep from * to last 3 [1: 3] sts, P2 [1: 2], K1 [0: 1].
Row 9: K3 [1: 3], *K4, P1, K3, rep from * to last 4 [2: 4] sts, K4 [2: 4].
Row 10: Rep row 8.
Row 11: Rep row 7.
Row 12: Rep row 6.
Row 13: Rep row 5.
Row 14: Purl.
Rows 15 and 16: Knit.
This completes border section of yoke patt.
Rows 17 and 18: Purl.

Rows 19 and 20: Knit.
Rows 21 and 22: Purl.
Row 23: Knit.
Row 24: K1, P2, *K2, P2, rep from * to end.
Row 25: Knit.
Row 26: P1, K2, *P2, K2, rep from * to end.
Rows 27–30: Rep rows 23–26.
Rows 31–33: Rep rows 23–25.
Rows 34 and 35: Purl.
Rows 36 and 37: Knit.
Rows 38 and 39: Purl.
Rows 40 and 41: Knit.
Row 42: Purl.
Row 43: *K2, P2, rep from * to last 3 sts, K2, P1.
Row 44: Purl.
Row 45: *P2, K2, rep from * to last 3 sts, P2, K1.
Rows 46–49: Rep rows 42–45.
Rows 50–52: Rep rows 42–44.
Rows 17–52 form patt for rest of yoke.
Repeating rows 17–52 **only**, cont in yoke patt until back measures 24¾ [26: 26¾] in (63 [66: 68] cm), ending with RS facing for next row.
Shape back neck
Next row (RS): Patt 40 [42: 44] sts and turn, leaving rem sts on a holder.
Work each side of neck separately.
Keeping patt correct, bind off 4 sts at beg of row.
Break off yarn and leave rem 36 [38: 40] sts on a holder.
With RS facing, rejoin yarn to rem sts, bind off center 23 sts, patt to end.
Complete to match first side, reversing shapings.

FRONT

Work as given for back until 22 rows less have been worked than on back to beg of back neck shaping, ending with RS facing for next row.
Shape neck
Next row (RS): Patt 47 [49: 51] sts and turn, leaving rem sts on a holder.
Work each side of neck separately.
Keeping patt correct, dec 1 st at neck edge of next 6 rows, then on foll 5 alt rows. 36 [38: 40] sts.
Work 7 rows, ending with RS facing for next row.
Break off yarn and leave rem 36 [38: 40] sts on a holder.
With RS facing, rejoin yarn to rem sts, bind off center 9 sts, patt to end.
Complete to match first side, reversing shapings.

SLEEVES

Using size 6 (4mm) needles, cast on 42 sts.
Beg with a K row, work in St st for 6 rows, ending with

RS facing for next row.

Row 7 (RS): K2, *P2, K2, rep from * to end.

Row 8: P2, *K2, P2, rep from * to end.

Rows 7 and 8 form rib.

Cont in rib until sleeve measures 2½ in (6 cm) **allowing first few rows to roll to RS**, inc 1 st at end of last row and ending with RS facing for next row. 43 sts.

Change to size 8 (5mm) needles.

Work in garter st for 4 rows, inc 1 st at each end of 3rd of these rows. 45 sts.

Beg with a K row, work in St st for 2 rows.

Now work cuff border patt as foll:

Row 1 (RS): Inc in first st, K5, (P1, K7) 4 times, P1, K5, inc in last st. 47 sts.

Row 2: (K1, P5, K1, P1) 5 times, K1, P5, K1.

Row 3: K1, (P1, K3) 11 times, P1, K1.

Row 4: P2, (K1, P1, K1, P5) 5 times, K1, P1, K1, P2.

Row 5: Inc in first st, K2, (P1, K7) 5 times, P1, K2, inc in last st. 49 sts.

Row 6: P3, (K1, P1, K1, P5) 5 times, K1, P1, K1, P3.

Row 7: K2, (P1, K3) 11 times, P1, K2.

Row 8: P1, (K1, P5, K1, P1) 6 times.

Row 9: Inc in first st, (K7, P1) 5 times, K7, inc in last st. 51 sts.

Row 10: Purl.

Rows 11 and 12: Knit.

Row 13: Inc in first st, P to last st, inc in last st. 53 sts.

These 13 rows complete cuff border patt.

Beg with a P row, cont in St st, shaping sides by inc 1 st at each end of 4th and 8 foll 4th rows, then on 3 foll 6th rows. 77 sts.

Work 1 row, ending with RS facing for next row.

Now work sleeve top border patt as foll:

Row 1 (RS): Purl.

Rows 2 and 3: Knit.

Row 4: Purl.

Row 5: Inc in first st, K5, (P1, K7) 8 times, P1, K5, inc in last st. 79 sts.

Row 6: (K1, P5, K1, P1) 9 times, K1, P5, K1.

Row 7: K1, (P1, K3) 19 times, P1, K1.

Row 8: P2, (K1, P1, K1, P5) 9 times, K1, P1, K1, P2.

Row 9: K3, (P1, K7) 9 times, P1, K3.

Row 10: Rep row 8.

Row 11: Inc in first st, (P1, K3) 19 times, P1, inc in last st. 81 sts.

Row 12: (P1, K1, P5, K1) 10 times, P1.

Row 13: (P1, K7) 10 times, P1.

Row 14: Purl.

Rows 15 and 16: Knit.

Row 17: Inc in first st, P to last st, inc in last st. 83 sts.

Row 18: Purl.

Rows 19 and 20: Knit.

Rows 21 and 22: Purl.

Row 23: Inc in first st, K to last st, inc in last st. 85 sts.

Row 24: Purl.

Row 25: K1, (P2, K2) 21 times.

Row 26: Purl.

Row 27: P1, (K2, P2) 21 times.

Rows 28–31: Rep rows 24–27.

Rows 32–34: Rep rows 24–26.

Row 35: Purl.

Row 36: Knit.

These 36 rows complete sleeve top border patt.

Beg with a K row, work in St st for 4 rows, ending with RS facing for next row.

Bind off.

FINISHING

Press as described on page 148.

Join right shoulder seam as foll:

Slip sts left on front and back right shoulder holders onto spare needles with points of both needles at side seam edge. Using a 3rd needle and holding front and back tog with WS facing, rejoin yarn and K tog first st of back with first st of front, *K tog next st of back with next st of front, lift 2nd st on right needle over first st and off right needle, rep from * to end, fastening off last st.

Join left shoulder seam in same way.

Neckband

With RS facing and using size 6 (4mm) circular needle, pick up and knit 21 sts down left side of neck, 9 sts from front, 21 sts up right side of neck, then 33 sts from back. 84 sts.

Round 1 (RS): *K2, P2, rep from * to end.

Rep this round 10 times more.

Round 12: Knit.

Rep last round 7 times more.

Bind off.

See page 148 for finishing instructions, setting in sleeves using the straight bind-off method, reversing seam for first 6 rows of sleeve (for St st roll) and leaving side seams open for first 23 rows.

Sugar Plum

LOUISA HARDING

SIZE AND YARN

One size

Rowan Pure Wool DK

A	Avocado	019	4	x 50 g
B	Port	037	3	x 50 g
C	Indigo	010	5	x 50 g
D	Damson	030	5	x 50 g
E	Marine	008	3	x 50 g
F	Pomegranate	029	4	x 50 g

Originally knitted and photographed (above) in Rowan Designer DK in shades 660, 661, 672, 659, 663, and 70

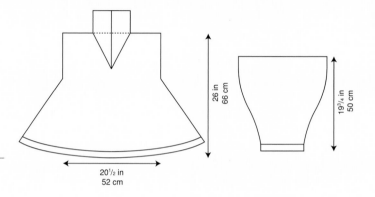

NEEDLES

1 pair size 3 (3.25mm) needles
1 pair size 6 (4mm) needles
Cable needle

NEW YARN SUBSTITUTIONS

In theory, this should be a really easy design to find a substitute yarn for, as the gauge is that of a standard double-knitting-weight yarn. But we wanted to keep the colors as close to the original as possible, so we chose Rowan Pure Wool DK. This yarn comes in a myriad of different colors, so we didn't really have any problems finding shades that worked together.

GAUGE

22 sts and 30 rows to 4 in (10 cm) measured over St st using size 6 (4mm) needles.

SPECIAL ABBREVIATIONS

Cr3L = slip next 2 sts onto cable needle and leave at front of work, P1, then K2 from cable needle; **Cr3R** = slip next st onto cable needle and leave at back of work, K2, then P1 from cable needle; **C2F** = slip next st onto cable needle and leave at front of work, K1, then K1 from cable needle; **C4F** = slip next 2 sts onto cable needle and leave at front of work, K2, then K2 from cable needle; **C3B** = slip next st onto cable needle and leave at back of work, K2, then K1 from cable needle; **C3F** = slip next 2 sts onto cable needle and leave at front of work, K1, then K2

from cable needle; **MB** = make bobble as foll—K into front, back, and front again of next st, (turn, K3) 3 times, turn, sl 1, K2tog, psso.

Pattern note: Back and front are worked in vertical stripes of color. Use a separate ball of yarn for each vertical stripe, twisting yarns together where they meet on WS to avoid holes forming.

BACK

Using size 3 (3.25mm) needles, cast on as foll—using yarn E cast on 40 sts, using yarn C cast on 40 sts, using yarn D cast on 40 sts, using yarn B cast on 40 sts, using yarn F cast on 40 sts, using yarn A cast on 40 sts. 240 sts.

Keeping colors correct as set by cast-on edge, work in garter st for 11 rows, ending with **WS** facing for next row.

Row 12 (WS): Keeping colors correct as set, (K18, M1, K4, M1, K18) 6 times. 252 sts.

Change to size 6 (4mm) needles.

Next row (RS): Using yarn F K42, using yarn B K42, using yarn D K42, using yarn C K42, using yarn E K42, using yarn A K42.

Next row: Using yarn A P42, using yarn E P42, using yarn C P42, using yarn D P42, using yarn B P42, using yarn F P42.

As this garment is knitted in vertical bands of color, it's really important that you remember to twist the two colors together where they meet so that holes don't appear along the line between the colors. To do this, work up to the color-change point in the row and let this color drop. Now pick up the next color, taking it under and around the previous color, so that the previous color is "caught" in the edge of the first stitch in the new color. But take care when you work back across the stitches—don't pull the edge stitches of each color too tight or you will distort your knitting and create messy lines along the color joins.

These 2 rows set position of vertical stripes for rest of back. Keeping vertical stripes correct, now work in patt as foll:

Row 1 (RS): ★K11, P1, (K2, P2) 4 times, K2, P1, K11, rep from ★ to end.

Row 2: ★P11, K1, (P2, K2) 4 times, P2, K1, P11, rep from ★ to end.

Row 3: ★K11, (P1, Cr3L) twice, P1, C2F, P1, (Cr3R, P1) twice, K11, rep from ★ to end.

Row 4: ★P11, (K2, P2) twice, K1, P2, K1, (P2, K2) twice, P11, rep from ★ to end.

Row 5: ★K11, P2, Cr3L, P1, Cr3L, K2, Cr3R, P1, Cr3R, P2, K11, rep from ★ to end.

Row 6: ★P11, K3, P2, K2, P6, K2, P2, K3, P11, rep from ★ to end.

Row 7: ★K11, P3, Cr3L, P1, Cr3L, Cr3R, P1, Cr3R, P3, K11, rep from ★ to end.

Row 8: ★P11, K4, P2, K2, P4, K2, P2, K4, P11, rep from ★ to end.

Row 9: ★K11, P2, MB, P1, K2, P2, C4F, P2, K2, P1, MB, P2, K11, rep from ★ to end.

Row 10: Rep row 8.

Row 11: ★K11, P3, Cr3R, P1, C3B, C3F, P1, Cr3L, P3, K11, rep from ★ to end.

Row 12: Rep row 6.

Row 13: ★K11, P2, Cr3R, P1, Cr3R, K2, Cr3L, P1, Cr3L, P2, K11, rep from ★ to end.

Row 14: Rep row 4.

Row 15: ★K11, (P1, Cr3R) twice, P1, C2F, P1, (Cr3L, P1) twice, K11, rep from ★ to end.

Row 16: ★P11, place marker on needle, K1, (P2, K2) 4 times, P2, K1, place marker on needle, P11, rep from ★ to end.
These 16 rows form patt.
Keeping patt and colors correct and slipping markers from left needle to right needle on every row, cont as foll:

Row 17 (RS): (K to within 2 sts of marker, sl 1, K1, psso, slip marker onto right needle, patt to next marker, slip marker onto

right needle, K2tog) 6 times, K to end. 240 sts.
Work 15 rows.
Rep last 16 rows 6 times more, then row 17 again. 156 sts.
Work even until all 16 patt rows have been worked 12 times in total, ending with RS facing for next row.
Work 3 rows, ending with **WS** facing for next row.

Shape shoulders
Next row (WS): ★P3, (K2, P2tog) twice, K1, P2, K1, (P2tog, K2) twice, P3, rep from ★ to end.
Bind off rem 132 sts, placing markers either side of center 44 sts to denote back neck.

FRONT
Work as given for back until all 16 patt rows have been worked 8 times in total, ending with RS facing for next row.
Work 6 rows, ending with RS facing for next row.

Shape for collar
Next row (RS): Patt 77 sts, place marker on needle, using yarn A K1, using yarn F K1, place 2nd marker on needle, patt 77 sts.
Next row: Patt to marker, slip marker onto right needle, using yarn F P1, using yarn A P1, slip marker onto right needle, patt to end.
Move markers 1 st closer to side edges (4 sts now between markers).
Next row (RS): Patt to marker, slip marker onto right needle, using yarn A K2, using yarn F K2, slip marker onto right needle, patt to end.
Next row: Patt to marker, slip marker onto right needle, using yarn F P2, using yarn A P2, slip marker onto right needle, patt to end.
Move markers 1 st closer to side edges (6 sts now between markers).
Next row (RS): Patt to marker, slip marker onto right needle, using yarn A K3, using yarn F K3, slip marker onto right needle, patt to end.
Next row: Patt to marker, slip marker onto right needle, using yarn F P3, using yarn A P3, slip marker onto right needle, patt to end.
Move markers 1 st closer to side edges (8 sts now between markers).

Divide for neck
Row 1 (RS): Patt to marker, slip marker onto right needle, using yarn A K2, inc twice in next st, K1 and turn, leaving rem sts on a holder. 80 sts.
Work each side of neck separately.
Row 2: Using yarn A K2, P4, slip marker onto right needle, patt to end.
Move marker 1 st closer to side edge.
Row 3: Patt to marker, slip marker onto right needle, using yarn A K3, inc twice in next st, K1, P2. 82 sts.
Row 4: Using yarn A K2, P2, K2, P3, slip marker onto right

needle, patt to end.

Move marker 1 st closer to side edge.

Row 5: Patt to marker, slip marker onto right needle, using yarn A K4, P2, K2, P2.

Row 6: Using yarn A K2, P2, K2, P4, slip marker onto right needle, patt to end.

Last 2 rows set the sts—working from side seam edge: sts up to marker in patt, first 3 sts beyond marker in St st using yarn A, then rem sts at front opening edge in 2x2 rib using yarn A.

Moving marker one st closer to side seam edge after every WS row and keeping sts correct, cont as set until there are 52 sts in patt beyond marker and 30 sts in St st and rib using yarn A. Remove marker.

Cont as set until front matches back to shoulder dec row, ending with **WS** facing for next row.

Shape shoulder

Next row (WS): Patt 30 sts, *P3, (K2, P2tog) twice, K1, P2, K1, (P2tog, K2) twice, P3, rep from * once more. 74 sts.

Bind off 44 sts at beg of next row. 30 sts.

Cont as set on these 30 sts only for 4¾ in (12 cm) more for back collar extension, ending with RS facing for next row. Bind off in patt.

With RS facing, rejoin yarns to rem sts and cont as foll:

Row 1 (RS): Using yarn F K1, inc twice in next st, K2, slip marker onto right needle, patt to end. 80 sts.

Row 2: Patt to marker, slip marker onto right needle, using yarn F P4, K2.

Move marker 1 st closer to side edge.

Row 3: Using yarn F P2, K1, inc twice in next st, K3, slip marker onto right needle, patt to end.

Row 4: Patt to marker, slip marker onto right needle, using yarn F P3, K2, P2, K2.

Move marker 1 st closer to side edge.

Row 5: Using yarn F P2, K2, P2, K4, slip marker onto right needle, patt to end.

Row 6: Patt to marker, slip marker onto right needle, using yarn F P4, K2, P2, K2.

Last 2 rows set the sts—working from side seam edge: sts up to marker in patt, first 3 sts beyond marker in St st using yarn F, then rem sts at front opening edge in 2x2 rib using yarn F. Complete to match first side, reversing shapings.

LEFT SLEEVE

Using size 3 (3.25mm) needles and yarn F, cast on 50 sts.

Work in garter st for 11 rows, ending with **WS** facing for next row.

Row 12 (WS): K23, M1, K4, M1, K23. 52 sts.

Change to size 6 (4mm) needles.

Break off yarn F and join in yarn C.

Beg with a K row, work in St st for 2 rows, ending with RS facing for next row.

Now work in patt as foll:

Row 1 (RS): K16, P1, (K2, P2) 4 times, K2, P1, K16.

Row 2: P16, K1, (P2, K2) 4 times, P2, K1, P to end.

Row 3: K16, (P1, Cr3L) twice, P1, C2F, P1, (Cr3R, P1) twice, K to end.

Row 4: P16, (K2, P2) twice, K1, P2, K1, (P2, K2) twice, P to end.

Row 5: Inc in first st, K15, P2, Cr3L, P1, Cr3L, K2, Cr3R, P1, Cr3R, P2, K to last st, inc in last st. 54 sts.

Row 6: P17, K3, P2, K2, P6, K2, P2, K3, P to end.

Row 7: K17, P3, Cr3L, P1, Cr3L, Cr3R, P1, Cr3R, P3, K to end.

Row 8: P17, K4, P2, K2, P4, K2, P2, K4, P to end.

Row 9: Inc in first st, K16, P2, MB, P1, K2, P2, C4F, P2, K2, P1, MB, P2, K to last st, inc in last st. 56 sts.

Row 10: P18, K4, P2, K2, P4, K2, P2, K4, P to end.

Row 11: K18, P3, Cr3R, P1, C3B, C3F, P1, Cr3L, P3, K to end.

Row 12: P18, K3, P2, K2, P6, K2, P2, K3, P to end.

Row 13: Inc in first st, K17, P2, Cr3R, P1, Cr3R, K2, Cr3L, P1, Cr3L, P2, K to last st, inc in last st. 58 sts.

Row 14: P19, (K2, P2) twice, K1, P2, K1, (P2, K2) twice, P to end.

Row 15: K19, (P1, Cr3R) twice, P1, C2F, P1, (Cr3L, P1) twice, K to end.

Row 16: P19, K1, (P2, K2) 4 times, P2, K1, P to end.

These 16 rows form patt and beg sleeve shaping.

Cont in patt, shaping sides by inc 1 st at each end of next and every foll 4th row until there are 116 sts.

Work even until all 16 patt rows have been worked 9 times in total, ending with RS facing for next row.

Work 6 rows, ending with RS facing for next row.

Bind off.

RIGHT SLEEVE

Work as given for left sleeve, **but** using yarn A instead of yarn F, and yarn D instead of yarn C.

FINISHING

Press as described on page 148.

Sew both shoulder seams using backstitch, or mattress stitch if preferred.

Sew together bound-off edges of back collar extensions, then sew one edge to back neck.

See page 148 for finishing instructions, setting in sleeves using the straight bind-off method.

Russian Jacket

LOUISA HARDING

SIZES AND YARN

		S	M	L	
To fit bust		34	36	38	in
		86	91	97	cm

Rowan Scottish Tweed DK and Kid Classic

A	Twd	Oatmeal	025	17	17	18	x 50 g
B	Kid	Tattoo	856	1	1	1	x 50 g
C	Kid	Nightly	846	1	1	1	x 50 g
D	Kid	Spruce	853	1	1	1	x 50 g
E	Kid	Teal	862	1	1	1	x 50 g

Originally knitted and photographed (above) in Rowan Fox Tweed DK in Wren 850 (A), Rowan Kid Silk in Steel Blue 991 (B), Holly 990 (D), and Opal 976 (E), and Rowan Designer DK in Airforce 65 (C).

NEEDLES

1 pair size 3 (3.25mm) needles
1 pair size 6 (4mm) needles
1 pair size 9 (5.5mm) needles
1 pair size 10½ (6.5mm) needles

BUTTONS—4

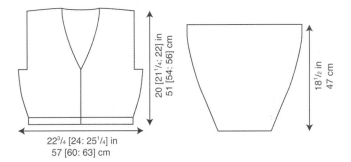

20 [21¼: 22] in
51 [54: 56] cm

22¾ [24: 25¼] in
57 [60: 63] cm

18½ in
47 cm

NEW YARN SUBSTITUTIONS

This jacket uses the same yarn for the body as for the colorwork collar and cuffs. But, to create a thicker, firmer fabric for the main sections, the yarn is used double here. Our substitute choice of Rowan Scottish Tweed DK works perfectly as a replacement, echoing both the feel and color effect of the original yarn. Extra texture is added by working the colorful scrolling leaves, tendrils, and flowers that adorn the collar and cuffs in fluffy Rowan Kid Classic on the Scottish Tweed DK background (right). However, if you wanted, you could choose shades of Scottish Tweed DK for these areas, too, making the entire jacket tweedy.

GAUGE

Body: 13 sts and 19 rows to 4 in (10 cm) measured over St st using size 10½ (6.5mm) needles and yarn A DOUBLE.

Collar and cuffs: 21 sts and 28 rows to 4 in (10 cm) measured over patterned St st using size 6 (4mm) needles and yarns A, B, C, D, and E SINGLE.

Pattern note: Back, front, and sleeves are knitted using TWO strands of yarn A held together throughout. Collar and cuffs are knitted using ONE strand of yarn throughout.

BACK

Using size 9 (5.5mm) needles and yarn A DOUBLE, cast on 63 [67: 71] sts.

Row 1 (RS): K1, *P1, K1, rep from * to end.

Row 2: Rep row 1.

These 2 rows form seed st.

Work in seed st for 4 rows more, inc 1 st at end of last row and ending with RS facing for next row. 64 [68: 72] sts.

Change to size 10½ (6.5mm) needles.

Beg with a K row, work in St st, inc 1 st at each end of 3rd and 4 foll 10th rows. 74 [78: 82] sts.

Work even until back measures 9¾ [11: 11¾] in (25 [28: 30] cm), ending with RS facing for next row.

Shape armholes

Bind off 5 sts at beg of next 2 rows. 64 [68: 72] sts.

Work even until armhole measures 10¼ in (26 cm), ending with RS facing for next row.

Shape shoulders and back neck

Bind off 7 [8: 8] sts at beg of next 2 rows. 50 [52: 56] sts.

Next row (RS): Bind off 7 [8: 8] sts, K until there are 9 [9: 11] sts on right needle and turn, leaving rem sts on a holder.

Work each side of neck separately.

Bind off 2 sts at beg of row.

Bind off rem 7 [7: 9] sts.

With RS facing, rejoin yarn to rem sts, bind off center 18 sts, K to end.

Complete to match first side, reversing shapings.

LEFT FRONT

Using size 9 (5.5mm) needles and yarn A DOUBLE, cast on 31 [33: 35] sts.

Work in seed st as given for back for 6 rows, inc 1 st at end of last row and ending with RS facing for next row. 32 [34: 36] sts.

Change to size 10½ (6.5mm) needles.

Beg with a K row, work in St st, inc 1 st at beg of 3rd and 4 foll 10th rows. 37 [39: 41] sts.

Work even until left front matches back to beg of armhole shaping, ending with RS facing for next row.

Shape armhole and front slope

Bind off 5 sts at beg and dec 1 st at end of next row. 31 [33: 35] sts.

Dec 1 st at end of 4th and every foll 4th row until 21 [23: 25] sts rem.

Work even until left front matches back to beg of shoulder shaping, ending with RS facing for next row.

Shape shoulder

Bind off 7 [8: 8] sts at beg of next and foll alt row.

Work 1 row.

Bind off rem 7 [7: 9] sts.

RIGHT FRONT

Using size 9 (5.5mm) needles and yarn A DOUBLE, cast on 31 [33: 35] sts.

Work in seed st as given for back for 6 rows, inc 1 st at beg of last row and ending with RS facing for next row. 32 [34: 36] sts.

Change to size 10½ (6.5mm) needles.

Beg with a K row, work in St st, inc 1 st at end of 3rd and 4 foll 10th rows. 37 [39: 41] sts.

Complete to match left front, reversing shapings.

SLEEVES

Using size 10½ (6.5mm) needles and yarn A DOUBLE, cast on 30 sts.

Beg with a K row, work in St st, shaping sides by inc 1 st at each end of 7th and every foll 4th row until there are 68 sts.

Work even until sleeve measures 18½ in (47 cm), ending with RS facing for next row.

Bind off.

COLLAR

Using size 6 (4mm) needles and yarn A SINGLE, cast on 76 sts. Beg and ending rows as indicated and using the **intarsia** technique as described on page 148, work in patt from chart, which is worked entirely in St st beg with a K row, as foll:

Work 1 row.

Cast on 3 sts at beg of next 6 rows, taking extra sts into patt. 94 sts.

Inc 1 st at each end of next 38 rows, ending with **WS** facing for next row. 170 sts.

Keeping chart correct, now shape outer edge of collar as foll:

Row 46 (WS): Patt 162 sts, wrap next st (by slipping next st from left needle to right needle, taking yarn to opposite side of work between needles and then slipping same st back onto left needle—when working back across wrapped sts, work the wrapped st and the wrapping loop tog as one st) and turn.

Row 47: Patt 154 sts, wrap next st and turn.
Row 48: Patt 148 sts, wrap next st and turn.
Row 49: Patt 142 sts, wrap next st and turn.
Row 50: Patt 136 sts, wrap next st and turn.
Row 51: Patt 130 sts, wrap next st and turn.
Row 52: Patt 124 sts, wrap next st and turn.
Row 53: Patt 118 sts, wrap next st and turn.
Row 54: Patt 114 sts, wrap next st and turn.
Row 55: Patt 110 sts, wrap next st and turn.
Row 56: Patt 106 sts, wrap next st and turn.
Row 57: Patt 102 sts, wrap next st and turn.
Row 58: Patt 98 sts, wrap next st and turn.
Row 59: Patt 94 sts, wrap next st and turn.
Row 60: Patt 90 sts, wrap next st and turn.
Row 61: Patt 86 sts, wrap next st and turn.
Break off contrasting yarn and cont using yarn A SINGLE **only**.
Row 62: Purl to end.
Row 63: Purl to end (to form fold line).
Row 64: P86, wrap next st and turn.
Row 65: K90, wrap next st and turn.
Row 66: P94, wrap next st and turn.
Row 67: K98, wrap next st and turn.
Row 68: P102, wrap next st and turn.
Row 69: K106, wrap next st and turn.
Row 70: P110, wrap next st and turn.
Row 71: K114, wrap next st and turn.
Row 72: P118, wrap next st and turn.
Row 73: K124, wrap next st and turn.
Row 74: P130, wrap next st and turn.
Row 75: K136, wrap next st and turn.
Row 76: P142, wrap next st and turn.
Row 77: K148, wrap next st and turn.
Row 78: P154, wrap next st and turn.
Row 79: K162, wrap next st and turn.
Row 80: Purl to end.
Change to size 3 (3.25mm) needles.
Dec 1 st at each end of next 38 rows, ending with RS facing for
next row. 94 sts.
Bind off 3 sts at beg of next 6 rows.
Bind off rem 76 sts.

CUFFS (both alike)

Using size 6 (4mm) needles and yarn A SINGLE, cast on 56 sts.
Beg and ending rows as indicated, beg with chart row 17 and
using the **intarsia** technique as described on page 148, work in
patt from chart, which is worked entirely in St st beg with a K
row, as foll:
Work 2 rows.
Inc 1 st at each end of next and 4 foll 5th rows, taking inc sts
into patt. 66 sts.

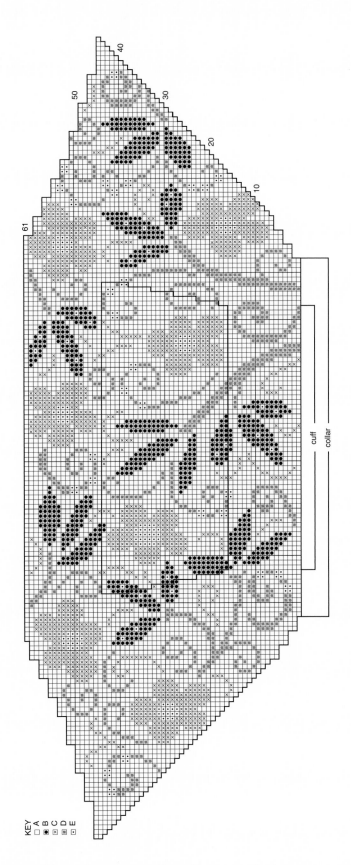

Work 5 rows, ending after chart row 44 and with RS facing for next row.

Break off contrasting yarns and cont using yarn A SINGLE **only**.

Row 29: Knit.

Row 30: Knit (to form fold line).

Change to size 3 (3.25mm) needles.

Beg with a K row, work in St st, dec 1 st at each end of 6th and 4 foll 5th rows. 56 sts.

Work 2 rows, ending with RS facing for next row. Bind off.

FINISHING

Press as described on page 148.

Sew both shoulder seams using backstitch, or mattress stitch if preferred.

Button band

Using size 10½ (6.5mm) needles and yarn A DOUBLE, cast on 6 sts.

Row 1 (RS): (K1, P1) 3 times.

Row 2: (P1, K1) 3 times.

These 2 rows form seed st.

Cont in seed st until button band, when slightly stretched, fits up left front opening edge from cast-on edge to a point 10 rows below beg of front slope shaping, ending with RS facing for next row.

Dec 1 st at end of next and foll 4 alt rows. 1 st.

Work 1 row, ending with RS facing for next row.

Fasten off.

Slip stitch button band in place.

Mark positions for 4 buttons on button band—first to come 1¾ in (4.5 cm) up from cast-on edge, last to come ⅜ in (1 cm) below beg of band shaping, and rem 2 buttons evenly spaced between.

Buttonhole band

Work to match button band with the addition of 4 buttonholes worked to correspond with positions marked for buttons as foll:

Buttonhole row (RS): Seed st 2 sts, bind off 2 sts (to make a buttonhole—cast on 2 sts over these bound-off sts on next row), seed st to end.

When band is complete, ending with RS facing for next row, fasten off.

Slip stitch buttonhole band in place.

See page 148 for finishing instructions, setting in sleeves using the square set-in method.

Sew together row-end edges of cuffs to form tubes. Fold cuffs along fold-line rows, then sew cast-on and bound-off edges of cuffs to cast-on edges of sleeves.

Positioning ends of fold-line row of collar level with first dec on bands, sew shaped row-end and bound-off edges of plain section of collar to front slope and back neck edges. Fold collar in half along fold-line row and slip stitch shaped row-end and bound-off edges of patterned section in place.

René

LOUISA HARDING

SIZES AND YARN

	S	M	L	
To fit bust	34	36	38	in
	86	91	97	cm

Rowan Pure Wool 4-Ply

| Port 437 | 5 | 6 | 6 | x 50 g |

Originally knitted and photographed (above) in Rowan
True 4-ply Botany in Plum 547

NEEDLES

1 pair size 2 (2.75mm) needles
1 pair size 3 (3.25mm) needles

BUTTONS—7

BEADS—approx 2,050 small pewter glass beads

NEW YARN SUBSTITUTION

The substitute yarn we have chosen here is identical to the
original yarn—it's a super-fine pure wool yarn. If you want to
knit your cardigan in a different color, Rowan Pure Wool 4-Ply
(below) comes in such a wide range of shades you should have
no problem finding a color that you like.

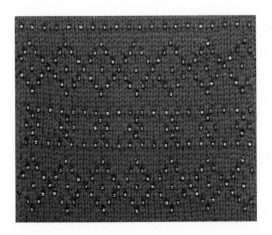

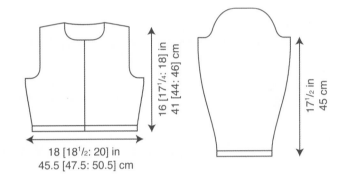

16 [17¼: 18] in
41 [44: 46] cm

18 [18½: 20] in
45.5 [47.5: 50.5] cm

17½ in
45 cm

GAUGE

28 sts and 36 rows to 4 in (10 cm) measured over St st using
size 3 (3.25mm) needles.

SPECIAL ABBREVIATIONS

bead 1 = place a bead by taking yarn to RS of work and
slipping bead up next to st just worked, slip next st purlwise
from left needle to right needle and take yarn back to WS of
work, leaving bead sitting in front of slipped st on RS.

Beading note: Before starting to knit, thread beads onto yarn.
To do this, thread a fine sewing needle (one that will easily pass
through the beads) with sewing thread. Knot ends of thread and
then pass end of yarn through this loop. Thread a bead onto
sewing thread and then gently slide it along and onto knitting
yarn. Continue in this way until required number of beads are
on yarn. Do not place beads on edge sts of rows as this will
interfere with seams.

BACK

Using size 2 (2.75mm) needles, cast on 115 [121: 129] sts.

Row 1 (RS): K1, *P1, K1, rep from * to end.

Row 2: Rep row 1.

These 2 rows form seed st.

Work in seed st for 6 rows more, ending with RS facing for next row.

Change to size 3 (3.25mm) needles.

Beg and ending rows as indicated, work in beaded patt from chart as foll:

Work 2 rows.

Inc 1 st at each end of next and 4 foll 10th rows. 125 [131: 139] sts.

Work 9 rows, thereby completing all 52 rows of chart and ending with RS facing for next row.

Beg with a K row, cont in St st, inc 1 st at each end of next row. 127 [133: 141] sts.

Work even until back measures 7¾ [9: 9¾] in (20 [23: 25] cm), ending with RS facing for next row.

Shape armholes

Bind off 4 sts at beg of next 2 rows, then 3 sts at beg of foll 4 rows. 107 [113: 121] sts.

Dec 1 st at each end of next 2 rows, then on foll 3 [4: 6] alt rows. 97 [101: 105] sts.

Work even until armhole measures 8¼ in (21 cm), ending with RS facing for next row.

Shape shoulders and back neck

Bind off 6 [6: 7] sts at beg of next 4 rows. 73 [77: 77] sts.

Next row (RS): Bind off 6 [6: 7] sts, K until there are 13 [15: 14] sts on right needle and turn, leaving rem sts on a holder. Work each side of neck separately.

Dec 1 st at neck edge of next 3 rows **and at same time** bind off 5 [6: 6] sts at beg of 2nd of these rows.

Bind off rem 5 [6: 5] sts.

With RS facing, rejoin yarn to rem sts, bind off center 35 sts, K to end.

Complete to match first side, reversing shapings.

LEFT FRONT

Using size 2 (2.75mm) needles, cast on 64 [67: 71] sts.

Row 1 (RS): *K1, P1, rep from * to last 0 [1: 1] st, K0 [1: 1].

Row 2: K0 [1: 1], *P1, K1, rep from * to end.

These 2 rows form seed st.

Work in seed st for 5 rows more, ending with **WS** facing for next row.

Row 8 (WS): Seed st 5 sts and slip these sts onto a holder, seed st to end. 59 [62: 66] sts.

Change to size 3 (3.25mm) needles.

Beg and ending rows as indicated, work in beaded patt from chart as foll:

Work 2 rows.

Inc 1 st at beg of next and 4 foll 10th rows. 64 [67: 71] sts.

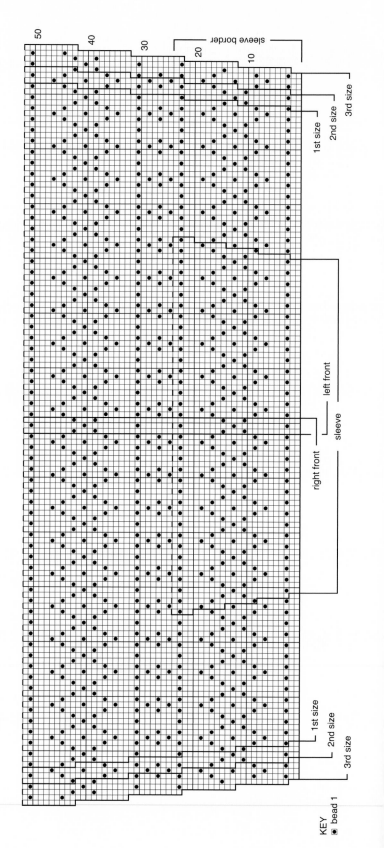

KEY
• bead 1

Work 9 rows, thereby completing all 52 rows of chart and ending with RS facing for next row.

Beg with a K row, cont in St st, inc 1 st at beg of next row. 65 [68: 72] sts.

Work even until left front matches back to beg of armhole shaping, ending with RS facing for next row.

Shape armhole

Bind off 4 sts at beg of next row, then 3 sts at beg of foll 2 alt rows. 55 [58: 62] sts.

Work 1 row.

Dec 1 st at armhole edge of next 2 rows, then on foll 3 [4: 6] alt rows. 50 [52: 54] sts.

Work even until 19 rows less have been worked than on back to beg of shoulder shaping, ending with **WS** facing for next row.

Shape neck

Bind off 7 sts at beg of next row, then 6 sts at beg of foll alt row. 37 [39: 41] sts.

Dec 1 st at neck edge of next 4 rows, then on foll 5 alt rows. 28 [30: 32] sts.

Work 2 rows, ending with RS facing for next row.

Shape shoulder

Bind off 6 [6: 7] sts at beg of next and foll 2 alt rows, then 5 [6: 6] sts at beg of foll alt row.

Work 1 row.

Bind off rem 5 [6: 5] sts.

RIGHT FRONT

Using size 2 (2.75mm) needles, cast on 64 [67: 71] sts.

Row 1 (RS): K0 [1: 1], *P1, K1, rep from * to end.

Row 2: *K1, P1, rep from * to last 0 [1: 1] st, K0 [1: 1].

These 2 rows form seed st.

Work in seed st for 5 rows more, ending with **WS** facing for next row.

Row 8 (WS): Seed st to last 5 sts and turn, leaving rem 5 sts on a holder. 59 [62: 66] sts.

Change to size 3 (3.25mm) needles.

Beg and ending rows as indicated, work in beaded patt from chart as foll:

Work 2 rows.

Inc 1 st at end of next and 4 foll 10th rows. 64 [67: 71] sts.

Complete to match left front, reversing shapings.

SLEEVES

Using size 2 (2.75mm) needles, cast on 61 sts.

Work in seed st as given for back for 8 rows, ending with RS facing for next row.

Change to size 3 (3.25mm) needles.

Beg and ending rows as indicated, work in beaded patt from chart as foll:

Inc 1 st at each end of 3rd and 3 foll 6th rows. 69 sts.

Work 3 rows, ending after chart row 24 and with RS facing for next row.

Beg with a K row, cont in St st, shaping sides by inc 1 st at each end of 3rd and every foll 6th row to 83 sts, then on every foll 8th row until there are 99 sts.

Work even until sleeve measures 17½ in (45 cm), ending with RS facing for next row.

Shape sleeve cap

Bind off 4 sts at beg of next 2 rows, then 3 sts at beg of foll 4 rows. 79 sts.

Dec 1 st at each end of next 6 rows, then on foll 6 alt rows, then on 4 foll 4th rows. 47 sts.

Work 1 row, ending with RS facing for next row.

Dec 1 st at each end of next and foll 4 alt rows, then on foll 5 rows, ending with RS facing for next row. 27 sts.

Work 1 row.

Bind off 3 sts at beg of next 2 rows.

Bind off rem 21 sts.

FINISHING

Press as described on page 148.

Sew both shoulder seams using backstitch, or mattress stitch.

Button band

Slip 5 sts from left front holder onto size 2 (2.75mm) needles and rejoin yarn with RS facing.

Cont in seed st as set until button band, when slightly stretched, fits up left front opening edge to neck shaping, ending with RS facing for next row.

Break off yarn and leave these 5 sts on another holder.

Slip stitch button band in place.

Mark positions for 6 buttons on button band—first to come 1 in (2.5 cm) up from cast-on edge, last to come ⅝ in (1.5 cm) below neck shaping, and rem 4 buttons evenly spaced between.

Buttonhole band

Slip 5 sts from right front holder onto size 2 (2.75mm) needles and rejoin yarn with **WS** facing.

Work as given for button band with the addition of 6 buttonholes worked to correspond with positions marked for buttons as foll:

Buttonhole row (RS): Seed st 2 sts, yo, work 2 tog (to make a buttonhole), seed st 1 st.

KNITTER'S TIP

Take care when you press this cardigan—or any beaded design. While you can safely steam press the pure wool yarn, the glass beads need extra care to avoid any chance of them breaking. Make sure you press the beaded areas from the wrong side, covering the work with a cloth and gently lowering your iron onto this cloth.

When band is complete, ending with RS facing for next row, do NOT break off yarn.

Slip stitch buttonhole band in place.

Collar

With RS facing and using size 2 (2.75mm) needles, seed st 5 sts of buttonhole band, pick up and knit 30 sts up right side of neck, 35 sts from back, and 30 sts down left side of neck, then seed st 5 sts of button band. 105 sts.

Work in seed st as set by bands for 3 rows, ending with RS facing for next row.

Row 4 (RS): Seed st 2 sts, yo, work 2 tog (to make 7th buttonhole), seed st to end.

Work in seed st for 2 rows more, ending with **WS** of body, RS of collar facing for next row.

Bind off 4 sts at beg of next 2 rows. 97 sts.

Now work in collar patt as foll:

Row 1 (RS of collar, WS of body): Seed st 3 sts, K to last 3 sts, seed st 3 sts.

Row 2: Seed st 3 sts, P to last 3 sts, seed st 3 sts.

Row 3: Seed st 3 sts, bead 1, K to last 4 sts, bead 1, seed st 3 sts.

Row 4: Rep row 2.

Row 5: Seed st 3 sts, M1, K to last 3 sts, M1, seed st 3 sts.

Row 6: Rep row 2.

(Rep rows 3–6) 5 times more, ending with RS of collar facing for next row. 109 sts.

Next row (RS): Seed st 3 sts, bead 1, ★K1, bead 1, rep from ★ to last 3 sts, seed st 3 sts.

Next row: Rep row 2.

Now work in seed st across all sts for 3 rows, ending with **WS** of collar facing for next row.

Bind off in seed st (on **WS**).

See page 148 for finishing instructions, setting in sleeves using the set-in method.

About Louisa Harding

Louisa Harding trained in textile design at Brighton University and was sent to Rowan Yarns for a three-month student work placement before her final degree show. While working at the Mill, Louisa submitted some designs for the Rowan magazine of the time and was delighted to have them accepted.

After graduation Louisa worked for a Canadian designer but returned to the UK in 1990. It wasn't long after her arrival home that she was asked to go back to the Rowan Mill and help in the design room.

For a few years Louisa worked alongside Kim Hargreaves producing designs for the Rowan magazines. She then became the key designer for the Jaeger brand. While on maternity leave Louisa came up with the idea of her "Miss Bea" books which were published by Rowan.

Louisa has gone on to create her own yarn label, "Louisa Harding," and has created a wide range of brochures and books.

Flighty

KIM HARGREAVES

SIZES AND YARN

		S	M	L	
To fit bust		34	36	38	in
		86	91	97	cm

One-color version
Rowan Classic Siena

Oak	659	4	4	4	x 50 g

Four-color version
Rowan Classic Siena

A Sloe	670	1	1	1	x 50 g
B Alpine	671	1	1	1	x 50 g
C Shadow	667	1	1	1	x 50 g
D Rosette	664	1	1	1	x 50 g

or

Rowan Purelife Organic Cotton 4-Ply

A Medium Indigo	758	1	1	1	x 50 g
B Chlorophyll	753	1	1	1	x 50 g
C Brazilwood	756	1	1	1	x 50 g
D Yellowwood	752	1	1	1	x 50 g

Originally knitted and photographed (above) in Rowan 4-Ply Cotton, four-color version in Marine 102 (A), Monsoon 109 (B), Vine 103 (C), and Bonny 104 (D), and one-color version in Straw 110

NEEDLES

1 pair size 1 (2.25mm) needles
1 pair size 3 (3mm) needles

BUTTONS—5

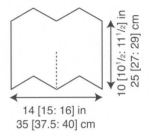

NEW YARN SUBSTITUTIONS

This little summer top was originally knitted in a super-fine pure cotton yarn that's no longer available. We chose cotton Rowan Classic Siena (below) as the substitute and new softer colors that keep the mood of the original.

Rowan Purelife Organic Cotton 4-Ply would work just as well as a substitute for the original yarn. Why not knit your top in these soft pastel shades to create a light and airy summer feel?

GAUGE

28 sts and 38 rows to 4 in (10 cm) measured over St st using size 3 (3mm) needles.

One-color version

Work as given for four-color version (see page 80), but using same color throughout.

Four color version

STRIPE SEQUENCE

Using yarn A, work 10 [12: 14] rows.
★★Work 6 rows B, 6 rows C, 4 rows D, 6 rows C, 6 rows B.★★
Using yarn A, work 10 [14: 18] rows.
Rep from ★★ to ★★ once.
Using yarn A, work 10 [12: 14] rows.

FRONT

Using size 1 (2.25mm) needles and yarn A, cast on 96 [104: 112] sts.
Work in garter st for 6 rows, ending with RS facing for next row.
Change to size 3 (3mm) needles.
Beg with first row of stripe sequence, now work in stripe sequence as given above throughout and cont as foll:
Beg with a K row, work in St st for 2 rows, ending with RS facing for next row.
Now work in chevron patt as foll:
Row 1 (RS): K1, K2tog, K20 [22: 24], M1, K1 (mark this st), M1, K22 [24: 26], K2tog tbl, K2tog, K22 [24: 26], M1, K1 (mark this st), M1, K20 [22: 24], K2tog tbl, K1.
Row 2: Purl.
These 2 rows form chevron patt.
Work 10 rows.
Row 13 (RS): (Patt to within 2 sts of marked st, M1, K2, M1, K marked st, M1, K2, M1) twice, patt to end. 100 [108: 116] sts.
Work 9 rows.
Rep last 10 rows twice more, then row 13 again. 112 [120: 128] sts.
Work 41 [49: 57] rows, ending with RS facing for next row.
Change to size 1 (2.25mm) needles.
Using yarn A, work in garter st for 5 rows, ending with **WS** facing for next row.
Bind off knitwise (on **WS**).

BACK

Left side panel

Using size 1 (2.25mm) needles and yarn A, cast on 49 [53: 57] sts.
Work in garter st for 6 rows, ending with RS facing for next row.
Change to size 3 (3mm) needles.
Beg with first row of stripe sequence, now work in stripe sequence as given above throughout and cont as foll:
Beg with a K row, work in St st for 2 rows, ending with RS facing for next row.
Now work in chevron patt as foll:
Row 1 (RS): K1, K2tog, K22 [24: 26], M1, K1 (mark this st), M1, K20 [22: 24], K2tog tbl, K1.
Row 2: Purl.
These 2 rows form chevron patt.
★★★Work 10 rows.
Row 13 (RS): Patt to within 2 sts of marked st, M1, K2, M1,

K marked st, M1, K2, M1, patt to end. 51 [55: 59] sts.
Work 9 rows.
Rep last 10 rows twice more, then row 13 again. 57 [61: 65] sts.★★★
Work 9 rows, dec 1 st at end of last row and ending with RS facing for next row. 56 [60: 64] sts.
Break off yarn and leave sts on a holder.

Right side panel

Using size 1 (2.25mm) needles and yarn A, cast on 49 [53: 57] sts.
Work in garter st for 6 rows, ending with RS facing for next row.
Change to size 3 (3mm) needles.
Beg with first row of stripe sequence, now work in stripe sequence as given above throughout and cont as foll:
Beg with a K row, work in St st for 2 rows, ending with RS facing for next row.
Now work in chevron patt as foll:
Row 1 (RS): K1, K2tog, K20 [22: 24], M1, K1 (mark this st), M1, K22 [24: 26], K2tog tbl, K1.
Row 2: Purl.
These 2 rows form chevron patt.
Work as given for left side panel from ★★★ to ★★★.
Work 9 rows, dec 1 st at beg of last row and ending with RS facing for next row. 56 [60: 64] sts.

Join panels

Row 61 (RS): Patt 56 [60: 64] sts of right side panel, then patt across 56 [60: 64] sts of left side panel left on holder. 112 [120: 128] sts.
Work 31 [39: 47] rows, ending with RS facing for next row.
Change to size 1 (2.25mm) needles.
Using yarn A, work in garter st for 5 rows, ending with **WS** facing for next row.
Bind off knitwise (on **WS**).

SHOULDER STRAPS (make 2)

Using size 1 (2.25mm) needles and yarn A, cast on 6 sts.
Row 1 (RS): K1, M1, K2tog tbl, K2tog, M1, K1.
Row 2: K1, P4, K1.
These 2 rows form patt.
Cont in patt until shoulder strap measures 15¾ in (40 cm), ending with RS facing for next row. Bind off.

FINISHING

Press as described on page 148. Sew both side seams using backstitch, or mattress stitch if preferred.
Make 5 button loops along left side of back opening and sew on buttons to right side of opening to correspond. Sew shoulder straps to inside of upper edge at top of chevron points, adjusting length to fit.
See page 148 for finishing instructions.

Dew

KIM HARGREAVES

YARN

Rowan Classic Baby Alpaca DK

Springleaf   214   4   x 50 g

Originally knitted and photographed (above) in Rowan DK Soft in Sage 175

NEEDLES

1 pair size 8 (5mm) needles

NEW YARN SUBSTITUTION

For this cozy little scarf we chose a soft and fluffy alpaca yarn (below) as the substitute. The needles used are thicker than you would expect for this weight of yarn—but this, combined with the clever drop stitch pattern, helps create a light and lacy scarf that you'll love to snuggle up in.

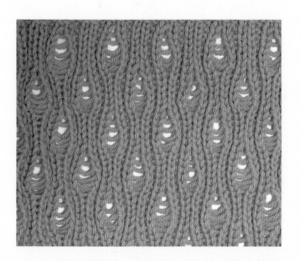

GAUGE

22 sts and 27 rows to 4 in (10 cm) measured over patt using size 8 (5mm) needles.

FINISHED SIZE

Finished scarf measures approx 10 in (26 cm) wide by 56 in (142 cm) long.

SCARF

Using size 8 (5mm) needles, cast on 52 sts.

Row 1 (RS): K1, (P2, K1, yo, K1, P2, K2) 6 times, P2, K1. 58 sts.

Now work in patt as foll:

Row 1 (WS): P1, (K2, P2, K2, P3) 6 times, K2, P1.

Row 2: K1, (P2, K3, P2, K2) 6 times, P2, K1.

Rows 3 and 4: Rep rows 1 and 2.

Row 5: Rep row 1.

Row 6: K1, (P2, K1, drop next st from left needle and allow it to unravel back down to row where yo was made, K1, P2, K1, yo, K1) 6 times, P2, K1.

Row 7: P1, (K2, P3, K2, P2) 6 times, K2, P1.

Row 8: K1, (P2, K2, P2, K3) 6 times, P2, K1.

Rows 9 and 10: Rep rows 7 and 8.

Row 11: Rep row 7.

Row 12: K1, (P2, K1, yo, K1, P2, K1, drop next st from left needle and allow it to unravel back down to row where yo was made, K1) 6 times, P2, K1.

Last 12 rows form patt.

Cont in patt until scarf measures approx 56 in (142 cm), ending after patt row 5 or 11 and with RS facing for next row.

Work 1 row more **but** omitting the "yo" needed for next patt rep. 52 sts.

Bind off in patt.

Dove

KIM HARGREAVES

SIZE AND YARN

One size
Rowan Felted Tweed DK
Bilberry   151   30   x 50 g
Originally knitted and photographed (above) in Rowan
DK Tweed in Mulberry 865

NEEDLES

1 short (24 in/60 cm) size 5 (3.75mm) circular needle
1 long (39½ in/100 cm) size 5 (3.75mm) circular needle
1 long (39½ in/100 cm) size 6 (4mm) circular needle

KNITTER'S TIP
Because of the number of stitches there are, this poncho is much easier to knit on a long circular needle. But, obviously, you won't be working in rounds. Simply use the circular needle as though it were two needles, working backward and forward in rows, and turning the work at the end of each row in the usual way.

NEW YARN SUBSTITUTION

This poncho was originally knitted in a firm tweedy yarn just
like Rowan Scottish Tweed DK. But we just loved the shade of
purple and this color isn't available in that yarn. So, instead, we
chose Rowan Felted Tweed DK (below). As this is quite a thin
yarn, we used it double to create a firm fabric that will hold its
shape. If you want to knit the poncho in Rowan Scottish Tweed
DK, you need 23 balls of yarn—and remember, only use one
strand of this yarn, not two.

GAUGE

21 sts and 29 rows to 4 in (10 cm) measured over St st using
size 6 (4mm) needles and yarn DOUBLE.

FINISHED SIZE

Finished poncho measures approx 48½ in (123 cm) wide and
approx 29½ in (75 cm) long from the shoulder point to the
lower edge (cast-on or bound-off edge).

PONCHO

The poncho is worked in one piece, beginning at the front
hem edge.
Using long size 5 (3.75mm) circular needle and yarn DOUBLE,
cast on 259 sts.
Row 1 (RS): K1, *P1, K1, rep from * to end.
Row 2: Rep row 1.
These 2 rows form seed st.
Work in seed st for 12 rows more, ending with RS facing for
next row.
Change to size 6 (4mm) circular needle.
Now work in patt as foll:
Row 1 (RS): Seed st 18 sts, K51, P1, K119, P1, K51, seed st
18 sts.
Row 2: Seed st 18 sts, P51, K1, P119, K1, P51, seed st 18 sts.
Last 2 rows form patt.
Cont in patt until front measures 26¾ in (68 cm), ending with

RS facing for next row.

Shape neck

Next row (RS): Patt 116 sts and turn, leaving rem sts on
a holder.

Work each side of neck separately.

Bind off 4 sts at beg of next row. 112 sts.

Dec 1 st at neck edge of next 5 rows, then on foll 4 alt rows.
103 sts.

Work 6 rows, ending with **WS** facing for next row.

Place markers at both ends of last row to denote
shoulder/overarm point.

Cast on 4 sts at beg of next row. 107 sts.

Work 1 row, ending with **WS** facing for next row.

Break off yarn and leave sts on a second holder.

With RS facing, rejoin yarns to rem sts, bind off center 27 sts,
patt to end. 116 sts.

Work 1 row.

Bind off 4 sts at beg of next row. 112 sts.

Dec 1 st at neck edge of next 5 rows, then on foll 4 alt rows.
103 sts.

Work 5 rows, ending with **WS** facing for next row.

Place markers at both ends of last row to denote shoulder/
overarm point.

Work 1 row.

Cast on 4 sts at beg of next row, ending with **WS** facing for
next row. 107 sts.

Join sections

Next row (WS): Patt 107 sts on needle, turn and cast on
45 sts, turn and patt across 107 sts left on second holder. 259 sts.

Cont in patt until work measures same from markers as from
top of seed st border to markers, ending with RS facing for
next row.

Change to long size 5 (3.75mm) circular needle.

Work in seed st across all sts for 14 rows, ending with RS facing
for next row.

Bind off in seed st.

FINISHING

Press as described on page 148.

Collar

With RS facing, using short size 5 (3.75mm) circular needle
and yarn DOUBLE, beg and ending at left shoulder marker,
pick up and knit 28 sts down left side of neck, 28 sts from front,
28 sts up right side of neck to other shoulder marker, then
60 sts from back. 144 sts.

Round 1 (RS): *K3, P3, rep from * to end.

Rep this round for 9 in (23 cm).

Bind off in rib.

See page 148 for finishing instructions.

Laurel Leaf

KIM HARGREAVES

SIZES AND YARN

	XS	S	M	L	XL	
To fit bust	32	34	36	38	40	in
	81	86	91	97	102	cm

Rowan Cotton Glace

		XS	S	M	L	XL	
A	Dawn Grey 831	8	8	9	9	9	x 50 g
B	Sky 749	2	2	2	2	2	x 50 g
C	Dijon 739	1	1	1	2	2	x 50 g
D	Umber 838	1	1	1	1	1	x 50 g

Originally knitted and photographed (above) in Rowan Cotton Glace in Fizz 722 (A), Pepper 796 (B), Mint 748 (C), and Pear 780 (D).

NEEDLES

1 pair size 2 (2.75mm) needles
1 pair size 3 (3.25mm) needles

BUTTONS—10

NEW YARN SUBSTITUTIONS

The colors used for this design are no longer available, but the new colors (below) echo the mood of the original cardigan.

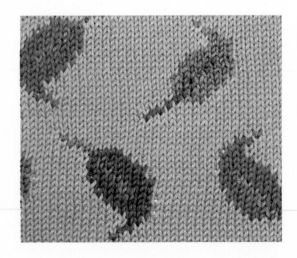

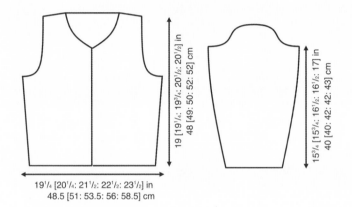

19 [19¼: 19¾: 20½: 20½] in
48 [49: 50: 52: 52] cm

19¼ [20¼: 21½: 22½: 23½] in
48.5 [51: 53.5: 56: 58.5] cm

15¾ [15¾: 16½: 16½: 17] in
40 [40: 42: 42: 43] cm

GAUGE

23 sts and 32 rows to 4 in (10 cm) measured over patterned St st using size 3 (3.25mm) needles.

BACK

Cast on 99 (105: 111: 117: 123) sts, using size 2 (2.75mm) needles and yarn B.
**★★Join in yarn A.
Using yarn A, knit 3 rows.
Row 4 (WS): Using yarn B, *P2tog, yo, rep from * to last st, P1.
Using yarn A, knit 2 rows.★★
Change to size 3 (3.25mm) needles.
Using the **intarsia** technique described on page 148, joining in and breaking off colors as required and beg with a K row, work in patt from body chart (see pages 86–87), which is worked entirely in St st, as foll:
Work 2 (2: 2: 4: 4) rows.
Inc 1 st at each end of next and every foll 14th row until there are 111 (117: 123: 129: 135) sts, taking inc sts into patt.
Work 11 (15: 15: 17: 17) rows, ending with chart row 84 (88: 88: 92: 92).
Shape armholes
Keeping chart correct, bind off 3 (4: 4: 5: 5) sts at beg of next 2 rows. 105 (109: 115: 119: 125) sts.

Dec 1 st at each end of next 7 (7: 9: 9: 11) rows, then on every foll alt row until 79 (81: 83: 85: 87) sts rem.

Work even until chart row 148 (152: 156: 160:162) has been completed, ending with RS facing for next row.

Shape shoulders and back neck

Keeping chart correct, bind off 7 (8: 8: 8: 8) sts at beg of next 2 rows. 65 (65: 67: 69: 71) sts.

Next row (RS): Bind off 7 (8: 8: 8: 8) sts, patt until there are 12 (11: 11: 12: 12) sts on right needle and turn, leaving rem sts on a holder.

Work each side of neck separately.

Bind off 4 sts at beg of next row.

Bind off rem 8 (7: 7: 8: 8) sts.

With RS facing, rejoin yarn to rem sts, bind off center 27 (27: 29: 29: 31) sts, patt to end.

Work to match first side, reversing shapings.

LEFT FRONT

Cast on 49 (53: 55: 59: 61) sts, using size 2 (2.75mm) needles and yarn B.

Work as for back from ★★ to ★★, inc 1 (0: 1: 0: 1) st at end of last row. 50 (53: 56: 59: 62) sts.

Change to size 3 (3.25mm) needles and work in patt from body chart as foll:

Work 2 (2: 2: 4: 4) rows.

Inc 1 st at beg of next and every foll 14th row until there are 56 (59: 62: 65: 68) sts, taking inc sts into patt.

Work 11 (15: 15: 17: 17) rows, ending with chart row 84 (88: 88: 92: 92).

Shape armhole

Keeping chart correct, bind off 3 (4: 4: 5: 5) sts at beg of next row. 53 (55: 58: 60: 63) sts.

Work 1 row.

Dec 1 st at armhole edge of next 7 (7: 9: 9: 11) rows, then on every foll alt row until 40 (41: 42: 43: 44) sts rem.

Work 11 (9: 9: 7: 5) rows, ending with chart row 116 (120: 122: 126: 126).

Shape neck

Keeping chart correct, dec 1 st at neck edge of next 9 rows, then on every foll alt row until 22 (23: 23: 24: 24) sts rem.

Work 5 rows, ending with chart row 148 (152: 156: 160: 162).

Shape shoulder

Keeping chart correct, bind off 7 (8: 8: 8: 8) sts at beg of next and foll alt row.

Work 1 row. Bind off rem 8 (7: 7: 8: 8) sts.

RIGHT FRONT

Cast on 49 (53: 55: 59: 61) sts, using size 2 (2.75mm) needles and yarn B.

Work as for back from ★★ to ★★, inc 1 (0: 1: 0: 1) st at beg of last row. 50 (53: 56: 59: 62) sts.

Change to size 3 (3.25mm) needles and work in patt from body chart as foll:

Work 2 (2: 2: 4: 4) rows.

Inc 1 st at end of next and every foll 14th row until there are 56 (59: 62: 65: 68) sts, taking inc sts into patt.

Complete to match left front, reversing shapings.

SLEEVES

Cast on 47 (47: 47: 51: 51) sts, using size 2 (2.75mm) needles and yarn B.

Work as for back from ★★ to ★★.

Change to size 3 (3.25mm) needles and work in patt from sleeve chart as foll:

Work 2 rows.

Inc 1 st at each end of next and every foll 10th row to 63 (55: 51: 63: 59) sts, then on every foll 8th row until there are 73 (75: 77: 79: 81) sts, taking inc sts into patt.

Work 11 rows, ending with chart row 124 (124: 128: 128: 132).

Shape sleeve cap

Keeping chart correct, bind off 3 (4: 4: 5: 5) sts at beg of next 2 rows. 67 (67: 69: 69: 71) sts.

Dec 1 st at each end of next 3 rows, then on foll 3 alt rows. 55 (55: 57: 57: 59) sts.

Work 3 rows, ending with RS facing for next row.

Dec 1 st at each end of next and every foll 4th row until 47 (47: 49: 49: 51) sts rem, then on every foll alt row until 35 sts rem.

Dec 1 st at each end of next 3 rows. 29 sts.

Bind off 4 sts at beg of next 2 rows.

Bind off rem 21 sts.

FINISHING

Press all pieces as described on page 148.

Sew both shoulder seams using backstitch, or mattress stitch.

Neck border

With RS facing, using size 2 (2.75mm) needles and yarn A, pick up and knit 31 (31: 34: 34: 36) sts up right side of neck, 35 (35: 37: 37: 39) sts from back, and 31 (31: 34: 34: 36) sts down left side of neck. 97 (97: 105: 105: 111) sts.

Rows 1 and 2: Using yarn A, knit.

Row 3 (WS): Using yarn B, *P2tog, yo, rep from * to last st, P1.

Rows 4 and 5: Using yarn A, knit.

Row 6: Using yarn B, knit.

Bind off knitwise (on **WS**) using yarn B.

Front borders (both alike)

With RS facing, using size 2 (2.75mm) needles and yarn A, pick up and knit 91 (93: 95: 97: 97) sts along one front opening edge between cast-on edge and top of neck border.

Work rows 1 to 6 as for neck border.

Bind off knitwise (on **WS**) using yarn B.

See page 148 for finishing instructions, and use eyelet holes of right front border as buttonholes.

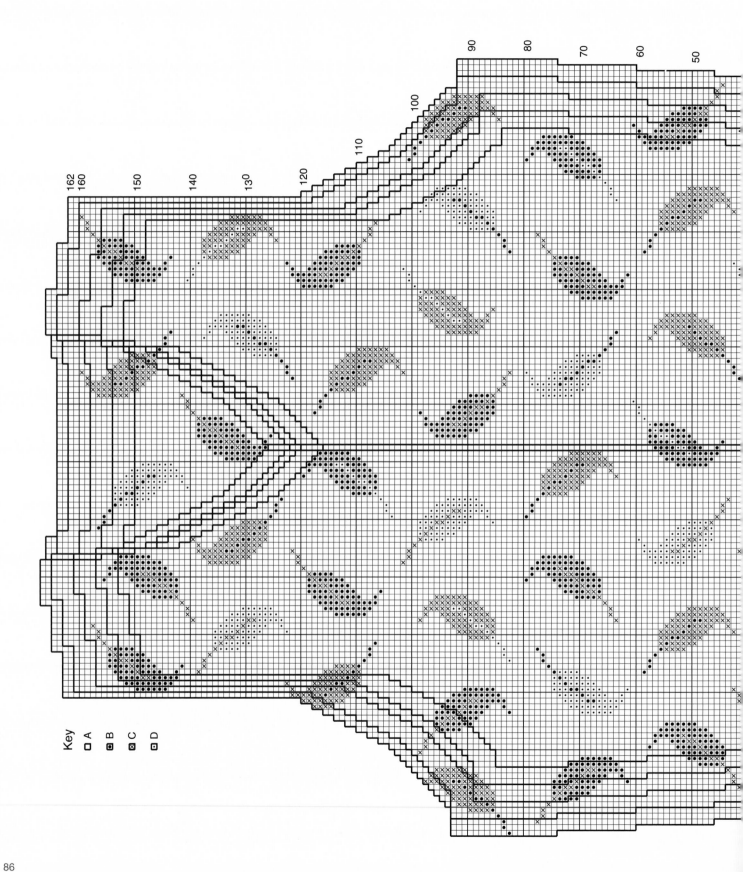

Key
□ A
◙ B
⊠ C
◘ D

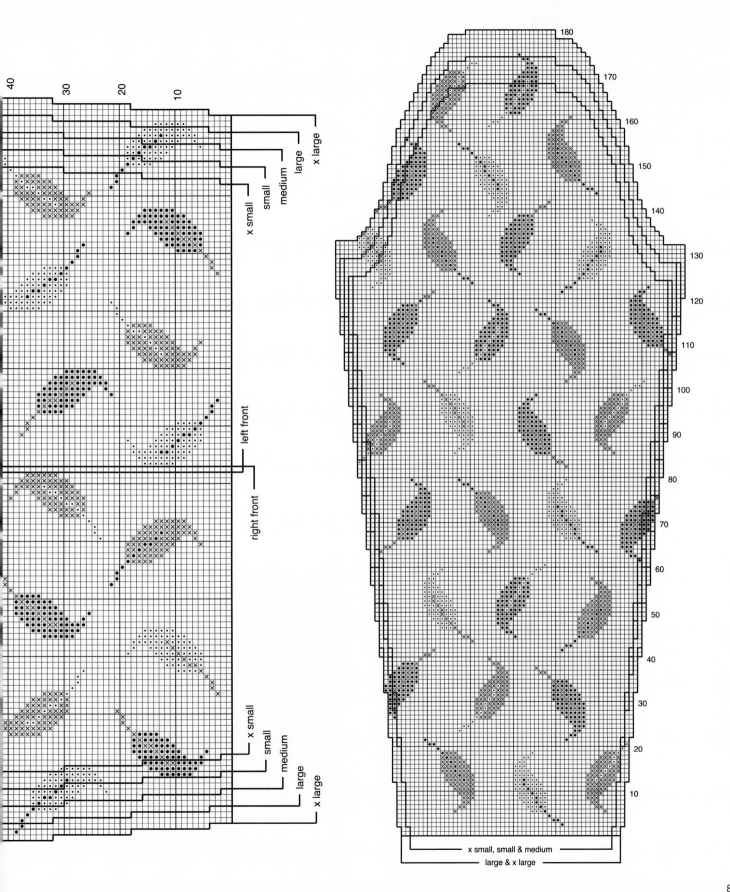

Champagne Please

BRANDON MABLY

SIZES AND YARN

		XS	S	M	L	XL	
To fit bust		32	34	36	38	40	in
		81	86	91	97	102	cm

Rowan Cotton Glace

		XS	S	M	L	XL	
A	Oyster	730	7	8	8	8	9	x 50 g
B	Sky	749	3	3	3	3	3	x 50 g
C	Candy Floss	747	2	2	2	2	2	x 50 g
D	Heather	828	2	2	2	2	3	x 50 g
E	Chalk	827	2	2	2	3	3	x 50 g

Originally knitted and photographed (above) in Rowan Cotton Glace in Pear 780 (A), Steel 798 (B), Oyster 730 (C), Pixie 723 (D), and Fizz 722 (E).

NEEDLES
1 pair size 2 (2.75mm) needles
1 pair size 3 (3.25mm) needles

BUTTONS—5

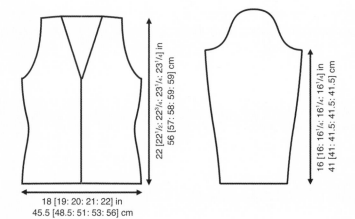

22 [22¹⁄₂: 22³⁄₄: 23¹⁄₄: 23³⁄₄] in
56 [57: 58: 59: 59] cm

18 [19: 20: 21: 22] in
45.5 [48.5: 51: 53: 56] cm

16 [16: 16¹⁄₄: 16¹⁄₄: 16¹⁄₄] in
41 [41: 41.5: 41.5: 41.5] cm

NEW YARN SUBSTITUTIONS
This cardigan was originally knitted in Rowan Cotton Glace—a yarn that's still available. But, as some of the original shades are no longer available, we chose new colors (right) that match the original ones as best we could and that reflect the mood of the original.

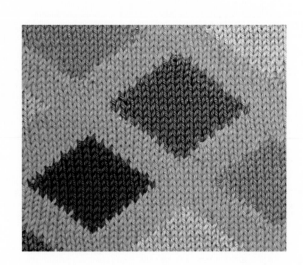

KNITTER'S TIP
Take care when knitting the diamonds on this cardigan. They may, at a glance, look symmetrical—but they aren't. Make sure you follow the chart accurately so that all the diamonds fit together as they should.

GAUGE

23 sts and 32 rows to 4 in (10 cm) measured over patterned St st using size 3 (3.25mm) needles.

BACK

Cast on 105 (111: 117: 123: 129) sts, using size 2 (2.75mm) needles and yarn A and work in seed st as foll:

Row 1: K1, *P1, K1, rep from * to end.

Row 2: Rep row 1.

Work 6 rows more in seed st.

Change to size 3 (3.25mm) needles.

Using the **intarsia** technique described on page 148, joining in and breaking off colors as required and beg with a K row, work in patt from body chart (see pages 90–91), which is worked entirely in St st, as foll:

Patt 8 (10: 10: 12: 12) rows.

Dec 1 st at each end of next and every foll 4th row until 87 (93: 99: 105: 111) sts rem.

Work 11 rows.

Inc 1 st at each end of next and every foll 6th row to 99 (105: 111: 117: 123) sts, then on every foll 4th row to 105 (111: 117: 123: 129) sts, taking inc sts into patt.

Work 13 rows, thus ending with chart row 108 (110: 110: 112: 112).

Shape armholes

Keeping chart correct, bind off 4 (4: 5: 5: 6) sts at beg of next 2 rows. 97 (103: 107: 113: 117) sts.

Dec 1 st at each end of next 5 (7: 7: 9: 9) rows, then on every foll alt row until 73 (75: 77: 79: 81) sts rem.

Work even until chart row 172 (174: 178: 180: 182) has been completed, thus ending with **RS** facing for next row.

Shape shoulders and back neck

Bind off 6 (6: 7: 7: 7) sts at beg of next 2 rows. 61 (63: 63: 65: 67) sts.

Next row (RS): Bind off 6 (6: 7: 7: 7) sts, patt until there are 10 (11: 10: 11: 12) sts on right needle and turn, leaving rem sts on a holder.

Work each side of neck separately.

Bind off 4 sts at beg of next row.

Bind off rem 6 (7: 6: 7: 8) sts.

With RS facing, rejoin yarn to rem sts, bind off center 29 sts, patt to end.

Work to match first side, reversing shapings.

LEFT FRONT

Cast on 57 (59: 63: 65: 69) sts, using size 2 (2.75mm) needles and yarn A.

Work 7 rows in seed st as for back.

Row 8 (WS): Patt 5 sts and slip these 5 sts onto a holder for button border, M1, patt to last 0 (1: 0: 1: 0) st, (inc in last st) 0 (1: 0: 1: 0) times. 53 (56: 59: 62: 65) sts.

Change to size 3 (3.25mm) needles and work in patt from body chart as foll:

Patt 8 (10: 10: 12: 12) rows.

Dec 1 st at beg of next and every foll 4th row until 44 (47: 50: 53: 56) sts rem.

Work 11 rows.

Inc 1 st at beg of next and every foll 6th row to 50 (53: 56: 59: 62) sts, then on every foll 4th row to 53 (56: 59: 62: 65) sts, taking inc sts into patt.

Work 13 rows, thus ending with chart row 108 (110: 110: 112: 112).

Shape armhole

Keeping chart correct, bind off 4 (4: 5: 5: 6) sts at beg of next row. 49 (52: 54: 57: 59) sts.

Work 1 row.

Dec 1 st at armhole edge on next 5 (4: 4: 2: 2) rows. 44 (48: 50: 55: 57) sts.

Work 1 (0: 0: 0: 0) row, thus ending with chart row 116.

Shape front slope

2nd, 3rd, 4th, and 5th sizes only

Dec 1 st at armhole edge of next (2: 2: 6: 6) rows **and at same time** dec 1 st at front slope edge on next and foll (0: 0: 2: 2) alt rows. (45: 47: 46: 48) sts.

All sizes

Dec 1 st at both ends of next and foll 6 (7: 8: 8: 8) alt rows. 30 (29: 29: 28: 30) sts.

5th size only

Work 1 row.

Dec 1 st at armhole edge only on next row. 29 sts.

All sizes

Work 1 row.

Dec 1 st at front slope edge only on next and foll 4 (2: 1: 0: 0) alt rows, then on every foll 4th row until 18 (19: 20: 21: 22) sts rem.

Work even until chart row 172 (174: 178: 180: 182) has been completed, thus ending with RS facing for next row.

Shape shoulder

Bind off 6 (6: 7: 7: 7) sts at beg of next and foll alt row.

Work 1 row.

Bind off rem 6 (7: 6: 7: 8) sts.

RIGHT FRONT

Cast on 57 (59: 63: 65: 69) sts, using size 2 (2.75mm) needles and yarn A.

Work 4 rows in seed st as for back.

Row 5 (RS) (buttonhole row): Patt 2 sts, yo (to make a buttonhole), work 2 tog, patt to end.

Work 2 rows more in seed st.

Row 8 (WS): (Inc in first st) 0 (1: 0: 1: 0) times, patt to last 5 sts, M1 and turn, leaving last 5 sts on a holder for buttonhole border. 53 (56: 59: 62: 65) sts.

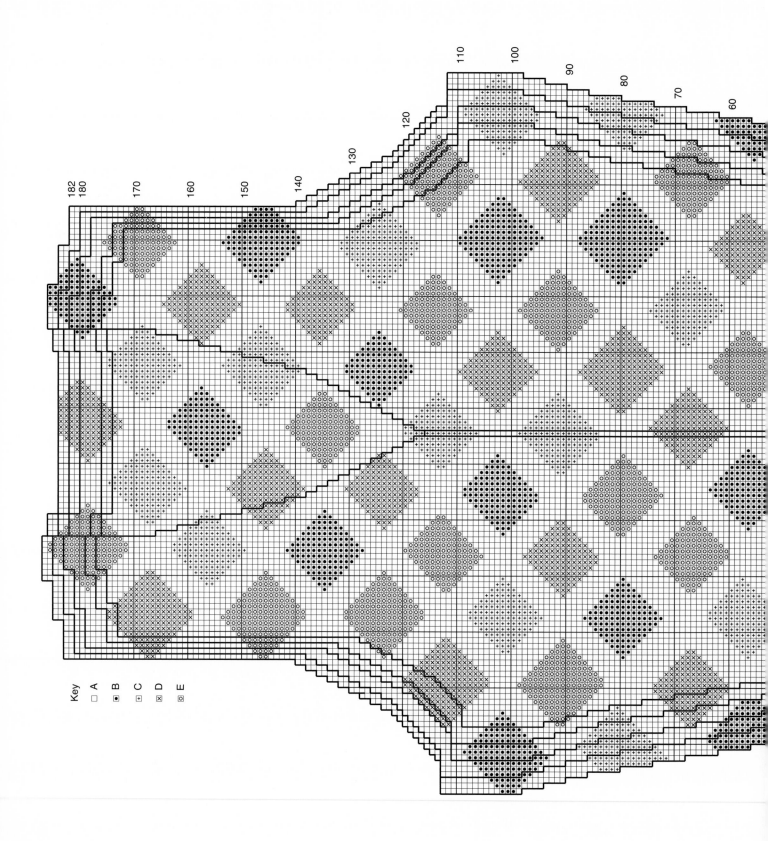

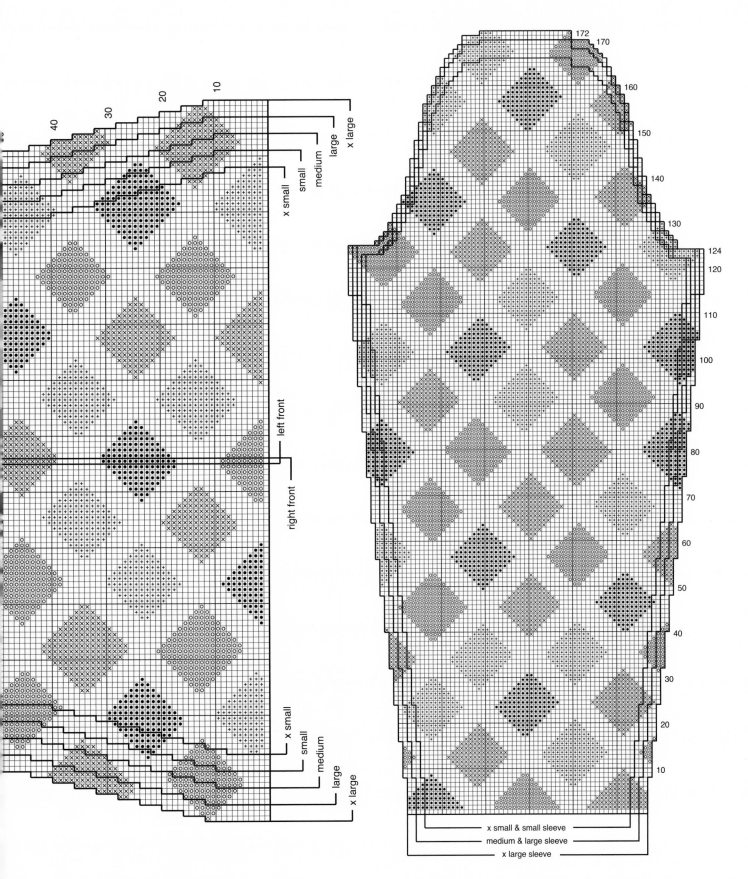

40
30
20
10

x large
large
medium
small
x small

left front
right front

x small
small
medium
large
x large

172
170
160
150
140
130
124
120
110
100
90
80
70
60
50
40
30
20
10

x small & small sleeve
medium & large sleeve
x large sleeve

Change to size 3 (3.25mm) needles and work in patt from body chart as foll:

Patt 8 (10: 10: 12: 12) rows.

Dec 1 st at end of next and every foll 4th row until 44 (47: 50: 53: 56) sts rem.

Complete to match left front, reversing shapings.

SLEEVES

Cast on 47 (47: 51: 51: 55) sts, using size 2 (2.75mm) needles and yarn A.

Work 8 rows in seed st as for back.

Change to size 3 (3.25mm) needles and work in patt from sleeve chart as foll:

Work 8 rows.

Inc 1 st at each end of next and every foll 8th row to 65 (75: 67: 77: 71) sts, taking inc sts into patt.

1st, 3rd, 4th, and 5th sizes only

Inc 1 st at each end of every foll 10th row to 73 (77: 79: 81) sts.

All sizes

Work 9 rows, thus ending with chart row 122 (122: 124: 124: 124).

Shape sleeve cap

Keeping chart correct, bind off 4 (4: 5: 5: 6) sts at beg of next 2 rows. 65 (67: 67: 69: 69) sts.

Dec 1 st at each end of next 3 rows, then on foll 4 alt rows. 51 (53: 53: 55: 55) sts.

Work 3 rows, ending with RS facing for next row.

Dec 1 st at each end of next and every foll 4th row until 41 (45: 43: 47: 45) sts rem, then on every foll alt row until 35 sts rem.

Dec 1 st at each end on next 3 rows. 29 sts.

Bind off 4 sts at beg of next 2 rows.

Bind off rem 21 sts.

FINISHING

Press all pieces as described on page 148.

Sew shoulder seams using backstitch.

Button border

Slip 5 sts left on holder for button border onto size 2 (2.75mm) needles and rejoin yarn A with RS facing.

Cont in seed st as set until border, when slightly stretched, fits up left front opening edge to shoulder and then across to center back neck, ending with RS facing for next row.

Bind off.

Slip stitch border in place.

Mark positions for 5 buttons on this border—lowest button level with buttonhole already worked in right front, top button ⅜ in (1 cm) below start of front slope shaping and rem 3 buttons evenly spaced between.

Buttonhole border

Work as for button border, rejoining yarn with **WS** facing and with the addition of 4 buttonholes more to correspond with positions marked for buttons worked as foll:

Buttonhole row (RS): Patt 2 sts, yo (to make a buttonhole), work 2 tog, patt 1 st.

Slip stitch border in place, sewing together bound-off ends of borders at center back neck.

See page 148 for finishing instructions, setting in sleeves using the set-in method.

About Brandon Mably

Brandon admits that he was not a star pupil at school and found it difficult to settle to one hobby or interest as a child. However, his love of color and design always remained a constant throughout his young life.

It was a chance meeting with Kaffe Fassett at a London bus stop that became a pivotal moment in Brandon's working life. Kaffe invited Brandon to visit his design studio, and an intrigued Brandon went along for a look. "As soon as I walked in I knew it felt right. I loved the color and the creativity." Brandon started spending all his free time in the studio and eventually was fortunate enough to be given a job there.

Brandon soon discovered he had a natural flare for designing and an instinct for working with color. His first solo knitting book was *Brilliant Knits*, followed in 2006 by *Knitting Color*.

Brandon regularly contributes to the Rowan magazines. He is also an inspirational and enthusiastic workshop tutor who teaches and lectures all over the world.

Emmeline

SARAH DALLAS

SIZES AND YARN

		XS	S	M	L	XL	
To fit bust		32	34	36	38	40	in
		81	86	91	97	102	cm
Rowan Scottish Tweed DK							
A Storm Grey	004	7	8	8	8	9	x 50 g
B Skye	003	1	1	1	1	1	x 50 g
C Sunset	011	1	1	1	1	1	x 50 g
D Oatmeal	025	1	1	1	1	1	x 50 g
E Purple Heather	030	1	1	1	1	1	x 50 g
F Lewis Grey	007	1	1	1	1	1	x 50 g

Originally knitted and photographed (above) in Rowan
Kid Classic in Silver 821 (A), Glacier 822 (B), Juicy 827 (C),
Chamois 820 (D), Crushed Velvet 825 (E), and Galaxy 824 (F).

NEEDLES

1 pair size 6 (4mm) needles
1 pair size 8 (5mm) needles

BUTTONS—6

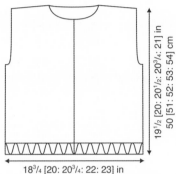

18³/₄ [20: 20³/₄: 22: 23] in
47 [50: 52: 55.5: 57.5] cm

19¹/₂ [20: 20¹/₂: 20³/₄: 21] in
50 [51: 52: 53: 54] cm

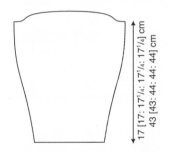

17 [17: 17¹/₄: 17¹/₄: 17¹/₄] in
43 [43: 44: 44: 44] cm

NEW YARN SUBSTITUTIONS

The original yarn used for this cardigan is still available, but
the color range has changed and a lot of the original shades are
no longer available. We wanted to keep the mottled color effect
of the original, so we chose a different yarn (right) rather than
new colors. However, if you wanted to knit this design in
the original Kid Classic yarn, you will need 5 (6: 6: 6: 7) balls
of the main color (yarn A) and one ball of each of the five
contrasting colors.

GAUGE

19 sts and 25 rows to 4 in (10 cm) measured over St st using
size 8 (5mm) needles.

BACK

Cast on 179 (187: 195: 211: 219) sts, using size 6 (4mm) needles
and yarn C.

Break off yarn C and join in yarn F.

Work bell ruffle as foll:

Row 1 (RS): P3, *K5, P3, rep from * to end.

Row 2: K3, *P5, K3, rep from * to end.

Rows 3 and 4: Rep rows 1 and 2.

Row 5: P3, *K1, sl 1, K2tog, psso, K1, P3, rep from * to end.
135 (141: 147: 159: 165) sts.

Row 6: K3, *P3, K3, rep from * to end.

Row 7: P3, *K3, P3, rep from * to end.

Row 8: Rep row 6.

Row 9: P3, *sl 1, K2tog, psso, P3, rep from * to end. 91 (95:
99: 107: 111) sts.

Row 10: K3, *P1, K3, rep from * to end.

These 10 rows complete bell ruffle.

Cont using yarn F and purl 4 rows, dec 1 (0: 0: 1: 1) st at each
end of first of these rows. 89 (95: 99: 105: 109) sts.

Change to size 8 (5mm) needles.

Using the **Fair Isle** technique described on page 148, starting and
ending rows as indicated and beg with a K row, work 11 rows
from body chart, which is worked entirely in St st.

Break off all contrasting colors and cont in yarn A as foll:

Beg with a P row, cont in St st until back measures 11¾ (12¼:
12¼: 12½: 12½) in/30 (31: 31: 32: 32) cm from cast-on edge,
ending with RS facing for next row.

Shape armholes

Bind off 4 sts at beg of next 2 rows. 81 (87: 91: 97: 101) sts.

Next row (RS): K3, K3tog, K to last 6 sts, K3tog tbl, K3.

Next row: Purl.

Rep last 2 rows once more. 73 (79: 83: 89: 93) sts.

Work even until armhole measures 7¾ (7¾: 8¼: 8¼: 8½) in/
20 (20: 21: 21: 22) cm, ending with RS facing for next row.

Shape shoulders and back neck

Bind off 7 (8: 8: 9: 10) sts at beg of next 2 rows. 59 (63: 67: 71:
73) sts.

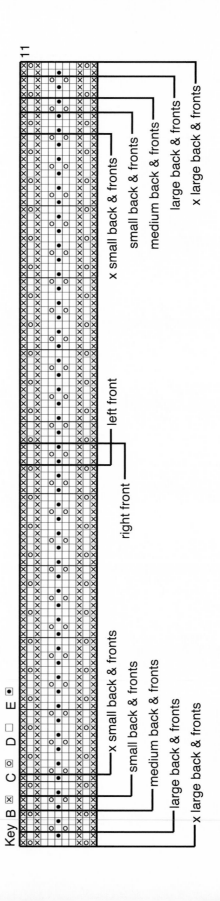

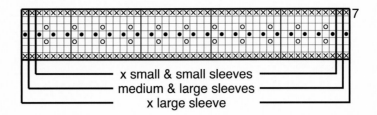

x small & small sleeves
medium & large sleeves
x large sleeve

Next row (RS): Bind off 7 (8: 8: 9: 10) sts, K until there are 11 (11: 13: 13: 13) sts on right needle and turn, leaving rem sts on a holder.

Work each side of neck separately.

Bind off 4 sts at beg of next row.

Bind off rem 7 (7: 9: 9: 9) sts.

With RS facing, rejoin yarn to rem sts, bind off center 23 (25: 25: 27: 27) sts, K to end.

Work to match first side, reversing shapings.

LEFT FRONT

Cast on 91 (99: 99: 107: 115) sts, using size 6 (4mm) needles and yarn C.

Break off yarn C, join in yarn F and work the 10 bell ruffle rows as for back. 47 (51: 51: 55: 59) sts.

Cont using yarn F and purl 4 rows, dec 1 (2: 0: 1: 3) sts evenly across first of these rows. 46 (49: 51: 54: 56) sts.

Change to size 8 (5mm) needles.

Starting and ending rows as indicated and beg with a K row, work 11 rows from body chart.

Break off all contrast colors and cont in yarn A as foll:

Beg with a P row, cont in St st until left front matches back to beg of armhole shaping, ending with RS facing for next row.

Shape armhole

Bind off 4 sts at beg of next row. 42 (45: 47: 50: 52) sts.

Work 1 row.

Next row (RS): K3, K3tog, K to end.

Next row: Purl.

Rep last 2 rows once more. 38 (41: 43: 46: 48) sts.

Work even until 17 (17: 17: 19: 19) rows less have been worked than on back to start of shoulder shaping, ending with **WS** facing for next row.

Shape neck

Bind off 9 (10: 10: 10: 10) sts at beg of next row. 29 (31: 33: 36: 38) sts.

Dec 1 st at neck edge on next 5 rows, then on foll 3 (3: 3: 4: 4) alt rows. 21 (23: 25: 27: 29) sts.

Work 5 rows, ending with RS facing for next row.

Shape shoulder

Bind off 7 (8: 8: 9: 10) sts at beg of next and foll alt row.

Work 1 row.

Bind off rem 7 (7: 9: 9: 9) sts.

RIGHT FRONT

Work to match left front, reversing shapings.

SLEEVES

Cast on 43 (43: 45: 45: 47) sts, using size 6 (4mm) needles and yarn C.

Work 6 rows in garter st.

Change to size 8 (5mm) needles.

Using the **Fair Isle** technique described on page 148, starting and ending rows as indicated, work 7 rows from sleeve chart.

Break off all contrasting colors and cont in yarn A as foll:

Beg with a P row, cont in St st, inc 1 st at each end of 2nd and every foll 6th row until there are 63 (63: 65: 65: 63) sts, then on every foll 4th row until there are 77 (77: 81: 81: 85) sts.

Work even until sleeve measures 17 (17: 17¼: 17¼: 17¼) in/ 43 (43: 44: 44: 44) cm from cast-on edge, ending with RS facing for next row.

Shape sleeve cap

Bind off 4 sts at beg of next 2 rows. 69 (69: 73: 73: 77) sts.

Next row (RS): Knit.

Next row: Purl.

Next row: K3, K3tog, K to last 6 sts, K3tog tbl, K3.

Next row: Purl.

Rep last 4 rows once more.

Bind off rem 61 (61: 65: 65: 69) sts.

FINISHING

Press all pieces as described on page 148.

Sew both shoulder seams using backstitch.

Button band

With RS facing, using size 6 (4mm) needles and yarn C, pick up and knit 82 (84: 86: 86: 88) sts evenly down left front opening edge, from neck shaping to cast-on edge.

Knit 2 rows.

Bind off knitwise (on **WS**).

Buttonhole band

With RS facing, using size 6 (4mm) needles and yarn C, pick up and knit 82 (84: 86: 86: 88) sts evenly up right front opening edge, from cast-on edge to neck shaping.

Next row (WS): K2, ★yo, K2tog, K12, rep from ★ 4 times more, yo, K2tog, K8 (10: 12: 12: 14).

Knit 1 row.

Bind off knitwise (on **WS**).

Neckband

With RS facing, size 6 (4mm) needles and yarn C, starting and ending at bound-off edge of front bands, pick up and knit 30 (31: 31: 34: 34) sts up right side of neck, 31 (33: 33: 35: 35) sts from back, and 30 (31: 31: 34: 34) sts down left side of neck. 91 (95: 95: 103: 103) sts.

Knit 2 rows.

Bind off knitwise (on **WS**).

See page 148 for finishing instructions, setting in sleeves using the set-in method.

About Sarah Dallas

Sarah Dallas is senior tutor in fashion and textiles at London's prestigious Royal College of Art where she has also been a fellow since 1992. It was Sarah who first set up the fashion knitwear course at the RCA.

Prior to that, Sarah designed and produced her own ready-to-wear label for 12 years and has also worked as a consultant for several leading UK stores as well as selling designs to other fashion stores abroad, such as Nieman Marcus in New York.

Sarah's association with Rowan spans almost the full 30 years of Rowan's history and she has regularly contributed to its publications. Sarah's first book was the very successful *Vintage Knitting* for Ebury. She has subsequently created two highly regarded books for Rowan, *Sarah Dallas Knitting* and *Scottish Inspirations*.

Surf

MARTIN STOREY

SIZES AND YARN

	Women's sizes			Men's sizes			
	S	M	L	M	L	XL	
To fit bust/chest							
	34	36	38	40	42	44	in
	86	91	97	102	107	112	cm
Rowan Denim							
	23	24	26	27	28	30	x 50 g

Photographed in Ecru 324

NEEDLES

1 pair size 3 (3.25mm) needles
1 pair size 5 (3.75mm) needles
1 pair size 6 (4mm) needles
2 double-pointed size 3 (3.25mm) needles
Size 3 (3.25mm) circular needle
Cable needle

GAUGE

Before washing: 20 sts and 28 rows to 4 in (10 cm) measured over St st using size 6 (4mm) needles.

Gauge note: Rowan Denim will shrink in length when washed for the first time. Allowances have been made in the pattern for shrinkage (see size diagram for after-washing measurements).

SPECIAL ABBREVIATIONS

C6B = Cable 6 back Slip next 3 sts onto cable needle and leave at back of work, K3, then K3 from cable needle.
C6F = Cable 6 front Slip next 3 sts onto cable needle and leave at front of work, K3, then K3 from cable needle.
C8B = Cable 8 back Slip next 4 sts onto cable needle and leave at back of work, K4, then K4 from cable needle.
C9B = Cable 9 back Slip next 5 sts onto cable needle and leave at back of work, K4, slip P st from cable needle back onto left needle and P this st, then K4 from cable needle.
C9F = Cable 9 front Slip next 5 sts onto cable needle and leave at front of work, K4, slip P st from cable needle back onto left needle and P this st, then K4 from cable needle.

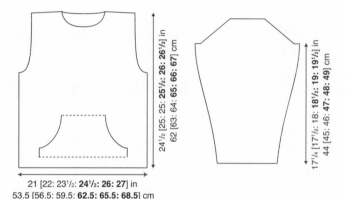

24½ [25: 25: **26: 26½**] in
62 [63: 64: **65: 66: 67**] cm

21 [22: 23½: **24½: 26: 27**] in
53.5 [56.5: 59.5: **62.5: 65.5: 68.5**] cm

17¼ [17½: 18: **18½: 19: 19½**] in
44 [45: 46: **47: 48: 49**] cm

Pattern note: The pattern instructions are written for three women's sizes followed by three men's sizes in **bold**. Where only one figure appears for one of the groups, it applies to all sizes in that group.

BACK

Cast on 107 (113: 119: **125: 131: 137**) sts, using size 5 (3.75mm) needles.
Beg with a K row, work in St st for 10 rows.
Row 11 (RS): Purl (to form hem fold line).
Beg with a P row, work in St st for 10 rows more, ending with **WS** facing for next row.
Row 22 (WS): P1 (4: 7: **10: 13: 16), *M1P, P3, rep from * to last 1 (4: 7: **10: 13: 16**) sts, M1P, P1 (4: 7: **10: 13: 16**).
143 (149: 155: **161: 167: 173**) sts.
Change to size 6 (4mm) needles and work as foll:
Row 1 (RS): K1 (0: 1: **0: 1: 0**), (P1, K1) 6 (8: 9: **11: 12: 14**) times, work next 117 sts as row 1 of chart for body (see page 98), (K1, P1) 6 (8: 9: **11: 12: 14**) times, K1 (0: 1: **0: 1: 0**).
Row 2: K1 (0: 1: **0: 1: 0**), (P1, K1) 6 (8: 9: **11: 12: 14**) times, work next 117 sts as row 2 of chart for body, (K1, P1) 6 (8: 9: **11: 12: 14**) times, K1 (0: 1: **0: 1: 0**).

These 2 rows set the sts—center 117 sts in patt foll chart with edge sts in seed st.★★★

Keeping sts correct as set, repeating the 28 patt rows throughout, work even until back measures 20½ in (52 cm) from cast-on edge, ending with RS facing for next row.

Shape armholes

Keeping patt correct, bind off 4 (4: 5: **5: 6: 6**) sts at beg of next 2 rows. 135 (141: 145: **151: 155: 161**) sts.

Dec 1 st at each end of next 3 (5: 5: **7: 7: 9**) rows, then on foll 4 (4: 5: **5: 6: 6**) alt rows. 121 (123: 125: **127: 129: 131**) sts. Work even until armhole measures 10¼ (10½: 11: **11½: 12: 12½**) in/26 (27: 28: **29.5: 30.5: 32**) cm, ending with RS facing for next row.

Shape shoulders

Keeping patt correct, bind off 5 sts at beg of next 12 rows. Bind off rem 61 (63: 65: **67: 69: 71**) sts, dec 11 sts evenly across row.

POCKET LINING

Cast on 71 sts, using size 6 (4mm) needles.

Row 1 (RS): P1, *K1, P1, rep from * to end.

Row 2: Rep row 1.

These 2 rows form seed st.

Work in seed st for 17 rows more, ending with WS facing

for next row.

Row 20 (WS): Seed st 3 sts, M1, (seed st 4 sts, M1) 4 times, seed st 33 sts, (M1, seed st 4 sts), 4 times, M1, seed st 3 sts. 81 sts. Break off yarn and leave sts on a holder.

FRONT

Cast on 107 (113: 119: **125: 131: 137**) sts, using size 5 (3.75mm) needles.

Beg with a K row, work in St st for 10 rows.

Row 11 (RS): Purl (to form hem fold line).

Beg with a P row, work in St st for 5 rows more, ending with RS facing for next row.

Row 17 (eyelet row) (RS): K50 (53: 56: **59: 62: 65**), K2tog, yo, K3, yo, K2tog tbl, K to end.

Beg with a P row, work in St st for 4 rows more, ending with **WS** facing for next row.

Work as given for back from ★★ to ★★★.

Keeping sts correct as set, repeating the 28 patt rows throughout, work 18 rows more, ending with RS facing for next row.

Shape pocket front

Next row (RS): Patt 122 (125: 128: **131: 134: 137**) sts and turn, leaving rem 21 (24: 27: **30: 33: 36**) sts on a holder for right side of front.

Next row: Patt 101 sts and turn, leaving rem 21 (24: 27: **30:**

BODY CHART

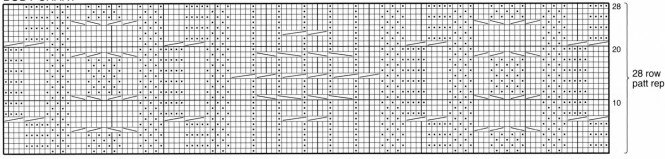

Key

□ K on RS, P on WS

▣ P on RS, K on WS

⟋ C8B

⟋ C6B

⟍ C6F

⟋ C9B

⟍ C9F

SLEEVE CHART

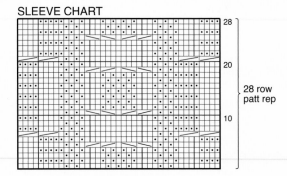

28 row patt rep

33: 36) sts on a second holder for left side of front.

Keeping patt correct, work on center 101 sts only for pocket front as foll:

Dec 1 st at each end of next 13 rows, then on foll 9 alt rows. 57 sts.

Work 22 rows more, ending with **WS** facing for next row.

Break off yarn and leave sts on a third holder.

Work pocket back

With RS facing, slip 21 (24: 27: **30: 33: 36**) sts of left side of front onto right needle, rejoin yarn, and keeping patt correct as set by side fronts, work across 81 sts of pocket lining as foll— patt 18 sts, seed st 45 sts, patt 18 sts, then patt across 21 (24: 27: **30: 33: 36**) sts of right side of front. 123 (129: 135: **141: 147: 153**) sts.

Keeping sts correct as set, work 53 rows more, ending with RS facing for next row.

Next row (RS): Patt 42 (45: 48: **51: 54: 57**) sts, M1, (patt 2 sts, M1) 19 times, patt to end. 143 (149: 155: **161: 167: 173**) sts.

Join sections

With WS facing, patt across first 43 (46: 49: **52: 55: 58**) sts, then holding WS of pocket front against RS of pocket back, patt tog first st of pocket front with next st of pocket back, patt tog rem 56 sts of pocket front with sts of pocket back, then patt rem 43 (46: 49: **52: 55: 58**) sts of left side of front. 143 (149: 155: **161: 167: 173**) sts.

Work even until front matches back to beg of armhole shaping, ending with RS facing for next row.

Shape armholes

Keeping patt correct, bind off 4 (4: 5: **5: 6: 6**) sts at beg of next 2 rows. 135 (141: 145: **151: 155: 161**) sts.

Dec 1 st at each end of next 3 (5: 5: **7: 7: 9**) rows, then on foll 4 (4: 5: **5: 6: 6**) alt rows. 121 (123: 125: **127: 129: 131**) sts.

Work even until 14 (**16**) rows less have been worked than on back to start of shoulder shaping, ending with RS facing for next row.

Shape neck

Next row (RS): Patt 48 (**49**) sts and turn, leaving rem sts on a holder.

Work each side of neck separately.

Bind off 7 sts at beg of next row. 41 (**42**) sts.

Dec 1 st at neck edge of next 10 rows, then on foll 0 (**1**) alt rows. 31 sts.

Work 2 rows, ending with RS facing for next row.

Shape shoulder

Bind off 5 sts at beg and dec 1 st at end of next row. 25 sts.

Work 1 row.

Bind off 5 sts at beg of next and foll 3 alt rows.

Work 1 row.

Bind off rem 5 sts.

With RS facing, rejoin yarn to rem sts, bind off center 25 (27: 29: **29: 31: 33**) sts dec 7 sts evenly across, patt to end.

Complete to match first side, reversing shapings.

SLEEVES

Cast on 50 (**58**) sts, using size 3 (3.25mm) needles.

Row 1 (RS): K3, *P4, K4, rep from * to last 7 sts, P4, K3.

Row 2: P3, *K4, P4, rep from * to last 7 sts, K4, P3.

These 2 rows form rib.

Work in rib for 21 rows more, ending with **WS** facing for next row.

Row 24 (WS): Rib 7 (**5**), *M1, P3 (**4**), rep from * to last 7 (**5**) sts, M1, P7 (**5**). 63 (**71**) sts.

Change to size 6 (4mm) needles and work as foll:

Row 1 (RS): (P1, K1) 6 (**8**) times, work next 39 sts as row 1 of chart for sleeve, (K1, P1) 6 (**8**) times.

Row 2: (P1, K1) 6 (**8**) times, work next 39 sts as row 2 of chart for sleeve, (K1, P1) 6 (**8**) times.

These 2 rows set the sts—center 39 sts in patt foll chart with edge sts in seed st.

Keeping sts correct as set, repeating the 28 patt rows throughout, cont as foll:

Inc 1 st at each end of 9th row (from beg of chart) and every foll 8th row to 83 (81: 71: **99: 93: 91**) sts, then on every foll 6th row until there are 93 (95: 99: **101: 105: 107**) sts.

Work even until sleeve measures 20¾ (21¼: 21½: **22¼: 22½: 23¼**) in/53 (54: 55: **56.5: 57.5: 59**) cm, ending with RS facing for next row.

Shape sleeve cap

Keeping patt correct, bind off 4 (4: 5: **5: 6: 6**) sts at beg of next 4 rows. 77 (79: 79: **81: 81: 83**) sts.

Dec 1 st at each end of every row until 23 sts rem.

Bind off.

FINISHING

Do NOT press.

Sew both shoulder seams using backstitch, or mattress stitch if preferred.

Collar

With RS facing and using size 3 (3.25mm) circular needle, starting and ending at left shoulder seam, pick up and knit 22 (**24**) sts down left side of neck, 18 (22: 22: **22: 22: 26**) sts from front, 22 (**24**) sts up right side of neck, then 50 (54: 54: **58: 58: 62**) sts from back. 112 (120: 120: **128: 128: 136**) sts.

Round 1 (RS): K1 (3: 3: 0), P4 (**1: 3: 3**), *K4, P4, rep from * to last 3 (1: 1: **7: 5: 5**) sts, K3 (1: 1: **4**), P0 (**3: 1: 1**).

This round forms rib.

Work in rib for 19 rounds more.

Round 21 (eyelet round) (RS): Rib 26 (28: 28: **30: 30: 32**), P2tog, yo, P1, K4, P1, yo, P2tog tbl, rib to end.

Work in rib for 3 rounds more.

Round 25 (RS): Purl (to form fold line).

Work in rib for 8 rounds more.

Bind off in rib.

Pocket borders (both alike)

With RS facing and using size 3 (3.25mm) needles, pick up and knit 45 sts evenly along curved pocket opening edge.

Row 1 (WS): K1, *P1, K1, rep from * to end.

Row 2: P1, *K1, P1, rep from * to end.

Rep last 2 rows twice more.

Bind off in rib.

Ties

Using double-pointed size 3 (3.25mm) needles, cast on 3 sts.

Next row (RS): K3—all 3 sts now on right needle, *slip sts to opposite end of needle and transfer this needle to left hand, without turning work and taking yarn quite tightly across back of work, K same 3 sts again—all 3 sts now on right needle again, rep from * until tie is 71 in (180 cm) long for hem tie, or 40 in (102 cm) long for collar tie.

Next row: K3tog and fasten off.

Machine wash all pieces before completing sewing together. Fold collar to inside along fold-line row and slip stitch in place.

KNITTER'S TIP

The ties through the neck and hem edges of this sporty sweater are knitted tubular cords. But there's no reason why you couldn't replace them with purchased cords, or twisted or crochet cords. And why not try knotting the ends of the cords, or adding those little "acorns" to give your sweater that really professional finish?

Sew pocket lining in place on inside, then neatly sew down ends of pocket borders.

See page 148 for finishing instructions, sewing in sleeves using the set-in method. Fold first 10 rows to inside around lower edge and slip stitch in place. Thread ties through neck and hem casings.

About Martin Storey

Martin Storey was born in Hull and taught to knit as a small child by an inspirational elementary school teacher who saw nothing unusual in teaching needlecrafts to boys and girls alike.

Martin studied fashion at Middlesex University which allowed him to cultivate his interest in hand knitting. The design department was a hot bed of the most influential and creative minds of the 1980s, and Martin mixed with the likes of fashion designers David Holler and Stevie Stewart—also known as Bodymap—as well as jewelers Dower and Hall.

After graduating Martin began working for a knitwear design company run by Jane and Patrick Gottelier, known as Artwork, which specializd in cotton denim yarns with natural fading qualities. Martin was involved in creating these sought-after signature denim knits which sold all over the world.

Martin left Artwork to become chief designer for the Jaeger brand which was taken under Rowan's wing in 1995. In 2005 he was chosen as the designer to spearhead the new brand of Rowan Classic.

Martin is also co-author/designer of several successful Rowan books, including *Classic Knits for Real Women* and *Classic Knits for Men*.

Able

KIM HARGREAVES

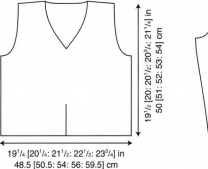
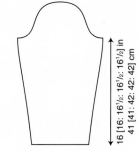

19½ [20: 20½: 20¾: 21¼] in
50 [51: 52: 53: 54] cm

19¼ [20¼: 21½: 22½: 23¾] in
48.5 [50.5: 54: 56: 59.5] cm

16 [16: 16½: 16½: 16½] in
41 [41: 42: 42: 42] cm

SIZES AND YARN

	XS	S	M	L	XL	
To fit bust	32	34	36	38	40	in
	81	86	91	97	102	cm
Rowan Summer Tweed						
	9	9	10	10	11	x 50 g

Photographed in Raffia 515

NEEDLES

1 pair size 6 (4mm) needles
1 pair size 8 (5mm) needles
Cable needle

KNITTER'S TIP

Rowan Summer Tweed is a wonderful luxury yarn, but it is fairly heavy. Make sure you match your gauge perfectly. If you knit just a little bit too loose, this sweater is going to sag and grow every time you wear it. And, because of the nature of this yarn, it is best stored folded rather than on a hanger.

GAUGE

18 sts and 26 rows to 4 in (10 cm) measured over seed stitch using size 8 (5mm) needles.

SPECIAL ABBREVIATIONS

C19B = Cable 19 back Slip next 11 sts onto cn and leave at back of work, K8, slip last 3 sts on cn back onto left needle and seed st these 3 sts, then K8 from cn.

Cr9R = Cross 9 right Slip next st onto cn and leave at back of work, K8, then seed st 1 st from cn.

Cr9L = Cross 9 left Slip next 8 sts onto cn and leave at front of work, seed st 1 st, then K8 from cn.

FRONT

First section

Cast on 47 (49: 52: 54: 57) sts, using size 6 (4mm) needles.

Row 1 (RS): Knit.
Row 2: K to last 11 sts, P8, K3.
Row 3: Knit.
Row 4: *K1, P1, rep from * to last 11 (11: 12: 12: 11) sts, K0 (0: 1: 1: 0), P8, K1, P1, K1.
Row 5: K1, P1, K9 (9: 10: 10: 9), *P1, K1, rep from * to end.
Last 2 rows set the sts—front opening edge 3 sts in seed st, next 8 sts in St st and side seam sts in seed st.
Keeping sts correct as set, cont as foll:
Work 3 rows more, ending with RS facing for next row.
Change to size 8 (5mm) needles.
Cont as set for 24 (26: 26: 28: 28) rows more, ending with RS facing for next row.
Break off yarn and leave sts on a holder.

Second section

Cast on 47 (49: 52: 54: 57) sts, using size 6 (4mm) needles.
Row 1 (RS): Knit.
Row 2: K3, P8, K to end.
Row 3: Knit.
Row 4: K1, P1, K1, P8, K0 (0: 1: 1: 0), *P1, K1, rep from * to end.
Row 5: *K1, P1, rep from * to last 11 (11: 12: 12: 11) sts, K9 (9: 10: 10: 9), P1, K1.
Last 2 rows set the sts—front opening edge 3 sts in seed st, next 8 sts in St st and side seam sts in seed st.
Keeping sts correct as set, cont as foll:

Work 3 rows more, ending with RS facing for next row.
Change to size 8 (5mm) needles.
Cont as set for 24 (26: 26: 28: 28) rows more, ending with RS facing for next row.

Join sections
Next row (RS): Seed st first 36 (38: 41: 43: 46) sts of second section, Cr9L, seed st 1 st, inc in next st, now work across sts of first section as foll—seed st first 2 sts, Cr9R, seed st to end. 95 (99: 105: 109: 115) sts.
Next row: Seed st 37 (39: 42: 44: 47) sts, P8, seed st 5 sts, P8, seed st to end.
Patt as foll:
Row 1 (RS): Seed st 37 (39: 42: 44: 47) sts, Cr9L, seed st 3 sts, Cr9R, seed st to end.
Row 2: Seed st 38 (40: 43: 45: 48) sts, P8, seed st 3 sts, P8, seed st to end.
Row 3: Seed st 38 (40: 43: 45: 48) sts, C19B, seed st to end.
Row 4: Rep row 2.
Row 5: Seed st 37 (39: 42: 44: 47), Cr9R, seed st 3 sts, Cr9L, seed st to end.
Row 6: Seed st 37 (39: 42: 44: 47) sts, P8, seed st 5 sts, P8, seed st to end.
Row 7: Seed st 36 (38: 41: 43: 46) sts, Cr9R, seed st 5 sts, Cr9L, seed st to end.
Row 8: Seed st 36 (38: 41: 43: 46) sts, P8, seed st 7 sts, P8, seed st to end.
Row 9: Seed st 36 (38: 41: 43: 46) sts, K8, seed st 7 sts, K8, seed st to end.
Rows 10–19: (Rep rows 8 and 9) 5 times.
Row 20: Rep row 8.
Row 21: Seed st 36 (38: 41: 43: 46) sts, Cr9L, seed st 5 sts, Cr9R, seed st to end.
Row 22: Rep row 6.
These 22 rows form patt.
Work in patt for 22 rows more, ending with RS facing for next row.
Front now measures approx 11¾ (12¼: 12¼: 12½: 12½) in/ 30 (31: 31: 32: 32) cm.

Shape armholes
Keeping patt correct, bind off 4 (5: 5: 6: 6) sts at beg of next 2 rows. 87 (89: 95: 97: 103) sts.
Dec 1 st at each end of next 5 (5: 6: 6: 6) rows. 77 (79: 83: 85: 91) sts.
Work 1 (1: 0: 0: 0) row, ending after patt row 8 and with RS facing for next row.

Divide for neck
Next row (RS): Work 2 tog, patt 20 (21: 23: 24: 27) sts, work 3 tog, patt 13 sts and turn, leaving rem sts on a holder. 35 (36: 38: 39: 42) sts.
Work each side of neck separately.
Next row: Seed st 3 sts, P8, seed st to last 0 (0: 0: 0: 2) sts,

(work2tog) 0 (0: 0: 0: 1) times.
Next row: Work 2 tog, seed st to last 11 sts, K8, seed st 3 sts. 34 (35: 37: 38: 40) sts.
Last 2 rows set the sts—8 sts from cable now worked in St st and all other sts in seed st.
Keeping sts correct as set, dec 1 st at armhole edge of 2nd and foll 0 (0: 1: 0: 1) alt row. 33 (34: 35: 37: 38) sts.
Work 3 (3: 1: 1: 1) rows, ending with RS facing for next row.
Next row (RS): (Work 2 tog) 0 (0: 0: 1: 1) times, patt to last 16 sts, work 3 tog, patt to end. 31 (32: 33: 34: 35) sts.
Working all neck decreases as set by last row, dec 2 sts at neck edge of every foll 8th (8th: 8th: 6th: 8th) row to 27 (28: 31: 32: 27) sts, then on every foll 10th (10th: 10th: 8th: -) row until 25 (26: 27: 26: -) sts rem.
Work even until armhole measures 7¾ (7¾: 8¼: 8¼: 8¾) in/ 20 (20: 21: 21: 22) cm, ending with RS facing for next row.

Shape shoulder
Bind off 4 (5: 5: 5: 5) sts at beg of next and foll alt row, then 5 (4: 5: 4: 5) sts at beg of foll alt row. 12 sts.
Cont as set on these 12 sts for 4 (4: 4: 4¼: 4¼) in/10 (10: 10: 11: 11) cm more for back neck border, ending with RS facing for next row.
Bind off.
With RS facing, rejoin yarn to rem sts and cont as foll:
Next row (RS): Work 2 tog, patt 12 sts, work 3 tog, patt to last 2 sts, work 2 tog.
Complete to match first side, reversing shapings.

BACK
Cast on 87 (91: 97: 101: 107) sts, using size 6 (4mm) needles.
Work in garter st for 3 rows, ending with **WS** facing for next row.
Row 4 (WS): K1, *P1, K1, rep from * to end.
Row 5: Rep row 4.
Rows 4 and 5 form seed st.
Work in seed st for 3 rows more, ending with RS facing for next row.
Change to size 8 (5mm) needles.
Cont in seed st until back matches front to beg of armhole shaping, ending with RS facing for next row.

Shape armholes
Keeping seed st correct, bind off 4 (5: 5: 6: 6) sts at beg of next 2 rows. 79 (81: 87: 89: 95) sts.
Dec 1 st at each end of next 5 (5: 7: 7: 9) rows, then on foll 3 alt rows. 63 (65: 67: 69: 71) sts.
Work even until 2 rows less have been worked than on front to beg of shoulder shaping, ending with RS facing for next row.

Shape back neck and shoulders
Next row (RS): Seed st 16 (17: 18: 17: 18) sts and turn, leaving rem sts on a holder.
Work each side of neck separately.
Dec 1 st at beg of next row. 15 (16: 17: 16: 17) sts.

Bind off 4 (5: 5: 5: 5) sts at beg and dec 1 st at end of next row.
Work 1 row.
Rep last 2 rows once more.
Bind off rem 5 (4: 5: 4: 5) sts.
With RS facing, rejoin yarn to rem sts, bind off center 31 (31: 31: 35: 35) sts, seed st to end.
Complete to match first side, reversing shapings.

SLEEVES

Cast on 51 (51: 53: 55: 55) sts, using size 6 (4mm) needles.
Work in garter st for 3 rows, ending with **WS** facing for next row.
Work in seed st as given for back for 3 rows, ending with RS facing for next row.
Change to size 8 (5mm) needles.
Cont in seed st, shaping sides by inc 1 st at each end of 15th (11th: 11th: 11th: 13th) and every foll 24th (18th: 18th: 18th: 16th) row to 59 (57: 57: 59: 67) sts, then on every foll – (20th: 20th: 20th: -) row until there are – (61: 63: 65: –) sts.
Work even until sleeve measures 16 (16: 16½: 16½: 16½) in/ 41 (41: 42: 42: 42) cm, ending with RS facing for next row.
Shape sleeve cap
Keeping seed st correct, bind off 4 (5: 5: 6: 6) sts at beg of next 2 rows. 51 (51: 53: 53: 55) sts.
Dec 1 st at each end of next 3 rows, then on foll 2 alt rows, then on every foll 4th row until 31 (31: 33: 33: 35) sts rem.
Work 1 row.
Dec 1 st at each end of next and every foll alt row until 27 sts rem, then on foll 3 rows, ending with RS facing for next row.
Bind off rem 21 sts.

FINISHING

Press as described on page 148.
Sew both shoulder seams using backstitch, or mattress stitch if preferred.
Sew together bound-off ends of back neck borders, then sew one edge to back neck.
Catch stitch front opening edges of cable in place on WS at lower edge.
See page 148 for finishing instructions, setting in sleeves using the set-in method.

Buena Vista

JEAN MOSS

SIZES AND YARN

	XS	S	M	L	XL	
To fit bust	32	34	36	38	40	in
	81	86	91	97	102	cm

Rowan Wool Cotton

			XS	S	M	L	XL	
A	Blue Wash	973	9	9	10	10	10	x 50 g
B	Citron	901	1	1	1	1	1	x 50 g
C	Clear	941	1	1	1	1	1	x 50 g
D	Flower	943	1	1	1	1	1	x 50 g

Originally knitted and photographed (above) in Rowan Calmer in Zeal 468 (A), Laurel 464 (B) and Pool 467 (C), and Rowan Summer Tweed in Brilliant 528 (D)

16¾ [17¾: 18¾: 19¾: 20¾] in
42 [44.5: 47: 49.5: 52] cm

16¼ [16½: 16¾: 17¼: 17¾] in
41 [42: 43: 44: 45] cm

9¾ [9¾: 10¼: 10¼: 10¼] in
25 [25: 26: 26: 26] cm

NEEDLES

1 pair size 7 (4.5mm) needles
Size 7 (4.5mm) circular needle

FASTENINGS—3 large decorative hooks and eyes

NEW YARN SUBSTITUTIONS

This neat and pretty bolero was originally knitted in Rowan Calmer and Rowan Summer Tweed. Both yarns are still in the Rowan range, but the colors have changed. We chose Rowan Wool Cotton (right) as a substitute yarn so we could recreate the original color effect. Our new colors are a little softer—but just as nice. Knitted in the original Rowan Calmer, this bolero was quite firm, but using Wool Cotton gives a much more fluid fabric that still holds its shape. If you want to use the original yarn—but different colors—you need 6 (6: 6: 7: 7) balls of Calmer in the main color (yarn A), and one ball of Calmer in each of the first two contrasting colors (yarns B and C). The third contrasting color (yarn D) was originally Summer Tweed and you need one ball of this.

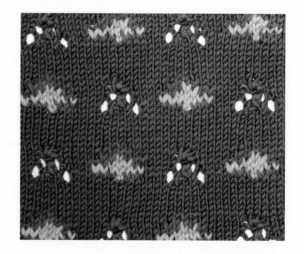

GAUGE

24 sts and 32 rows to 4 in (10 cm) measured over St st using size
7 (4.5mm) needles.

SPECIAL ABBREVIATIONS

Cluster 3 = Using yarn A, P tog next 3 sts leaving sts on left
needle, take yarn to back of work, K tog same 3 sts leaving sts on
left needle, bring yarn to front of work, P tog same 3 sts again,
slipping sts off left needle.

BACK

Cast on 101 (107: 113: 119: 125) sts, using size 7 (4.5mm)
needles and yarn A.

Using the **intarsia** technique as described on page 148 and
starting and ending rows as indicated, repeating the 24 row patt
repeat throughout, cont in patt from chart, which is worked
mainly in St st, as foll:

Work 3 rows, ending with **WS** facing for next row.

Dec 1 st at each end of next and every foll 3rd row until 89 (95:
101: 107: 113) sts rem.

Work 9 rows, ending with RS facing for next row.

Inc 1 st at each end of next and every foll 5th row until there are
101 (107: 113: 119: 125) sts.

Work even until back measures 9½ (9¾: 9¾: 10¼: 10¼) in/24 (25:
25: 26: 26) cm, ending with RS facing for next row.

Shape armholes

Keeping patt correct, bind off 5 (6: 6: 7: 7) sts at beg of next
2 rows. 91 (95: 101: 105: 111) sts.

Dec 1 st at each end of next 1 (1: 3: 3: 5) rows, then on foll
4 (5: 5: 6: 6) alt rows. 81 (83: 85: 87: 89) sts.

Work even until armhole measures 6¾ (6¾: 7: 7: 7½) in/
17 (17: 18: 18: 19) cm, ending with RS facing for next row.

Shape shoulders and back neck

Next row (RS): Bind off 8 (8: 9: 9: 9) sts, patt until there are
20 (20: 20: 20: 21) sts on right needle and turn, leaving rem sts
on a holder.

Work each side of neck separately.

Dec 1 st at beg of next row. 19 (19: 19: 19: 20) sts.

Bind off 8 (8: 9: 9: 9) sts at beg and dec 1 st at end of next row.
10 (10: 9: 9: 10) sts.

Dec 1 st at beg of next row.

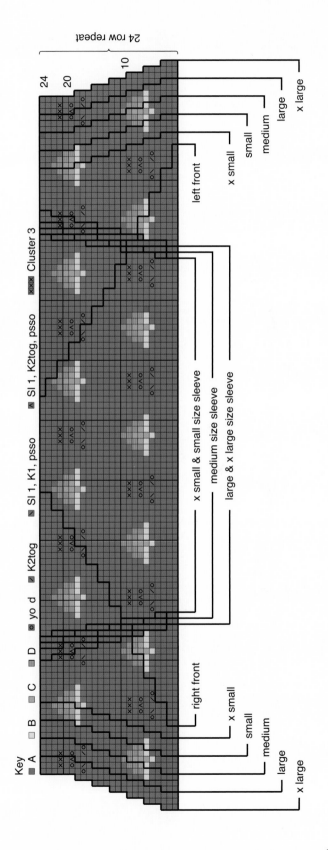

Bind off rem 9 (9: 8: 8: 9) sts.

With RS facing, rejoin yarn to rem sts, bind off center 25 (27: 27: 29: 29) sts, patt to end.

Complete to match first side, reversing shapings.

LEFT FRONT

Cast on 2 (5: 8: 11: 14) sts, using size 7 (4.5mm) needles and yarn A.

Starting and ending rows as indicated, cont in patt from chart as foll:

Work 1 row, ending with **WS** facing for next row.

Cast on 4 sts at beg of next and foll 5 alt rows, then 3 sts at beg of foll 4 alt rows **and at same time** dec 1 st at end (side seam edge) of 3rd row and at same edge on every foll 3rd row. 32 (35: 38: 41: 44) sts.

Work 1 row, ending with **WS** facing for next row.

Cast on 3 sts at beg of next and foll 3 alt rows. 44 (47: 50: 53: 56) sts.

Inc 1 st at side seam edge of next and every foll 5th row until there are 50 (53: 56: 59: 62) sts.

Work even until 20 rows less have been worked than on back to beg of armhole shaping, ending with RS facing for next row.

Shape front slope

Keeping patt correct, dec 1 st at end of next and every foll 4th row until 45 (48: 51: 54: 57) sts rem.

Work 3 rows, ending with RS facing for next row.

Shape armhole

Keeping patt correct, bind off 5 (6: 6: 7: 7) sts at beg and dec 1 st at end of next row. 39 (41: 44: 46: 49) sts.

Work 1 row.

Dec 1 st at armhole edge of next 1 (1: 3: 3: 5) rows, then on foll 4 (5: 5: 6: 6) alt rows **and at same time** dec 1 st at front slope edge of 3rd and every foll 4th row. 32 (32: 33: 33: 34) sts.

Dec 1 st at front slope edge of 2nd (4th: 2nd: 4th: 2nd) and every foll 4th row until 30 (28: 31: 29: 31) sts rem, then on every foll 6th row until 25 (25: 26: 26: 27) sts rem.

Work even until left front matches back to start of shoulder shaping, ending with RS facing for next row.

Shape shoulder

Bind off 8 (8: 9: 9: 9) sts at beg of next and foll alt row.

Work 1 row.

Bind off rem 9 (9: 8: 8: 9) sts.

RIGHT FRONT

Cast on 2 (5: 8: 11: 14) sts, using size 7 (4.5mm) needles and yarn A.

Starting and ending rows as indicated, cont in patt from chart as foll:

Work 2 rows, ending with RS facing for next row.

Cast on 4 sts at beg of next and foll 5 alt rows, then 3 sts at beg of foll 4 alt rows **and at same time** dec 1 st at end (side seam

edge) of 2nd row and at same edge on every foll 3rd row. 32 (35: 38: 41: 44) sts.

Complete to match left front, following chart for right front and reversing shapings.

SLEEVES

Cast on 59 (59: 61: 63: 63) sts, using size 7 (4.5mm) needles and yarn A.

Starting and ending rows as indicated, cont in patt from chart, shaping sides by inc 1 st at each end of 5th (3rd: 3rd: 3rd: 3rd) and every foll 6th (4th: 6th: 6th: 4th) row to 79 (63: 85: 87: 71) sts, then on every foll 8th (6th: –: –: 6th) row until there are 81 (83: –: –: 89) sts.

Work even until sleeve measures 9¾ (9¾: 10¼: 10¼: 10¼) in/ 25 (25: 26: 26: 26) cm, ending with RS facing for next row.

Shape sleeve cap

Keeping patt correct, bind off 5 (6: 6: 7: 7) sts at beg of next 2 rows. 71 (71: 73: 73: 75) sts.

Dec 1 st at each end of next 7 rows, then on every foll alt row until 25 sts rem, then on foll row, ending with RS facing for next row.

Bind off 3 sts at beg of next 4 rows.

Bind off rem 11 sts.

FINISHING

Press described on page 148.

Sew both shoulder seams using backstitch, or mattress stitch if preferred.

Sew side seams.

Body frill

With RS facing, using size 7 (4.5mm) circular needle and yarn A, starting and ending at base of left side seam, pick up and knit 100 (106: 113: 119: 124) sts across back cast-on edge, 63 (66: 69: 72: 75) sts along shaped edge of right front to straight row-end edge, 22 (24: 24: 26: 26) sts up straight row-end edge to start of front slope shaping, 62 (63: 64: 65: 67) sts up right front slope to shoulder, 31 (33: 33: 35: 35) sts from back, 62 (63: 64: 65: 67) sts down left front slope to start of front slope shaping, 22 (24: 24: 26: 26) sts down straight row-end edge to start of hem shaping, then 63 (66: 69: 72: 75) sts along shaped edge of left front to side seam. 425 (445: 460: 480: 495) sts.

★★Working in rounds, cont as foll:

Round 1 (RS): ★K into front, back, and front again of next st, K4, rep from ★ to end. 595 (623: 644: 672: 693) sts.

Round 2: Knit.

Round 3: ★K1, inc in next st, K4, inc in next st, rep from ★ to end. 765 (801: 828: 864: 891) sts.

Round 4: Knit.

Round 5: ★K3, inc in next st, K4, inc in next st, rep from ★ to end. 935 (979: 1,012: 1,056: 1,089) sts.

Round 6: Knit.

Bind off.

Sew sleeve seams.

Cuff frill

With RS facing, using size 7 (4.5mm) circular needle and yarn A, starting and ending at base of sleeve seam, pick up and knit 55 (55: 60: 60: 60) sts around cast-on edge of sleeve.

Complete as for body frill from ★★.

See page 148 for finishing instructions, setting in sleeves using the set-in method. Sew hooks and eyes to inside of fronts just next to pick-up row and level with start of front slope shaping.

About Jean Moss

Jean Moss is one of Britain's leading knitwear designers and she is known worldwide for her distinctive style and couture hand knits. Her innovative combinations of intricate textures, striking colorways, and sophisticated styling have been widely influential over the years.

A self-taught knitter, Jean has been producing her own unique collections and publications for over 20 years, as well as designing for Rowan Yarns and many international fashion houses such as Ralph Lauren, Laura Ashley, and Benetton. It was in the early 1980s, while working in Yorkshire for Ralph Lauren, that Jean met Stephen Sheard, who asked her to design for Rowan Magazine 4.

Jean is passionate about passing on her wealth of knowledge and runs an extensive workshop and lecturing programs both in the UK and in the US.

Powder Puff

KAFFE FASSETT

YARN
Rowan Kidsilk Haze

A	Majestic	589	1 x 25 g
B	Putty	626	2 x 25 g
C	Jelly	597	1 x 25 g
D	Flower	643	1 x 25 g
E	Candy Girl	606	1 x 25 g
F	Heavenly	592	2 x 25 g
G	Pearl	590	1 x 25 g

Use Kidsilk Haze DOUBLE throughout
Originally knitted and photographed (above) in Rowan Kidsilk Haze in Majestic 589 (A), Caramel Swirl 604 (B), Jelly 597 (C), Bebe 586 (D), Candy Girl 606 (E), Heavenly 592 (F), and Pearl 590 (G)

NEEDLES
1 pair size 3 (3mm) needles
1 pair size 5 (3.75mm) needles

NEW YARN SUBSTITUTIONS
Knitted in Kidsilk Haze, this clever scarf uses seven different colors. Unfortunately, a couple of the original colors are no longer available, so we have substituted new colors to recreate the original as closely as possible.

GAUGE
23 sts and 32 rows to 4 in (10 cm) measured over St st using size 5 (3.75mm) needles and yarn DOUBLE.

FINISHED SIZE
Finished scarf measures approx 10 in (25 cm) wide by 54 in (137 cm) long.

SCARF
Cast on 58 sts, using size 3 (3mm) needles and yarn A.
Work in garter st for 4 rows, ending with RS facing for next row.
Change to size 5 (3.75mm) needles.
Using the **intarsia** technique as described on page 148 and

joining in and breaking off colors as required, cont as foll:
Row 1 (RS): Using yarn E K16, using yarn F K13, using yarn G K13, using yarn B K16.
Row 2: Using yarn B K3, P13, using yarn G P13, using yarn F P13, using yarn E P13, K3.
Rows 3–18: (Rep rows 1 and 2) 8 times.
Row 19: Using yarn F K16, using yarn G K13, using yarn B K13, using yarn C K16.
Row 20: Using yarn C K3, P13, using yarn B P13, using yarn G P13, using yarn F P13, K3.
Rows 21–36: (Rep rows 19 and 20) 8 times.
Row 37: Using yarn G K16, using yarn B K13, using yarn C K13, using yarn D K16.
Row 38: Using yarn D K3, P13, using yarn C P13, using yarn B P13, using yarn G P13, K3.
Rows 39–54: (Rep rows 37 and 38) 8 times.
Row 55: Using yarn B K16, using yarn C K13, using yarn D K13, using yarn E K16.
Row 56: Using yarn E K3, P13, using yarn D P13, using yarn C P13, using yarn B P13, K3.
Rows 57–72: (Rep rows 55 and 56) 8 times.
Row 73: Using yarn C K16, using yarn D K13, using yarn E K13, using yarn F K16.
Row 74: Using yarn F K3, P13, using yarn E P13, using yarn D P13, using yarn C P13, K3.
Rows 75–90: (Rep rows 73 and 74) 8 times.
Row 91: Using yarn D K16, using yarn E K13, using yarn F K13, using yarn G K16.
Row 92: Using yarn G K3, P13, using yarn F P13, using yarn E P13, using yarn D P13, K3.
Rows 93–108: (Rep rows 91 and 92) 8 times.
(Rep rows 1–108) 3 times more, ending with RS facing for next row.
Change to size 3 (3mm) needles.
Break off all yarns and join in yarn A.
Work in garter st for 3 rows.
Bind off knitwise (on WS).

FINISHING
Press as described on page 148.

Rosebud

SASHA KAGAN

SIZES AND YARN

		XS	S	M	L	XL	
To fit bust		32	34	36	38	40	in
		81	86	91	97	102	cm

Rowan Wool Cotton

		XS	S	M	L	XL	
A Hiss	952	8	9	9	10	10	x 50 g
B Tender	951	2	2	2	2	2	x 50 g
C Flower	943	2	2	2	2	2	x 50 g
D Riviera	930	2	2	2	2	2	x 50 g
E Deepest Olive	907	2	2	2	2	2	x 50 g

NEEDLES

1 pair size 3 (3.25mm) needles
1 pair size 6 (4mm) needles

BUTTONS—9

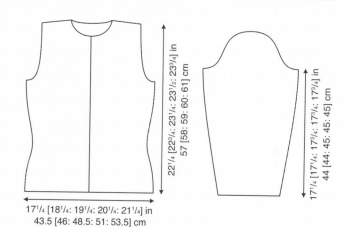

22¼ [22¾: 23¼: 23½: 23¾] in
57 [58: 59: 60: 61] cm

17¼ [18¼: 19¼: 20¼: 21¼] in
43.5 [46: 48.5: 51: 53.5] cm

17¼ [17¼: 17¾: 17¾: 17¾] in
44 [44: 45: 45: 45] cm

KNITTER'S TIP

Rowan Wool Cotton is a fine yarn for its weight and some knitters find they need to use a size smaller needle to obtain the correct gauge. It is therefore really important you check your gauge before you start. Knitted too loosely, this cardigan will sag out of shape as soon as you put it on. And you may find you run out of yarn, too.

GAUGE

24 sts and 30 rows to 4 in (10 cm) measured over lace and St st pattern using size 6 (4mm) needles.

BACK

Cast on 103 (109: 115: 121: 127) sts, using size 3 (3.25mm) needles and yarn A.
Row 1 (RS): K1, ★P1, K1, rep from ★ to end.
Row 2: Rep row 1.
These 2 rows form seed st.
Work in seed st for 6 rows more, inc 1 st at end of last row

and ending with RS facing for next row. 104 (110: 116: 122: 128) sts.
Change to size 6 (4mm) needles.
Using the **intarsia** technique as described on page 148, starting and ending rows as indicated, and repeating the 32 row repeat throughout, cont in patt from chart for back (see page 110) as foll:
Dec 1 st at each end of 5th and every foll 6th row until 92 (98: 104: 110: 116) sts rem.
Work 15 rows, ending with RS facing for next row.
Inc 1 st at each end of next and every foll 8th row until there are 104 (110: 116: 122: 128) sts, taking inc sts into patt.
Work even until back measures 14½ (15: 15: 15¼: 15¼) in/ 37 (38: 38: 39: 39) cm, ending with RS facing for next row.
Shape armholes
Keeping patt correct, bind off 3 (4: 4: 5: 5) sts at beg of next 2 rows. 98 (102: 108: 112: 118) sts.
Dec 1 st at each end of next 3 (3: 5: 5: 7) rows, then on foll 1 (2: 2: 3: 3) alt rows, then on foll 4th row. 88 (90: 92: 94: 96) sts.
Work even until armhole measures 7¾ (7¾: 8¼: 8¼: 8½) in/ 20 (20: 21: 21: 22) cm, ending with RS facing for next row.

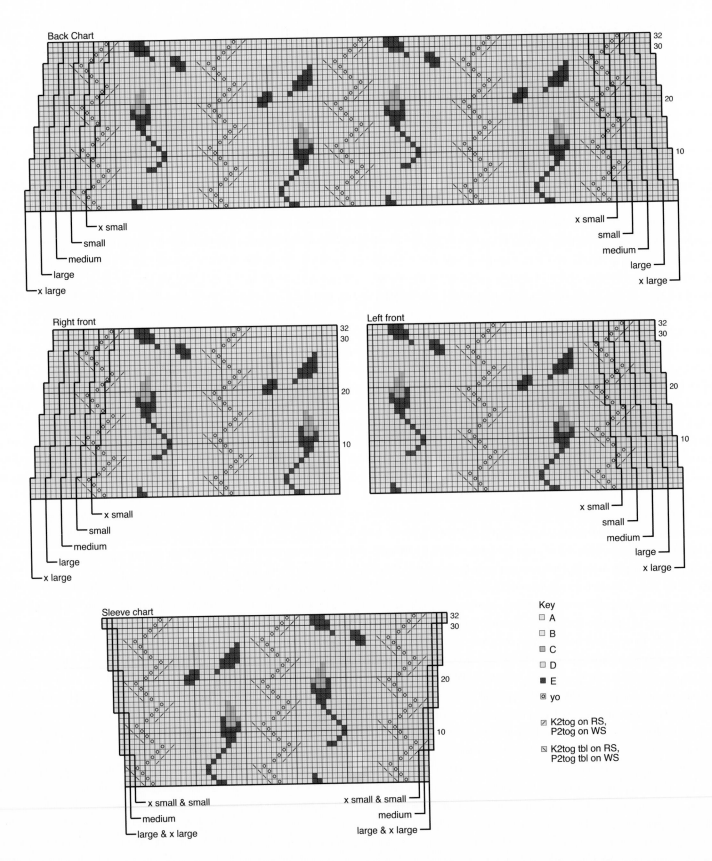

Back Chart

x small
small
medium
large
x large

x small
small
medium
large
x large

Right front

x small
small
medium
large
x large

Left front

x small
small
medium
large
x large

Sleeve chart

x small & small
medium
large & x large

x small & small
medium
large & x large

Key

☐ A
☐ B
☐ C
☐ D
■ E
⊙ yo

☑ K2tog on RS,
P2tog on WS

☒ K2tog tbl on RS,
P2tog tbl on WS

Shape shoulders and back neck

Bind off 8 (8: 9: 9: 9) sts at beg of next 2 rows. 72 (74: 74: 76: 78) sts.

Next row (RS): Bind off 8 (8: 9: 9: 9) sts, patt until there are 13 (13: 12: 12: 13) sts on right needle and turn, leaving rem sts on a holder.

Work each side of neck separately.

Bind off 4 sts at beg of next row.

Bind off rem 9 (9: 8: 8: 9) sts.

With RS facing, rejoin yarn to rem sts, bind off center 30 (32: 32: 34: 34) sts, patt to end.

Complete to match first side, reversing shapings.

LEFT FRONT

Cast on 55 (57: 61: 63: 67) sts, using size 3 (3.25mm) needles and yarn A.

Work in seed st as given for back for 7 rows, ending with **WS** facing for next row.

Row 8 (WS): Seed st 7 sts and slip these sts onto a holder, M1, seed st to last 0 (1: 0: 1: 0) st, (inc in last st) 0 (1: 0: 1: 0) times. 49 (52: 55: 58: 61) sts.

Change to size 6 (4mm) needles.

Starting and ending rows as indicated, cont in patt from chart for left front as foll:

Dec 1 st at beg of 5th and every foll 6th row until 43 (46: 49: 52: 55) sts rem.

Work 15 rows, ending with RS facing for next row.

Inc 1 st at beg of next and every foll 8th row until there are 49 (52: 55: 58: 61) sts, taking inc sts into patt.

Work even until left front matches back to beg of armhole shaping, ending with RS facing for next row.

Shape armhole

Keeping patt correct, bind off 3 (4: 4: 5: 5) sts at beg of next row. 46 (48: 51: 53: 56) sts.

Work 1 row.

Dec 1 st at armhole edge of next 3 (3: 5: 5: 7) rows, then on foll 1 (2: 2: 3: 3) alt rows, then on foll 4th row. 41 (42: 43: 44: 45) sts.

Work even until 15 (15: 15: 17: 17) rows less have been worked than on back to start of shoulder shaping, ending with **WS** facing for next row.

Shape neck

Keeping patt correct, bind off 5 (6: 6: 6: 6) sts at beg of next row, then 4 sts at beg of foll alt row. 32 (32: 33: 34: 35) sts.

Dec 1 st at neck edge of next 5 rows, then on foll 2 (2: 2: 3: 3) alt rows. 25 (25: 26: 26: 27) sts.

Work 3 rows, ending with RS facing for next row.

Shape shoulder

Bind off 8 (8: 9: 9: 9) sts at beg of next and foll alt row.

Work 1 row.

Bind off rem 9 (9: 8: 8: 9) sts.

RIGHT FRONT

Cast on 55 (57: 61: 63: 67) sts, using size 3 (3.25mm) needles and yarn A.

Work in seed st as given for back for 4 rows, ending with RS facing for next row.

Row 5 (buttonhole row) (RS): K1, P1, K2tog, yo, seed st to end.

Work in seed st for 2 rows more, ending with **WS** facing for next row.

Row 8 (WS): (Inc in first st) 0 (1: 0: 1: 0) times, seed st to last 7 sts, M1 and turn, leaving rem 7 sts on a holder. 49 (52: 55: 58: 61) sts.

Change to size 6 (4mm) needles.

Starting and ending rows as indicated, cont in patt from chart for right front as foll:

Dec 1 st at end of 5th and every foll 6th row until 43 (46: 49: 52: 55) sts rem.

Complete as given for left front, following chart for right front and reversing shapings.

SLEEVES

Cast on 55 (55: 57: 59: 59) sts, using size 3 (3.25mm) needles and yarn A.

Work in seed st as given for back for 8 rows, inc 1 st at end of last row and ending with RS facing for next row. 56 (56: 58: 60: 60) sts.

Change to size 6 (4mm) needles.

Starting and ending rows as indicated, cont in patt from chart for sleeves, shaping sides by inc 1 st at each end of 7th and every foll 8th row to 66 (76: 76: 78: 88) sts, then on every foll 10th (10th: 10th: 10th: -) row until there are 80 (82: 84: 86: -) sts.

Work even until sleeve measures 17¼ (17¼: 17¾: 17¾: 17¾) in/ 44 (44: 45: 45: 45) cm, ending with RS facing for next row.

Shape sleeve cap

Keeping patt correct, bind off 3 (4: 4: 5: 5) sts at beg of next 2 rows. 74 (74: 76: 76: 78) sts.

Dec 1 st at each end of next 5 rows, then on foll 2 alt rows, then on every foll 4th row until 54 (54: 56: 56: 58) sts rem.

Work 1 row, ending with RS facing for next row.

Dec 1 st at each end of next and every foll alt row to 46 sts, then on foll 3 rows, ending with RS facing for next row.

Bind off 6 sts at beg of next 4 rows.

Bind off rem 16 sts.

FINISHING

Press as described on page 148.

Sew both shoulder seams using backstitch, or mattress stitch.

Button band

Slip 7 sts left on left front holder onto size 3 (3.25mm) needles and rejoin yarn A with RS facing.

Cont in seed st as set until band, when slightly stretched, fits up left front opening edge to neck shaping, ending with RS facing for next row.

Break off yarn and leave sts on a holder.

Slip stitch band in position.

Mark positions for 9 buttons on this band—first to come level with buttonhole already worked in right front, last to come ⅜ in (1 cm) up from neck shaping, and rem 7 buttons evenly spaced between.

Buttonhole band

Slip 7 sts left on right front holder onto size 3 (3.25mm) needles and rejoin yarn A with **WS** facing.

Cont in seed st as set until band, when slightly stretched, fits up right front opening edge to neck shaping, ending with RS facing for next row and with the addition of 7 buttonholes more worked as foll:

Buttonhole row (RS): K1, P1, K2tog, yo, K1, P1, K1.

Do NOT break off yarn.

Neckband

With RS facing, using size 3 (3.25mm) needles and yarn A, seed st across 7 sts of buttonhole band, pick up and knit 23 (24: 24: 27: 27) sts up right side of neck, 39 (41: 41: 43: 43) sts from back, and 23 (24: 24: 27: 27) sts down left side of neck, then seed st across 7 sts of button band. 99 (103: 103: 111: 111) sts.

Work in seed st as set by front bands for 2 rows, ending with **WS** facing for next row.

Row 3 (WS): Seed st to last 4 sts, yo (to make 9th buttonhole), K2tog tbl, seed st to end.

Work in seed st for 2 rows more.

Bind off in seed st.

Belt

Cast on 7 sts, using size 3 (3.25mm) needles and yarn A.

Work in seed st as given for back until belt measures 53 in (135 cm).

Bind off.

See page 148 for finishing instructions, setting in sleeves using the set-in method.

About Sasha Kagan

Sasha Kagan's design trademarks are flowers and foliage which she stylizes in a unique and beautiful way. Indeed, she has a large garden abundant with native wild flowers and more formal planting at her home in Wales.

Sasha studied for a degree in fine art and printmaking and went on to study at the Royal College of Art in London. It was while there that she became interested in the work of William Morris and the creativity of the Arts and Crafts movement of the late 1800s. This is an influence that can still be seen in her knitted fabrics today.

Sasha regularly contributes her designs to Rowan magazines and continues to publish her own books and patterns. She also produces an impressive number of packaged kits and is a sought-after workshop tutor. She has lectured and taught throughout the world and was recently recognized as an influential figure in the knitting world at the Victoria and Albert Museum, London.

Veronica

MARION FOALE

SIZES AND YARN

	XS	S	M	L	XL	
To fit bust	32	34	36	38	40	in
	81	86	91	97	102	cm

Rowan Classic Cashsoft Aran

Haze 004	19	20	21	22	23	x 50 g

Originally knitted and photographed (above) in Rowan 4-Ply
Soft in Rain Cloud 387 used double

NEEDLES

1 pair size 3 (3.25mm) needles
1 pair size 5 (3.75mm) needles
1 pair size 6 (4mm) needles

BUTTONS—5

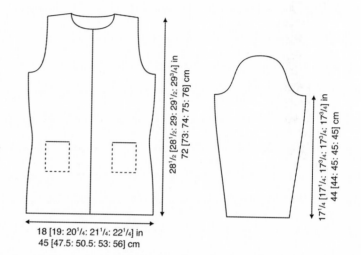

28½ [28½: 29: 29½: 29¾] in
72 [73: 74: 75: 76] cm

18 [19: 20¼: 21¼: 22¼] in
45 [47.5: 50.5: 53: 56] cm

17¼ [17¼: 17¾: 17¾: 17¾] in
44 [44: 45: 45: 45] cm

NEW YARN SUBSTITUTION

This jacket was originally knitted using two strands of a super-
fine pure wool yarn that's no longer available. It created a nice
firm fabric that held its shape well. We could have substituted
Rowan Pure Wool 4-Ply for the original yarn but, to make it
easier to knit, we chose instead to replace it with just one strand
of soft and squishy Rowan Classic Cashsoft Aran (right). Knitted
to a slightly tighter gauge than would be normal, Cashsoft Aran
creates the perfect fabric. If, however, you prefer to knit it using
Rowan Pure Wool 4-Ply, you need 20 (21: 22: 23: 24) balls of
yarn. But remember to use this yarn double throughout.

GAUGE

22 sts and 32 rows to 4 in (10 cm) measured over patt using size 6 (4mm) needles.

BACK

Left back

Cast on 57 (60: 63: 66: 69) sts, using size 5 (3.75mm) needles.

Row 1 (RS): K2, *P1, K1, rep from * to last 1 (0: 1: 0: 1) st, P1 (0: 1: 0: 1).

Row 2: K1 (0: 1: 0: 1), *P1, K1, rep from * to end.

Row 3: *K1, P1, rep from * to last 1 (0: 1: 0: 1) st, K1 (0: 1: 0: 1).

Row 4: P1 (0: 1: 0: 1), *K1, P1, rep from * to last 2 sts, K2.

Rep last 4 rows twice more, ending with RS facing for next row.

Change to size 6 (4mm) needles.

Row 13 (RS): Patt 7 sts, *K3, P2, rep from * to last 0 (3: 1: 4: 2) sts, K0 (3: 1: 3: 2), P0 (0: 0: 1: 0).

Row 14: P to last 7 sts, patt 7 sts.

These 2 rows set the sts—back opening edge 7 sts still in moss st and rem sts now in patt.

Cont as set for 26 rows more, ending with RS facing for next row.

Dec 1 st at end of next row. 56 (59: 62: 65: 68) sts.

Work 7 rows more, ending with RS facing for next row.

Break off yarn and leave sts on a holder.

Right back

Cast on 57 (60: 63: 66: 69) sts, using size 5 (3.75mm) needles.

Row 1 (RS): P1 (0: 1: 0: 1), *K1, P1, rep from * to last 2 sts, K2.

Row 2: *K1, P1, rep from * to last 1 (0: 1: 0: 1) st, K1 (0: 1: 0: 1).

Row 3: K1 (0: 1: 0: 1), *P1, K1, rep from * to end.

Row 4: K2, *P1, K1, rep from * to last 1 (0: 1: 0: 1) st, P1 (0: 1: 0: 1).

Rep last 4 rows twice more, ending with RS facing for next row.

Change to size 6 (4mm) needles.

Row 13 (RS): P0 (0: 0: 1: 0), K0 (3: 1: 3: 2), *P2, K3, rep from * to last 7 sts, patt 7 sts.

Row 14: Patt 7 sts, P to end.

These 2 rows set the sts—back opening edge 7 sts still in moss st and rem sts now in patt.

Cont as set for 26 rows more, ending with RS facing for next row.

Dec 1 st at beg of next row. 56 (59: 62: 65: 68) sts.

Work 7 rows more, ending with RS facing for next row.

Join sections

Row 49 (RS): Patt first 49 (52: 55: 58: 61) sts of right back, holding RS of right back against WS of left back P tog first st of left back with next st of right back, P tog next 2 sts of each section, (K tog next 2 sts of each section) 3 times, (P tog next 2 sts of each section) twice, patt rem 49 (52: 55: 58: 61) sts of left back. 105 (111: 117: 123: 129) sts.

Now working all sts in patt, cont as follows:

Work 1 row, ending with RS facing for next row.

Counting in from both ends of last row, place markers on 33rd (36th: 39th: 42nd: 45th) st in from both ends of row.

Row 51 (dec row) (RS): (Patt to within 2 sts of marked st, K2tog, K marked st, K2 tog tbl) twice, patt to end. 101 (107: 113: 119: 125) sts.

Work 9 rows.

Row 61 (dec row) (RS): Work 2 tog, (patt to within 2 sts of marked st, K2tog, K marked st, K2 tog tbl) twice, patt to last 2 sts, work 2 tog. 95 (101: 107: 113: 119) sts.

Work 9 rows.

Rep last 20 rows twice more. 75 (81: 87: 93: 99) sts.

Row 111 (inc row) (RS): (Patt to marked st, M1, K marked st, M1) twice, patt to end. 79 (85: 91: 97: 103) sts.

Work 9 rows.

Rep last 10 rows 4 times more, then the first of these rows (the inc row) again. 99 (105: 111: 117: 123) sts.

Work even until back measures 20½ (20¾: 20¾: 21¼: 21¼) in/ 52 (53: 53: 54: 54) cm, ending with RS facing for next row.

Shape armholes

Keeping patt correct, bind off 5 (6: 6: 7: 7) sts at beg of next 2 rows. 89 (93: 99: 103: 109) sts.

Dec 1 st at each end of next 5 (5: 7: 7: 9) rows, then on foll 2 (3: 3: 4: 4) alt rows, then on every foll 4th row until 71 (73: 75: 77: 79) sts rem.

Work even until armhole measures 7¾ (7¾: 8¼: 8¼: 8½) in/ 20 (20: 21: 21: 22) cm, ending with RS facing for next row.

Shape shoulders and back neck

Bind off 7 (7: 7: 7: 8) sts at beg of next 2 rows. 57 (59: 61: 63: 63) sts.

Next row (RS): Bind off 7 (7: 7: 7: 8) sts, patt until there are 11 (11: 12: 12: 11) sts on right needle and turn, leaving rem sts on a holder.

Work each side of neck separately.

Bind off 4 sts at beg of next row.

Bind off rem 7 (7: 8: 8: 7) sts.

With RS facing, rejoin yarn to rem sts, bind off center 21 (23: 23: 25: 25) sts, patt to end.

Complete to match first side, reversing shapings.

POCKET LININGS (make 2)

Cast on 27 sts, using size 6 (4mm) needles.

Row 1 (RS): K1, *P1, K1, rep from * to end.

Rows 2 and 3: P1, ★K1, P1, rep from ★ to end.
Row 4: Rep row 1.
Rep last 4 rows 9 times more.
Break off yarn and leave sts on a holder.

LEFT FRONT

Cast on 59 (62: 65: 68: 71) sts, using size 5 (3.75mm) needles.
Row 1 (RS): P1 (0: 1: 0: 1), ★K1, P1, rep from ★ to last 2 sts, K2.
Row 2: K2, ★K1, P1, rep from ★ to last 1 (0: 1: 0: 1) st, K1 (0: 1: 0: 1).
Row 3: K1 (0: 1: 0: 1), ★P1, K1, rep from ★ to last 2 sts, K2.
Row 4: K2, ★P1, K1, rep from ★ to last 1 (0: 1: 0: 1) st, P1 (0: 1: 0: 1).
Rep last 4 rows twice more, ending with RS facing for next row.
Change to size 6 (4mm) needles.
Row 13 (RS): P0 (0: 0: 1: 0), K0 (3: 1: 3: 2), ★P2, K3, rep from ★ to last 14 sts, patt 14 sts.
Row 14: Patt 14 sts, P to end.
These 2 rows set the sts—front opening edge 14 sts still in moss st and rem sts now in patt.
Cont as set for 26 rows more, ending with RS facing for next row.
Dec 1 st at beg of next row. 58 (61: 64: 67: 70) sts.
Work 13 rows more, ending with RS facing for next row.
Place pocket
Row 55 (RS): Patt 10 (13: 16: 19: 22) sts, slip next 27 sts onto a holder and in their place patt across 27 sts of first pocket lining, patt to end.
Work 5 rows, ending with RS facing for next row.
Counting in from beg of last row, place marker on 26th st in from beg of row.
Row 61 (dec row) (RS): Work 2 tog, patt to within 2 sts of marked st, K2tog, K marked st, K2 tog tbl, patt to end. 55 (58: 61: 64: 67) sts.
Work 19 rows.
Rep last 20 rows once more, then first of these rows (the dec row) again. 49 (52: 55: 58: 61) sts.
Work 9 rows.
Row 111 (inc row) (RS): Patt to marked st, M1, K marked st, M1, patt to end. 51 (54: 57: 60: 63) sts.
Work 9 rows.
Rep last 10 rows once more, then the first of these rows (the inc row) again. 55 (58: 61: 64: 67) sts.
Work even until left front matches back to beg of armhole shaping, ending with RS facing for next row.
Shape armhole
Keeping patt correct, bind off 5 (6: 6: 7: 7) sts at beg of next row. 50 (52: 55: 57: 60) sts.
Work 1 row.
Dec 1 st at each end of next 5 (5: 7: 7: 9) rows, then on foll 2 (3: 3: 4: 4) alt rows, then on every foll 4th row until 41 (42: 43: 44: 45) sts rem.

Work even until 25 (25: 25: 27: 27) rows less have been worked than on back to start of shoulder shaping, ending with **WS** facing for next row.
Shape neck
Next row (WS): Bind off 5 sts, patt until there are 8 (9: 9: 9: 9) sts on right needle and slip these sts onto a holder, patt to end. 28 (28: 29: 30: 31) sts.
Keeping patt correct, dec 1 st at neck edge of next and foll 6 (6: 6: 7: 7) alt rows. 21 (21: 22: 22: 23) sts.
Work 11 rows, ending with RS facing for next row.
Shape shoulder
Bind off 7 (7: 7: 7: 8) sts at beg of next and foll alt row.
Work 1 row.
Bind off rem 7 (7: 8: 8: 7) sts.
Mark positions for 5 buttons along left front opening edge—first to come in row 71, last to come 1¼ in (3 cm) below neck shaping, and rem 3 buttons evenly spaced between.

RIGHT FRONT

Cast on 59 (62: 65: 68: 71) sts, using size 5 (3.75mm) needles.
Row 1 (RS): K2, ★P1, K1, rep from ★ to last 1 (0: 1: 0: 1) st, P1 (0: 1: 0: 1).
Row 2: K1 (0: 1: 0: 1), ★P1, K1, rep from ★ to last 2 sts, K2.
Row 3: K2, ★K1, P1, rep from ★ to last 1 (0: 1: 0: 1) st, K1 (0: 1: 0: 1).
Row 4: P1 (0: 1: 0: 1), ★K1, P1, rep from ★ to last 2 sts, K2.
Rep last 4 rows twice more, ending with RS facing for next row.
Change to size 6 (4mm) needles.
Row 13 (RS): Patt 14 sts, ★K3, P2, rep from ★ to last 0 (3: 1: 4: 2) sts, K0 (3: 1: 3: 2), P0 (0: 0: 1: 0).
Row 14: P to last 14 sts, patt to end.
These 2 rows set the sts—front opening edge 14 sts still in moss st and rem sts now in patt.
Cont as set for 26 rows more, ending with RS facing for next row.
Dec 1 st at end of next row. 58 (61: 64: 67: 70) sts.
Work 13 rows more, ending with RS facing for next row.
Place pocket
Row 55 (RS): Patt 21 sts, slip next 27 sts onto a holder and in their place patt across 27 sts of second pocket lining, patt to end.
Work 5 rows, ending with RS facing for next row.
Counting in from end of last row, place marker on 26th st in from end of row.
Row 61 (dec row) (RS): Patt to within 2 sts of marked st, K2tog, K marked st, K2 tog tbl, patt to last 2 sts, work 2 tog. 55 (58: 61: 64: 67) sts.
Work 9 rows.
Row 71 (buttonhole row) (RS): Patt 5 sts, work 2 tog, yo, patt to end.
Working 4 buttonholes more in this way to correspond with positions marked on left front for buttons, complete to match left front, reversing shapings.

SLEEVES

Cast on 49 (49: 51: 53: 53) sts, using size 3 (3.25mm) needles.

Row 1 (RS): K1, *P1, K1, rep from * to end.

Row 2: P1, *K1, P1, rep from * to end.

Row 3: Rep row 2.

Row 4: Rep row 1.

Rep these 4 rows 3 times more, then rows 1 and 2 again, ending with RS facing for next row.

Change to size 6 (4mm) needles.

Row 19 (RS): K1 (1: 2: 3: 3), *P2, K3, rep from * to last 3 (3: 4: 5: 5) sts, P2, K1 (1: 2: 3: 3).

Row 20: Purl.

Last 2 rows form patt.

Cont in patt, inc 1 st at each end of 3rd and every foll 10th (8th: 8th: 8th: 8th) row to 69 (59: 57: 59: 69) sts, then on every foll 12th (10th: 10th: 10th: 10th) row until there are 71 (73: 75: 77: 79) sts, taking inc sts into patt.

Work even until sleeve measures 17¼ (17¼: 17¾: 17¾: 17¾) in/ 44 (44: 45: 45: 45) cm, ending with RS facing for next row.

Shape sleeve cap

Keeping patt correct, bind off 5 (6: 6: 7: 7) sts at beg of next 2 rows. 61 (61: 63: 63: 65) sts.

Dec 1 st at each end of next 5 rows, then on foll 2 alt rows, then on every foll 4th row until 37 (37: 39: 39: 41) sts rem.

Work 1 row, ending with RS facing for next row.

Dec 1 st at each end of next and every foll alt row to 29 sts, then on foll 3 rows, ending with RS facing for next row. 23 sts.

Bind off 4 sts at beg of next 2 rows.

Bind off rem 15 sts.

FINISHING

Press described on page 148.

Sew both shoulder seams using backstitch, or mattress stitch if preferred.

Collar

With RS facing and using size 5 (3.75mm) needles, slip 8 (9: 9: 9: 9) sts from right front holder onto right needle, rejoin yarn and pick up and knit 24 (24: 24: 26: 26) sts up right side of neck, 29 (31: 31: 33: 33) sts from back, 24 (24: 24: 26: 26) sts down left side of neck, then patt 8 (9: 9: 9: 9) sts from left front holder. 93 (97: 97: 103: 103) sts.

Row 1 (RS of collar, WS of body): K2, *P1, K1, rep from * to last 3 sts, P1, K2.

Row 2: K3, *P1, K1, rep from * to last 2 sts, K2.

Row 3: Rep row 2.

Row 4: Rep row 1.

These 4 rows set the sts—2 sts in garter st at each end of row and moss st between.

Keeping sts correct as set, work 1 row.

Row 6: K2, M1, patt to last 2 sts, M1, K2.

Work 3 rows.

Rep last 4 rows until collar measures 4 in (10 cm).

Bind off in patt.

Pocket tops (both alike)

Slip 27 sts from pocket holder onto size 5 (3.75mm) needles and rejoin yarn with RS facing.

Beg with row 1, work in moss st as given for sleeves for 8 rows.

Bind off in patt.

See page 148 for finishing instructions, setting in sleeves using the set-in method.

Electra

LOUISA HARDING

SIZES AND YARN

	XS	S	M	L	XL	
To fit bust	32	34	36	38	40	in
	81	86	91	97	102	cm

Rowan Felted Tweed DK and Kidsilk Haze

A Felted Tweed DK in Rage 150

	2	2	2	2	3	x 50 g

B Felted Tweed DK in Phantom 153

	1	1	1	1	1	x 50 g

C *Kidsilk Haze in Blood 627

	1	1	1	1	1	x 25 g

D Felted Tweed DK in Camel 157

	1	1	1	1	1	x 50 g

*Use Kidsilk Haze DOUBLE throughout

Originally knitted and photographed (above) in Rowan Yorkshire Tweed DK in Revel 342 (A), Rowan Felted Tweed in Midnight 133 (B) and Melody 142 (D), and Rowan Kidsilk Haze in Splendour 579 (C)

NEEDLES

1 pair size 6 (4mm) needles
1 pair size 7 (4.5mm) needles
1 pair size 3 (3.25mm) needles

NEW YARN SUBSTITUTIONS

Here we've substituted yarns for the ones that are no longer available and for the colors that have been discontinued. Rowan Felted Tweed DK is quite a fine yarn and here (right) it's knitted fairly loosely to create a fluid fabric and to accentuate the tactile qualities of the yarn. Rowan Kidsilk Haze is used sparingly in the design to provide a subtle contrast of texture.

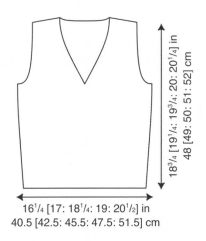

18³/₄ [19¹/₄: 19³/₄: 20: 20¹/₄] in
48 [49: 50: 51: 52] cm

16¹/₄ [17: 18¹/₄: 19: 20¹/₂] in
40.5 [42.5: 45.5: 47.5: 51.5] cm

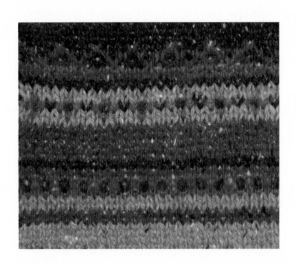

GAUGE

20 sts and 27 rows to 4 in (10 cm) measured over patterned St st using size 7 (4.5mm) needles.

BACK

Using size 6 (4mm) needles and yarn D, cast on 75 [79: 85: 89: 97] sts.

Break off yarn D and join in yarn A.

Row 1 (RS): K1 [0: 0: 0: 0], P1 [1: 1: 0: 1], *K2, P1, rep from *

to last 1 [0: 0: 2: 0] sts, K1 [0: 0: 2: 0].

Row 2: P1 [0: 0: 0: 0], K1 [1: 1: 0: 1], *P2, K1, rep from * to last 1 [0: 0: 2: 0] sts, P1 [0: 0: 2: 0].

These 2 rows form rib.

Work in rib for 28 rows more, inc 1 st at each end of last row and ending with RS facing for next row. 77 [81: 87: 91: 99] sts.

Change to size 7 (4.5mm) needles.

Beg and ending rows as indicated, using the **Fair Isle** technique as described on page 148 and repeating the 34 row patt repeat throughout, cont in patt from chart, which is worked entirely in St st, as foll:

Inc 1 st at each end of 17th and foll 16th row, taking inc sts into patt. 81 [85: 91: 95: 103] sts.

Work even until back measures 11¾ [12¼: 12¼: 12½: 12½] in (30 [31: 31: 32: 32] cm), ending with RS facing for next row.

Shape armholes

Keeping patt correct, bind off 3 [4: 4: 5: 6] sts at beg of next

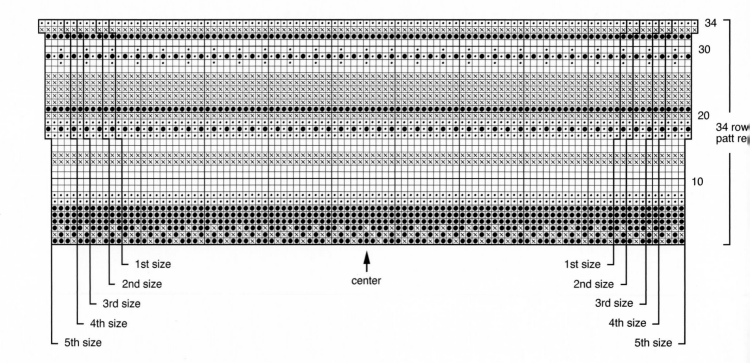

KEY
⊠ A
◉ B
⊡ C
☐ D

2 rows, then 3 sts at beg of foll 2 rows. 69 [71: 77: 79: 85] sts.

Dec 1 st at each end of next 1 [1: 3: 3: 5] rows, then on foll 2 alt rows, then on foll 4th row. 61 [63: 65: 67: 69] sts.

Work even until armhole measures 7 [7: 7½: 7½: 7¾] in (18 [18: 19: 19: 20] cm), ending with RS facing for next row.

Shape shoulders and back neck

Bind off 5 [5: 6: 6: 6] sts at beg of next 2 rows. 51 [53: 53: 55: 57] sts.

Next row (RS): Bind off 5 [5: 6: 6: 6] sts, patt until there are 9 [9: 8: 8: 9] sts on right needle and turn, leaving rem sts on a holder.

Work each side of neck separately.

Bind off 3 sts at beg of next row.

Bind off rem 6 [6: 5: 5: 6] sts.

With RS facing, rejoin yarns to rem sts, bind off center 23 [25: 25: 27: 27] sts, patt to end.

Complete to match first side, reversing shapings.

FRONT

Work as given for back until 2 rows less have been worked than on back to beg of armhole shaping.

Divide for neck

Next row (RS): Patt 40 [42: 45: 47: 51] sts and turn, leaving rem sts on a holder.

Work each side of neck separately.

Work 1 row, ending with RS facing for next row.

Shape armhole

Keeping patt correct, bind off 3 [4: 4: 5: 6] sts at beg of next row, then 3 sts at beg of foll alt row **and at same time** dec 1 st at neck edge on next and foll alt row. 32 [33: 36: 37: 40] sts.

Work 1 row.

Dec 1 st at armhole edge of next 1 [1: 3: 3: 5] rows, then on foll 2 alt rows, then on foll 4th row **and at same time** dec 1 st at front slope edge of next and foll 4 [4: 4: 5: 5] alt rows. 23 [24: 25: 25: 26] sts.

Dec 1 st at front slope edge **only** on 4th [2nd: 2nd: 2nd: 2nd] and foll 0 [1: 0: 0: 0] alt rows, then on 6 [6: 7: 7: 7] foll 4th rows. 16 [16: 17: 17: 18] sts.

Work even until front matches back to beg of shoulder shaping, ending with RS facing for next row.

Shape shoulder

Bind off 5 [5: 6: 6: 6] sts at beg of next and foll alt row.

Work 1 row.

Bind off rem 6 [6: 5: 5: 6] sts.

With RS facing, slip center st onto a holder, rejoin yarns to rem sts, patt to end.

Complete to match first side, reversing shapings.

FINISHING

Press as described on page 148.

Sew right shoulder seam using backstitch, or mattress stitch.

Neckband

With RS facing, using size 3 (3.25mm) needles and yarn A, pick up and knit 44 [44: 47: 47: 50] sts down left front slope, inc in st left on holder and place marker between these 2 sts, pick up and knit 44 [44: 47: 47: 50] sts up right front slope, then 30 [30: 30: 33: 33] sts from back. 120 [120: 126: 129: 135] sts.

Row 1 (WS): P1, *K1, P2, rep from * to last 2 sts, K1, P1.

Row 2: K1, *P1, K2, rep from * to last 2 sts, P1, K1.

These 2 rows form rib.

Row 3 (WS): Rib to within 2 sts of marker, P2tog tbl, slip marker onto right needle, P2tog, rib to end.

Row 4: Rib to within 2 sts of marker, K2tog, slip marker onto right needle, K2tog tbl, rib to end.

Row 5: Rep row 3.

Break off yarn A and join in yarn D.

Bind off in rib.

Armhole borders (both alike)

With RS facing, using size 3 (3.25mm) needles and yarn A, pick up and knit 86 [86: 92: 92: 101] sts evenly all round armhole edge.

Row 1 (WS): P2, *K1, P2, rep from * to end.

Row 2: K2, *P1, K2, rep from * to end.

These 2 rows form rib.

Work in rib for 3 rows more, ending with RS facing for next row.

Break off yarn A and join in yarn D.

Bind off in rib.

See page 148 for finishing instructions.

Hydrangea Top

KAFFE FASSETT

SIZES AND YARN

	XXS	XS	S	M	L	XL	XXL	XXXL	
To fit bust									
	32	34	36	38	40	42	44	46	in
	81	86	91	97	102	107	112	117	cm

Rowan Classic Siena

A Grasshopper 663									
	1	1	1	1	1	1	1	1	x 50 g
B Shadow 667									
	4	4	5	5	6	6	6	7	x 50 g
C Rosette 664									
	1	1	1	1	1	1	1	1	x 50 g
D Flounce 662									
	1	1	1	2	2	2	2	2	x 50 g
E Chilli 666									
	1	1	1	1	1	1	1	1	x 50 g

Originally knitted and photographed (above) in Rowan 4-Ply Cotton in Fennel 135 (A), Ardour 130 (B), Orchid 120 (C), Cheeky 133 (D), and Bloom 132 (E)

NEEDLES

1 pair size 2 (2.75mm) needles
1 pair size 3 (3mm) needles

NEW YARN SUBSTITUTIONS

The original Rowan 4-Ply Cotton used for this neat top, and the colorful cardigan on page 122, is no longer available. To keep the summery feel of these two garments we chose to alter the colors slightly, rather than change the yarn to a more wintery woolly one. Rowan Classic Siena (right) is the perfect substitute for the original yarn and we hope you agree our new colors effectively recreate the bright summery mood.

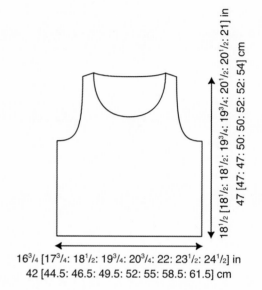

16³/4 [17³/4: 18¹/2: 19³/4: 20³/4: 22: 23¹/2: 24¹/2] in
42 [44.5: 46.5: 49.5: 52: 55: 58.5: 61.5] cm

18¹/2 [18¹/2: 18¹/2: 19³/4: 19³/4: 20¹/2: 20¹/2: 21] in
47 [47: 47: 50: 50: 52: 52: 54] cm

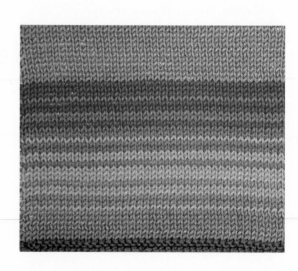

GAUGE

28 sts and 38 rows to 4 in (10 cm) measured over St st using size 3 (3mm) needles.

BACK

Using size 2 (2.75mm) needles and yarn A, cast on 118 [124: 130: 138: 146: 154: 164: 172] sts.

Work in garter st for 2 rows, ending with RS facing for next row.

Change to size 3 (3mm) needles.

Beg with a K row and joining in and breaking off colors as required, work in striped St st as foll:

Rows 1 to 6: Using yarn B.

Row 7: Using yarn C.

Rows 8 and 9: Using yarn B.

Rows 10 and 11: Using yarn C.

Row 12: Using yarn B.

Rows 13–15: Using yarn C.

Row 16: Using yarn D.

Rows 17 and 18: Using yarn C.

Rows 19 and 20: Using yarn D.

Row 21: Using yarn C.

Rows 22 and 23: Using yarn D.

Row 24: Using yarn E.

Rows 25 and 26: Using yarn D.

Rows 27 and 28: Using yarn E.

Row 29: Using yarn D.

Rows 30–32: Using yarn E.

Break off contrasting colors and cont in St st using yarn B **only**.

Work even until back measures 11 [11: 10¾: 12: 11½: 12¼: 12: 12½] in (28 [28: 27: 30: 29: 31: 30: 32] cm), ending with RS facing for next row.

Shape armholes

Bind off 9 [10: 10: 11: 11: 12: 12: 13] sts at beg of next 2 rows. 100 [104: 110: 116: 124: 130: 140: 146] sts.

Dec 1 st at each end of next 9 [9: 11: 11: 13: 13: 15: 15] rows, then on foll 4 [5: 5: 6: 5: 6: 7: 8] alt rows. 74 [76: 78: 82: 88: 92: 96: 100] sts.★★

Work even until armhole measures 7½ [7½: 7¾: 7¾: 8¼: 8¼: 8½: 8½] in (19 [19: 20: 20: 21: 21: 22: 22] cm), ending with RS facing for next row.

Shape back neck and shoulders

Next row (RS): K10 [11: 12: 14: 16: 18: 20: 22] and turn, leaving rem sts on a holder.

Work each side of neck separately.

Bind off 4 sts at beg of next row.

Bind off rem 6 [7: 8: 10: 12: 14: 16: 18] sts.

With RS facing, rejoin yarn to rem sts, bind off center 54 [54: 54: 54: 56: 56: 56: 56] sts, K to end.

Complete to match first side, reversing shapings.

FRONT

Work as given for back to ★★.

Work 7 [5: 7: 3: 7: 5: 3: 1] rows, ending with RS facing for next row.

Shape neck

Next row (RS): K22 [23: 24: 27: 29: 31: 34: 36] and turn, leaving rem sts on a holder.

Work each side of neck separately.

Dec 1 st at neck edge of next 7 rows, then on foll 9 [9: 9: 10: 10: 10: 11: 11] alt rows. 6 [7: 8: 10: 12: 14: 16: 18] sts.

Work even until front matches back to shoulder bind-off, ending with RS facing for next row.

Shape shoulder

Bind off rem 6 [7: 8: 10: 12: 14: 16: 18] sts.

With RS facing, rejoin yarn to rem sts, bind off center 30 [30: 30: 28: 30: 30: 28: 28] sts, K to end.

Complete to match first side, reversing shapings.

FINISHING

Press as described on page 148.

Sew right shoulder seam using backstitch, or mattress stitch if preferred.

Neckband

With RS facing, using size 2 (2.75mm) needles and yarn E, pick up and knit 35 [35: 35: 37: 37: 37: 39: 39] sts down left side of neck, 29 [29: 29: 27: 29: 29: 27: 27] sts from front, 35 [35: 35: 37: 37: 37: 39: 39] sts up right side of neck, then 50 [50: 50: 50: 52: 52: 52: 52] sts from back. 149 [149: 149: 151: 155: 155: 157: 157] sts.

★★★Work in garter st for 3 rows, ending with RS facing for next row.

Break off yarn E and join in yarn D.

Work in garter st for 4 rows, ending with RS facing for next row.

Break off yarn D and join in yarn A.

Work in garter st for 1 row, ending with **WS** facing for next row.

Bind off knitwise (on **WS**).

Sew left shoulder and neckband seam.

Armhole borders

With RS facing, using size 2 (2.75mm) needles and yarn E, pick up and knit 128 [130: 136: 138: 144: 146: 152: 154] sts evenly all around armhole edge.

Work as given for neckband from ★★★.

See page 148 for finishing instructions.

Hydrangea Cardigan

KAFFE FASSETT

SIZES AND YARN

	XXS	XS	S	M	L	XL	XXL	XXXL	
To fit bust									
	32	34	36	38	40	42	44	46	in
	81	86	91	97	102	107	112	117	cm

Rowan Classic Siena

A Grasshopper 663									
	3	3	4	4	4	4	5	5	x 50 g
B Shadow 667									
	8	8	9	9	9	9	10	10	x 50 g
C Rosette 664									
	3	3	3	3	3	3	3	3	x 50 g
D Flounce 662									
	2	2	2	2	2	2	3	3	x 50 g
E Chilli 666									
	2	2	2	3	3	3	3	3	x 50 g

Originally knitted and photographed (above) in Rowan 4-Ply Cotton in Fennel 135 (A), Ardour 130 (B), Orchid 120 (C), Cheeky 133 (D), and Bloom 132 (E).

NEEDLES

1 pair size 2 (2.75mm) needles
1 pair size 3 (3mm) needles

BUTTONS—7

KNITTER'S TIP

Although this cardigan is knitted in exactly the same yarn using the same needle size as the matching top (see page 120), you might have noticed that the gauges of the two garments are different. This is because the sleeveless top is knitted in plain stockinette stitch while the cardigan has an intarsia design all over it. On a colorwork design like this the knitting has a tendency to "pull in" a little—hence the slightly tighter gauge.

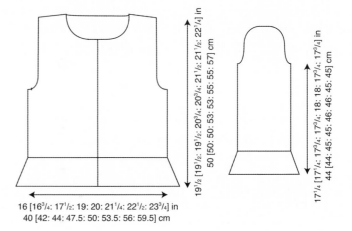

19½ [19½: 19½: 20¾: 21½: 21½: 22¼] in
50 [50: 50: 53: 55: 55: 57] cm

16 [16¾: 17½: 19: 20: 21¼: 22½: 23¾] in
40 [42: 44: 47.5: 50: 53.5: 56: 59.5] cm

17¼ [17¼: 17¾: 17¾: 18: 18: 17¾: 17¾] in
44 [44: 45: 45: 46: 46: 45: 45] cm

GAUGE

30 sts and 40 rows to 4 in (10 cm) measured over patterned St st using size 3 (3mm) needles.

BACK

Using size 2 (2.75mm) needles and yarn A, cast on 160 [168: 176: 188: 200: 212: 224: 236] sts.

★★Work in garter st for 2 rows, ending with RS facing for next row.

Change to size 3 (3mm) needles.

Beg with a K row and joining in and breaking off colors as required, work in striped St st as foll:

Rows 1–6: Using yarn B.
Row 7: Using yarn C.
Rows 8 and 9: Using yarn B.
Rows 10 and 11: Using yarn C.
Row 12: Using yarn B.
Rows 13–15: Using yarn C.
Row 16: Using yarn D.
Rows 17 and 18: Using yarn C.
Rows 19 and 20: Using yarn D.
Row 21: Using yarn C.
Rows 22 and 23: Using yarn D.

Row 24: Using yarn E.

Rows 25 and 26: Using yarn D.

Rows 27 and 28: Using yarn E.

Row 29: Using yarn D.

Rows 30 and 31: Using yarn E.★★

Row 32 (WS): Using yarn E, P1 [1: 1: 3: 1: 3: 1: 3], ★P2tog, P2, rep from ★ to last 3 [3: 3: 5: 3: 5:3: 5] sts, P2tog, P1 [1: 1: 3: 1: 3: 1: 3]. 120 [126: 132: 142: 150: 160: 168: 178] sts.

Beg and ending rows as indicated, using the **Fair Isle** technique as described on page 148 and repeating the 40 row patt repeat throughout, work in patt from chart, which is worked entirely in St st, as foll:

Work even until back measures 11¾ [11¾: 11¼: 12½: 12¼: 13: 12½: 13¼] in (30 [30: 29: 32: 31: 33: 32: 34] cm), ending with RS facing for next row.

Shape armholes

Keeping patt correct, bind off 5 [6: 6: 7: 7: 8: 8: 9] sts at beg of next 2 rows. 110 [114: 120: 128: 136: 144: 152: 160] sts.

Dec 1 st at each end of next 3 [3: 5: 5: 7: 7: 9: 9] rows, then on foll 2 [3: 2: 4: 4: 5: 5: 7] alt rows, then on 2 foll 4th rows. 96 [98: 102: 106: 110: 116: 120: 124] sts.

Work even until armhole measures 7¾ [7¾: 8¼: 8¼: 8½: 8½: 9: 9] in (20 [20: 21: 21: 22: 22: 23: 23] cm), ending with RS facing for next row.

Shape shoulders and back neck

Bind off 8 [8: 9: 9: 10: 11: 11: 12] sts at beg of next 2 rows. 80 [82: 84: 88: 90: 94: 98: 100] sts.

Next row (RS): Bind off 8 [8: 9: 9: 10: 11: 11: 12] sts, patt until there are 11 [12: 12: 14: 13: 14: 16: 16] sts on right needle and turn, leaving rem sts on a holder.

Work each side of neck separately.

Bind off 4 sts at beg of next row.

Bind off rem 7 [8: 8: 10: 9: 10: 12: 12] sts.

With RS facing, rejoin yarns to rem sts, bind off center 42 [42: 42: 42: 44: 44: 44: 44] sts, patt to end.

Complete to match first side, reversing shapings.

LEFT FRONT

Using size 2 (2.75mm) needles and yarn A, cast on 77 [81: 85: 91: 97: 103: 109: 115] sts.

Work as given for back from ★★ to ★★.

Row 32 (WS): Using yarn E, P1 [1: 1: 2: 1: 2: 1: 2], ★P2tog, P2, rep from ★ to last 4 [4: 4: 5: 4: 5: 4: 5] sts, P2tog, P2 [2: 2: 3: 2: 3: 2: 3]. 58 [61: 64: 69: 73: 78: 82: 87] sts.

Beg and ending rows as indicated, work in patt from chart as foll:

Work even until left front matches back to beg of armhole shaping, ending with RS facing for next row.

Shape armhole

Keeping patt correct, bind off 5 [6: 6: 7: 7: 8: 8: 9] sts at beg of next row. 53 [55: 58: 62: 66: 70: 74: 78] sts.

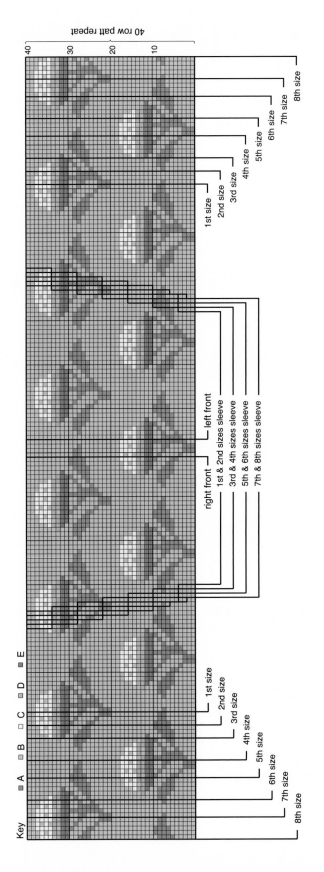

Work 1 row.

Dec 1 st at armhole edge of next 3 [3: 5: 5: 7: 7: 9: 9] rows, then on foll 2 [3: 2: 4: 4: 5: 5: 7] alt rows, then on 2 foll 4th rows. 46 [47: 49: 51: 53: 56: 58: 60] sts.

Work even until 25 [25: 25: 27: 27: 27: 29: 29] rows less have been worked than on back to beg of shoulder shaping, ending with **WS** facing for next row.

Shape neck

Keeping patt correct, bind off 11 [11: 11: 10: 11: 11: 10: 10] sts at beg of next row. 35 [36: 38: 41: 42: 45: 48: 50] sts.

Dec 1 st at neck edge of next 7 rows, then on foll 3 [3: 3: 4: 4: 4: 5: 5] alt rows, then on 2 foll 4th rows. 23 [24: 26: 28: 29: 32: 34: 36] sts.

Work 3 rows, ending with RS facing for next row.

Shape shoulder

Bind off 8 [8: 9: 9: 10: 11: 11: 12] sts at beg of next and foll alt row.

Work 1 row.

Bind off rem 7 [8: 8: 10: 9: 10: 12: 12] sts.

RIGHT FRONT

Work to match left front, reversing shapings.

SLEEVES

Using size 2 (2.75mm) needles and yarn A, cast on 83 [83: 85: 85: 87: 87: 91: 91] sts.

Work as given for back from ★★ to ★★.

Row 32 (WS): Using yarn E, P1 [1: 1: 1: 2: 2: 1: 1], ★P2tog, P2, rep from ★ to last 2 [2: 4: 4: 5: 5: 2: 2] sts, P2tog, P0 [0: 2: 2: 3: 3: 0: 0]. 62 [62: 64: 64: 66: 66: 68: 68] sts.

Beg and ending rows as indicated, work in patt from chart, shaping sides by inc 1 st at each end of 5th [5th: 5th: 5th: 5th: 5th: 5th: 3rd] and every foll 6th [6th: 6th: 6th: 6th: 6th: 6th: 4th] row to 84 [92: 90: 98: 96: 104: 110: 74] sts, then on every foll 8th [8th: 8th: 8th: 8th: 8th: –: 6th] row until there are 98 [100: 102: 104: 106: 108: –: 112] sts, taking inc sts into patt.

Work even until sleeve measures 17¼ [17¼: 17¾: 17¾: 18: 18: 17¾: 17¾] in (44 [44: 45: 45: 46: 46: 45: 45] cm), ending with RS facing for next row.

Shape sleeve cap

Keeping patt correct, bind off 5 [6: 6: 7: 7: 8: 8: 9] sts at beg of next 2 rows. 88 [88: 90: 90: 92: 92: 94: 94] sts.

Dec 1 st at each end of next 5 rows, then on every foll alt row to 44 sts, then on foll 7 rows, ending with RS facing for next row. 30 sts.

Bind off 10 sts at beg of next 2 rows.

Bind off rem 10 sts.

FINISHING

Press as described on page 148.

Sew both shoulder seams using backstitch, or mattress stitch if preferred.

Neckband

With RS facing, using size 2 (2.75mm) needles and yarn A, beg and ending at front opening edges, pick up and knit 32 [32: 32: 33: 34: 34: 35: 35] sts up right side of neck, 49 [49: 49: 49: 51: 51: 51: 51] sts from back, then 32 [32: 32: 33: 34: 34: 35: 35] sts down left side of neck. 113 [113: 113: 115: 119: 119: 121: 121] sts.

Work in garter st for 4 rows, ending with **WS** facing for next row.

Bind off knitwise (on **WS**).

Button band

With RS facing, using size 2 (2.75mm) needles and yarn A, pick up and knit 126 [126: 126: 132: 132: 138: 138: 144] sts down left front opening edge, from top of neckband to cast-on edge.

Work in garter st for 4 rows, ending with **WS** facing for next row.

Bind off knitwise (on **WS**).

Buttonhole band

Work to match button band, with the addition of 7 buttonholes in row 2 as foll:

Row 2 (RS): K2, ★yo, K2tog, K18 [18: 18: 19: 19: 20: 20: 21], rep from ★ 5 times more, yo, K2tog, K2.

See page 148 for finishing instructions, setting in sleeves using the set-in method.

Anice

SHARON MILLER

YARN

Rowan Kidsilk Haze

5   x 25 g

Photographed in Cream 634

NEEDLES

1 pair size 8 (5mm) needles

GAUGE

After pressing, 18 sts and 26 rows to 4 in (10 cm) measured over patt using size 8 (5mm) needles.

FINISHED SIZE

Finished shawl measures 22½ in (57 cm) by 78½ in (200 cm).

LOWER BORDER

Using size 8 (5mm) needles and waste yarn, cast on 11 sts. Break off waste yarn and join in main yarn.

Row 1 (RS): P1, yo, P1, yo, K2tog tbl, yo, K2tog tbl, P2, K2tog, yo, K1. 12 sts.

Row 2 and every foll alt row: Purl.

Row 3: P1, yo, P3, yo, K2tog tbl, yo, K2tog tbl, P1, K2tog, yo, K1. 13 sts.

Row 5: P1, yo, P5, yo, K2tog tbl, yo, K2tog tbl, K2tog, yo, K1. 14 sts.

Row 7: K2tog tbl, yo, K2tog tbl, P1, K2tog, yo, K2tog, yo, P2, K2tog, yo, K1. 13 sts.

Row 9: K2tog tbl, yo, sl 1, K2tog, psso, yo, K2tog, yo, P3, K2tog, yo, K1. 12 sts.

Row 11: K2tog tbl, P1, K2tog, yo, P4, K2tog, yo, K1. 11 sts.

Row 12: Rep row 2.

These 12 rows form patt.

Rep last 12 rows 10 times more, then row 1, ending after a RS row. 12 sts. Do NOT break off yarn.

MAIN SECTION

With 12 sts of lower border on right needle, with RS facing and using right needle, pick up and knit 66 sts evenly along straight row-end edge of lower border, unravel waste yarn used for cast-on and K these 11 sts. 89 sts on right needle.

Next row (WS): P11, place marker on needle, K4, inc in next st, (K6, inc in next st) 8 times, K5, place second marker on needle (there will be the 12 sts of the lower border beyond this marker) and turn.

Next row: K75 and turn.

Next row: K75 and turn.

Next row (RS): P2, K2tog, yo, K5, (K6, yo, sl 1, K2tog, psso, yo, K5) 4 times, K6, yo, K2tog tbl, P2, slip marker onto right needle, K1, yo, K2tog tbl, P2, K2tog, yo, K2tog, yo, P1, yo, P1. 99 sts.

Next row: Purl.

Sts between markers form center section, with sts beyond markers forming side borders.

Place center section chart

Keeping original 12 sts from lower border correct in patt as set by lower border, cont in patt as foll:

Row 1 (RS): Lower border patt to first marker, slip marker (onto right needle), work next 75 sts as row 1 of chart (see page 126), slip marker (onto right needle), K1, yo, K2tog tbl, P1, K2tog, yo, K2tog, yo, P3, yo, P1.

Row 2 and every foll alt row: Purl.

Row 3: Lower border patt to first marker, slip marker, work next 75 sts as row 3 of chart, slip marker, K1, yo, K2tog tbl, K2tog, yo, K2tog, yo, P5, yo, P1.

Row 5: Lower border patt to first marker, slip marker, work next 75 sts as row 5 of chart, slip marker, K1, yo, K2tog tbl, P2, yo, K2tog tbl, yo, K2tog tbl, P1, K2tog, yo, K2tog.

Row 7: Lower border patt to first marker, slip marker, work next 75 sts as row 7 of chart, slip marker, K1, yo, K2tog tbl, P3, yo, K2tog tbl, yo, sl 1, K2tog, psso, yo, K2tog.

Row 9: Lower border patt to first marker, slip marker, work next 75 sts as row 9 of chart, slip marker, K1, yo, K2tog tbl, P4, yo, K2tog tbl, P1, K2tog.

Row 11: Lower border patt to first marker, slip marker, work next 75 sts as row 11 of chart, slip marker, K1, yo, K2tog tbl, P2, K2tog, yo, K2tog, yo, P1, yo, P1.

Row 12: Rep row 2.

These 12 rows form patt for border at ends of RS rows.

Now keeping border patt sts beyond markers correct as now set and working center sts between markers foll chart, repeating the 60 row patt repeat, cont as foll:

Work chart rows 13–60.

Now (rep chart rows 1–60) 6 times more, then chart rows 1–58 again, ending with RS facing for next row.

Next row (RS): Lower border patt to first marker and slip these sts onto a holder, K75 and turn.

Next row: K75.

Next row: K75 and turn.

Next row: K75.

Next row: K4, K2tog, (K6, K2tog) 8 times, K5, slip marker, patt to end. (66 sts now in center section.)

Work top border

Next row (WS): P to within 1 st of marker, P2tog (this is last st of border with first st of center section) and turn.

Next row: Patt to end.

Next row: P to last st of border, P2tog (this is last st of border with next st of center section) and turn.

Rep last 2 rows until all sts of center section have been used up. 11 sts. Break off yarn, leaving a fairly long end.

FINISHING

Graft 11 sts left on needle together with 11 sts of border up other side of work left on holder. Pin out to measurements given, cover with damp cloths and leave to dry naturally.

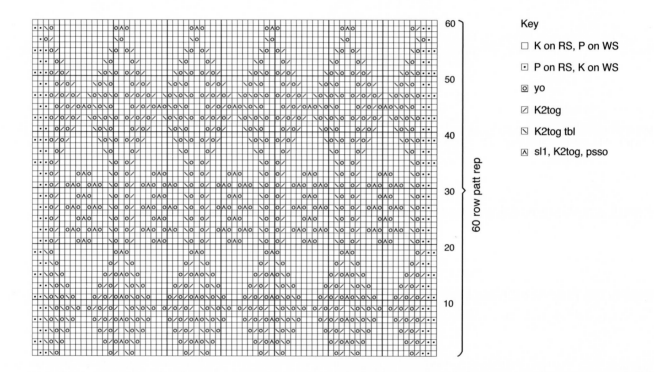

Key

☐ K on RS, P on WS

⊡ P on RS, K on WS

◎ yo

☑ K2tog

◩ K2tog tbl

◮ sl1, K2tog, psso

60 row patt rep

About Sharon Miller

Sharon Miller trained as a school teacher and taught for nine years. In 1986, after the birth of her son, she decided to change career direction and started designing knitwear.

Sharon has always been interested in textile history and especially in "heirloom knitting." After moving to Devon in 1986 she began to collect old needlecraft books. Through her collection she discovered the tradition of fine lace knitwear—known as white knitting—and began putting her own designs together. She started by experimenting with charting antique Shetland lace designs to make them easier to understand and knit. To enhance the stitch effects, Sharon uses very fine yarns. Thus it was the introduction of Kidsilk Haze into the Rowan range in 2001 that acted as the catalyst for her enormously popular Rowan design work.

Doon Coat

ERIKA KNIGHT

SIZES AND YARN

	S	M	L	XL	
To fit bust					
	32–34	36–38	40–42	44–46	in
	81–86	91–97	102–107	112–117	cm
Rowan Kid Classic					
	15	17	18	20	x 50 g

Photographed in Victoria 852

NEEDLES

1 pair size 6 (4mm) needles
1 pair size 7 (4.5mm) needles

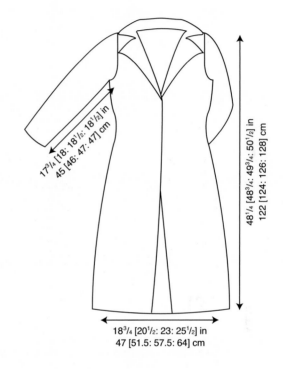

17³/₄ [18: 18¹/₂: 18¹/₂] in
45 [46: 47: 47] cm

48¹/₄ [48³/₄: 49³/₄: 50¹/₂] in
122 [124: 126: 128] cm

18³/₄ [20¹/₂: 23: 25¹/₂] in
47 [51.5: 57.5: 64] cm

GAUGE

22 sts and 28 rows to 4 in (10 cm) measured over St st using
size 7 (4.5mm) needles.

BACK

Using size 6 (4mm) needles, cast on 125 [135: 149: 163] sts.
Beg with a K row, work in St st for 4 rows, ending with RS
facing for next row.
Change to size 7 (4.5mm) needles.
Cont in St st until back measures 18½ [19: 19¼: 19½] in
(47 [48: 49: 50] cm), ending with RS facing for next row.
Next row (RS): K2, sl 1, K1, psso, K to last 4 sts, K2tog, K2.
Working all side seam shaping as set by last row, dec 1 st at each
end of 6th and every foll 6th row until 95 [105: 119: 133] sts rem.
Work 1 row, ending with RS facing for next row.
Shape belt openings
Next row (RS): K15 [17: 19: 21] and turn, leaving rem sts on
a holder.

Work 15 rows on these sts, ending with RS facing for next row.
Break off yarn and leave sts on a 2nd holder.
Return to sts left on first holder, rejoin yarn with RS facing,
K65 [71: 81: 91] and turn, leaving rem sts on holder.
Work 15 rows on these sts, ending with RS facing for next row.
Break off yarn and leave sts on a 3rd holder.
Return to sts left on first holder, rejoin yarn with RS facing,
K to end. 15 [17: 19: 21] sts.
Work 15 rows on these sts, ending with RS facing for next row.
Break off yarn and leave sts on a 4th holder.
Join sections
Rejoin yarn with RS facing and cont as foll:
Next row (RS): Work across 15 [17: 19: 21] sts on 2nd holder
as foll—K2, M1, K to end, K across 65 [71: 81: 91] sts on 3rd
holder; then K across 15 [17: 19: 21] sts on 4th holder as foll—
K to last 2 sts, M1, K2. 97 [107: 121: 135] sts.
Working all side seam shaping as set by last row, inc 1 st at
each end of 12th and every foll 12th row until there are

103 [113: 127: 141] sts.

Work 7 rows, ending with RS facing for next row. Back should measure 39 [39¼: 39¾: 40¼] in (99 [100: 101: 102] cm).

Shape armholes

Bind off 7 [8: 9: 10] sts at beg of next 2 rows. 89 [97: 109: 121] sts.

Dec 1 st at each end of next 3 [5: 5: 7] rows, then on foll 3 [3: 5: 6] alt rows. 77 [81: 89: 95] sts.

Work even until armhole measures 8¾ [9: 9½: 9¾] in (22 [23: 24: 25] cm), ending with RS facing for next row.

Shape shoulders and back neck

Next row (RS): Bind off 9 [10: 11: 13] sts, K until there are 12 [13: 15: 16] sts on right needle and turn, leaving rem sts on a holder.

Work each side of neck separately.

Bind off 3 sts at beg of next row.

Bind off rem 9 [10: 12: 13] sts.

With RS facing, rejoin yarn to rem sts, bind off center 35 [35: 37: 37] sts, K to end.

Complete to match first side, reversing shapings.

LEFT FRONT

Using size 6 (4mm) needles, cast on 68 [73: 80: 87] sts.

Row 1 (RS): K to last 12 sts, (P3, K3) twice.

Row 2: (P3, K3) twice, P to end.

These 2 rows set the sts—front opening edge 12 sts in rib with all other sts in St st.

Cont as set for 2 rows more, ending with RS facing for next row.

Change to size 7 (4.5mm) needles.

Cont as set until left front measures 18½ [19: 19¼: 19½] in (47 [48: 49: 50] cm), ending with RS facing for next row.

Next row (RS): K2, sl 1, K1, psso, patt to end.

Working all side seam shaping as set by last row, dec 1 st at beg of 6th and every foll 6th row until 53 [58: 65: 72] sts rem.

Work 1 row, ending with RS facing for next row.

Shape belt opening

Next row (RS): K15 [17: 19: 21] and turn, leaving rem sts on a holder.

Work 15 rows on these sts, ending with RS facing for next row. Break off yarn and leave sts on a 2nd holder.

Return to sts left on first holder, rejoin yarn with RS facing, patt to end. 38 [41: 46: 51] sts.

Work 15 rows on these sts, ending with RS facing for next row. Break off yarn and leave sts on a 3rd holder.

Join sections

Rejoin yarn with RS facing and cont as foll:

Next row (RS): Work across 15 [17: 19: 21] sts on 2nd holder as foll—K2, M1, K to end; then patt across 38 [41: 46: 51] sts on 3rd holder. 54 [59: 66: 73] sts.

Working all side seam shaping as set by last row, inc 1 st at beg of 12th and foll 12th row. 56 [61: 68: 75] sts.

Work 1 row, ending with RS facing for next row.

Shape front slope

Next row (RS): K to last 13 sts and turn, leaving rem 13 sts on a holder. 43 [48: 55: 62] sts.

Dec 1 st at front slope edge of 2nd and 2 [1: 2: 1] foll 4th row, then on foll 6th row **and at same time** inc 1 st at side seam edge of 10th row. 40 [46: 52: 60] sts.

Work 1 [5: 1: 5] rows, ending with RS facing for next row.

Shape armhole

Bind off 7 [8: 9: 10] sts at beg and dec 0 [1: 0: 1] st at end of next row. 33 [37: 43: 49] sts.

Work 1 row.

Dec 1 st at armhole edge of next 3 [5: 5: 7] rows, then on foll 3 [3: 5: 6] alt rows **and at same time** dec 1 st at front slope edge on 3rd [5th: 3rd: 5th] and every foll 6th row. 25 [27: 30: 33] sts.

Dec 1 st at front slope edge **only** on 6th [6th: 6th: 4th] and every foll 6th row until 18 [20: 23: 26] sts rem.

Work even until left front matches back to beg of shoulder shaping, ending with RS facing for next row.

Shape shoulder

Bind off 9 [10: 11: 13] sts at beg of next row.

Work 1 row.

Bind off rem 9 [10: 12: 13] sts.

RIGHT FRONT

Using size 6 (4mm) needles, cast on 68 [73: 80: 87] sts.

Row 1 (RS): (K3, P3) twice, K to end.

Row 2: P to last 12 sts, (K3, P3) twice.

These 2 rows set the sts—front opening edge 12 sts in rib with all other sts in St st.

Cont as set for 2 rows more, ending with RS facing for next row.

Change to size 7 (4.5mm) needles.

Cont as set until right front measures 18½ [19: 19¼: 19½] in (47 [48: 49: 50] cm), ending with RS facing for next row.

Next row (RS): Patt to last 4 sts, K2tog, K2.

Working all side seam shaping as set by last row, dec 1 st at end of 6th and every foll 6th row until 53 [58: 65: 72] sts rem.

Work 1 row, ending with RS facing for next row.

Shape belt opening

Next row (RS): Patt 38 [41: 46: 51] sts and turn, leaving rem sts on a holder.

Work 15 rows on these sts, ending with RS facing for next row. Break off yarn and leave sts on a 2nd holder.

Return to sts left on first holder, rejoin yarn with RS facing, K to end. 15 [17: 19: 21] sts.

Work 15 rows on these sts, ending with RS facing for next row. Break off yarn and leave sts on a 3rd holder.

Join sections

Rejoin yarn with RS facing and cont as foll:

Next row (RS): Patt across 38 [41: 46: 51] sts on 2nd holder; then work across 15 [17: 19: 21] sts on 3rd holder as foll—K to last 2 sts, M1, K2. 54 [59: 66: 73] sts.

Working all side seam shaping as set by last row, inc 1 st at end of 12th and foll 12th row. 56 [61: 68: 75] sts.

Work 1 row, ending with RS facing for next row.

Shape front slope

Next row (RS): Patt 13 sts and slip these sts onto a holder, K to end. 43 [48: 55: 62] sts.

Complete to match left front, reversing shapings.

SLEEVES

Using size 6 (4mm) needles, cast on 51 [53: 55: 55] sts.

Row 1 (RS): P0 [1: 2: 2], K3, *P3, K3, rep from * to last 0 [1: 2: 2] sts, P0 [1: 2: 2].

Row 2: K0 [1: 2: 2], P3, *K3, P3, rep from * to last 0 [1: 2: 2] sts, K0 [1: 2: 2].

These 2 rows form rib.

Work in rib for 2 rows more, ending with RS facing for next row.

Change to size 7 (4.5mm) needles.

Cont in rib, shaping sides by inc 1 st at each end of next and every 4th row to 59 [65: 69: 81] sts, then on every foll 6th row until there are 91 [95: 99: 103] sts, taking inc sts into rib.

Work even until sleeve measures 17¾ [18: 18½: 18½] in (45 [46: 47: 47] cm), ending with RS facing for next row.

Shape sleeve cap

Keeping rib correct, bind off 7 [8: 9: 10] sts at beg of next 2 rows. 77 [79: 81: 83] sts.

Dec 1 st at each end of next 7 rows, then on every foll alt row until 41 sts rem, then on foll 5 rows, ending with RS facing for next row. 31 sts.

Bind off 5 sts at beg of next 4 rows.

Bind off rem 11 sts.

FINISHING

Press as described on page 148.

Sew both shoulder seams using backstitch, or mattress stitch if preferred.

Left collar

Slip 13 sts from left front holder onto size 7 (4.5mm) needles and rejoin yarn with RS facing, patt to end.

Next row (WS of front, RS of collar): P3, K3, P3, K4.

This row sets the sts—front opening edge 9 sts in rib as set and rem sts in St st.

Inc 1 st at beg of next and every foll alt row until there are 35 sts, taking inc sts into St st.

Work 8 rows, ending with RS of collar facing for next row.

Bind off 25 sts at beg of next row. 10 sts.

Work 1 row.

Cast on 25 sts at beg of next row. 35 sts.

Now working all sts in St st, work even until collar, unstretched, fits up left front slope and across to center back neck, ending with RS facing for next row.

Bind off.

Right collar

Slip 13 sts from right front holder onto size 7 (4.5mm) needles and rejoin yarn with **WS** facing.

Next row (WS of front, RS of collar): K4, P3, K3, P3.

This row sets the sts—front opening edge 9 sts in rib as set and rem sts in St st.

Inc 1 st at end of next and every foll alt row until there are 35 sts, taking inc sts into St st.

Work 9 rows, ending with **WS** of collar facing for next row.

Bind off 25 sts at beg of next row. 10 sts.

Work 1 row.

Cast on 25 sts at beg of next row. 35 sts.

Now working all sts in St st, work even until collar, unstretched, fits up right front slope and across to center back neck, ending with RS facing for next row.

Bind off.

Belt

Using size 6 (4mm) needles, cast on 27 sts.

Row 1 (RS): K3, (P3, K3) 4 times.

Row 2: P3, (K3, P3) 4 times.

Rep these 2 rows until belt measures 67¾ [71½: 75½: 79½] in (172 [182: 192: 202] cm), ending with RS facing for next row.

Bind off in rib.

See page 148 for finishing instructions, setting in sleeves using the set-in method. Using photograph as a guide, thread belt through openings in back and fronts.

KNITTER'S TIP

This coat has a knitted belt threaded through slots made as the back and fronts are worked. But why not give your coat a slightly different look by threading a purchased leather belt through instead? Just make sure the belt you choose fits neatly through the slots without stretching them.

Earth Stripe Tunic

KAFFE FASSETT

SIZES AND YARN

	S	M	L	XL	
To fit bust					
	32–34	36–38	40–42	44–46	in
	81–86	91–97	102–107	112–117	cm

Rowan Kidsilk Haze

	S	M	L	XL	
A Hurricane 632					
	2	2	2	2	x 25 g
B Jacob 631 (or Putty 626)					
	2	2	2	3	x 25 g
C Elegance 577 (or Ember 644)					
	2	2	2	2	x 25 g
D Drab 588					
	4	4	4	4	x 25 g
E Candy Girl 606					
	1	1	1	1	x 25 g
F Meadow 581					
	2	2	2	3	x 25 g
G Majestic 589					
	5	5	6	6	x 25 g
H Trance 582					
	2	2	3	3	x 25 g
I Jelly 597					
	1	1	1	1	x 25 g
J Blushes 583					
	1	1	1	1	x 25 g

NEEDLES

1 pair size 3 (3.25mm) needles
1 pair size 6 (4mm) needles
Size 6 (4mm) circular needle

> ### KNITTER'S TIP
> The clever shaded stripe effect of this tunic, and its matching wrap (see page 133), is created by using two different shades of yarn for each stripe. This, in conjunction with the fluffy nature of the yarn, softens the appearance of the stripes so that they merge together forming a wonderful haze of color.

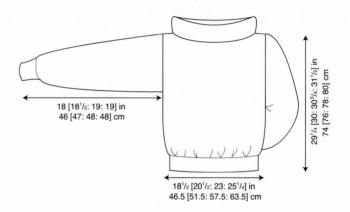

18 [18¹/₂: 19: 19] in
46 [47: 48: 48] cm

29¹/₄ [30: 30³/₄: 31¹/₂] in
74 [76: 78: 80] cm

18¹/₂ [20¹/₂: 23: 25¹/₄] in
46.5 [51.5: 57.5: 63.5] cm

GAUGE

24 sts and 28 rows to 4 in (10 cm) measured over St st using size 6 (4mm) needles and yarn DOUBLE.

STRIPE SEQUENCE

Rows 1–4: Using yarns G and H.
Rows 5–8: Using yarns D and G.
Rows 9 and 10: Using yarns B and F.
Rows 11–13: Using yarns G and J.
Row 14: Using yarns A and H.
Row 15: Using yarns H and I.
Rows 16–19: Using yarns F and G.
Rows 20–22: Using yarns C and D.
Row 23: Using yarns B and E.
Rows 24–26: Using yarns B and J.
Rows 27 and 28: Using yarns C and G.
Rows 29 and 30: Using yarns G and I.
Rows 31–35: Using yarns D and G.
Rows 36 and 37: Using yarns G and H.
Row 38: Using yarns B and E.
Rows 39 and 40: Using yarns G and J.
Rows 41 and 42: Using yarns C and G.
Rows 43 and 44: Using yarns C and I.
Rows 45–47: Using yarns D and H.

Row 48: Using yarns A and H.
Rows 49 and 50: Using yarns A and G.
Rows 51–53: Using yarns D and G.
Rows 54–58: Using yarns F and G.
Row 59: Using yarns F and I.
Rows 60 and 61: Using yarns C and G.
Row 62: Using yarns G and J.
Row 63: Using yarns D and G.
Row 64: Using yarns F and G.
Rows 65–69: Using yarns D and H.
Row 70: Using yarns A and B.
Rows 71 and 72: Using yarns F and G.
Rows 73 and 74: Using yarns G and H.
Rows 75 and 76: Using yarns D and H.
Rows 77 and 78: Using yarns C and D.
Rows 79 and 80: Using yarns C and I.
Row 81: Using yarns G and H.
Row 82: Using yarns F and G.
Rows 83–85: Using yarns G and J.
Rows 86–88: Using yarns B and E.
Row 89: Using yarns A and B.
Rows 90 and 91: Using yarns C and G.
Rows 92–95: Using yarns D and H.
Rows 96–102: Using yarns B and F.
Rows 103 and 104: Using yarns F and I.
Rows 105 and 106: Using yarns C and I.
Rows 107 and 108: Using yarns D and H.
Row 109: Using yarns A and B.
Rows 110–113: Using yarns D and G.
Rows 114 and 115: Using yarns G and J.
Row 116: Using yarns B and J.
Rows 117–120: Using yarns A and G.
Rows 121–123: Using yarns B and F.
Rows 124–126: Using yarns D and G.
Rows 127–132: Using yarns F and G.
Row 133: Using yarns B and E.
Row 134: Using yarns A and G.
Rows 135 and 136: Using yarns G and H.
Rows 137 and 138: Using yarns F and G.
Rows 139–142: Using yarns C and G.
Rows 143–146: Using yarns C and D.
Row 147: Using yarns C and I.
Row 148: Using yarns B and E.
Rows 149–151: Using yarns F and G.
Rows 152–154: Using yarns D and G.
Rows 155–157: Using yarns A and B.
Rows 158 and 159: Using yarns B and E.
Row 160: Using yarns B and J.
Row 161: Using yarns B and F.
Rows 162–167: Using yarns G and H.
Rows 168 and 169: Using yarns F and G.

Rows 170 and 171: Using yarns D and G.
Rows 172 and 173: Using yarns G and I.
Rows 174 and 175: Using yarns C and I.
Rows 176–179: Using yarns B and F.
Rows 180–182: Using yarns F and G.
Rows 183 and 184: Using yarns D and G.
Rows 185 and 186: Using yarns A and H.
These 186 rows form stripe sequence and are repeated as required.

BACK
Using size 3 (3.25mm) needles and yarns A and B held together, cast on 114 [126: 138: 154] sts.
Row 1 (RS): K2, ★P2, K2, rep from ★ to end.
Row 2: P2, ★K2, P2, rep from ★ to end.
These 2 rows form rib.
Keeping rib correct and joining in and breaking off colors as required, cont in rib in stripes as foll:
Rows 3–5: Using yarns C and D.
Rows 6 and 7: Using yarns A and E.
Rows 8 and 9: Using yarns A and G.
Rows 10–12: Using yarns B and F.
Rows 13–15: Using yarns C and D.
Rows 16 and 17: Using yarns A and H.
Rows 18–20: Using yarns A and E.
Rep last 20 rows once more, dec 1 [1: 0: 1] st at each end of last row and ending with RS facing for next row. 112 [124: 138: 152] sts.
Change to size 6 (4mm) needles.
Beg with a K row and stripe row 1, work in St st in stripe sequence (as given beginning on page 130) until back measures 29¼ [30: 30¾: 31½] in (74 [76: 78: 80] cm), ending with RS facing for next row.
Shape shoulders and back neck
Next row (RS): Bind off 7 [10: 13: 17] sts, K until there are 13 [16: 19: 22] sts on right needle and turn, leaving rem sts on a holder.
Work each side of neck separately.
Bind off 5 sts at beg of next row.
Bind off rem 8 [11: 14: 17] sts.
With RS facing, rejoin appropriate yarns to rem sts, bind off center 72 [72: 74: 74] sts, K to end.
Complete to match first side, reversing shapings.

FRONT
Work as given for back until 6 [6: 8: 8] rows less have been worked than on back to beg of shoulder shaping, ending with RS facing for next row.
Shape neck
Next row (RS): K32 [38: 46: 53] and turn, leaving rem sts on a holder.

Work each side of neck separately.

Bind off 8 sts at beg of next row, then 6 sts at beg of foll alt row. 18 [24: 32: 39] sts.

Dec 1 st at neck edge of next 2 [2: 4: 4] rows, ending with RS facing for next row. 16 [22: 28: 35] sts.

Shape shoulder

Bind off 7 [10: 13: 17] sts at beg and dec 1 st at end of next row.

Work 1 row.

Bind off rem 8 [11: 14: 17] sts.

With RS facing, rejoin appropriate yarns to rem sts, bind off center 48 [48: 46: 46] sts, K to end.

Complete to match first side, reversing shapings.

SLEEVES

Using size 3 (3.25mm) needles and yarns A and B held together, cast on 50 [54: 54: 58] sts.

Work in striped rib as given for back for 28 rows, ending with RS facing for next row.

Change to size 6 (4mm) needles.

Beg with row 1, work in stripe sequence (as given beginning on page 130) as foll:

Row 1 (RS): K2 [5: 4: 7], inc once in each of next 46 [44: 46: 44] sts, K to end. 96 [98: 100: 102] sts.

Beg with a **P** row, work in St st, shaping sides by inc 1 st at each end of 14th and foll 7 [7: 8: 10] alt rows, then on every foll 4th row until there are 140 [144: 148: 152] sts.

Work even until sleeve measures 18 [18½: 19: 19] in (46 [47: 48: 48] cm), ending with RS facing for next row.

Bind off.

FINISHING

Press as described on page 148.

Sew both shoulder seams using backstitch, or mattress stitch if preferred.

Collar

With **WS** facing, using size 6 (4mm) circular needle and yarns A and B held together, beg and ending at right shoulder seam, pick up and knit 23 [23: 25: 25] sts down right side of neck, 48 [48: 46: 46] sts from front, 23 [23: 25: 25] sts up left side of neck, then 82 [82: 84: 84] sts from back. 176 [176: 180: 180] sts.

Working in rounds of St st (by working every round as a K round) and beg with row 1, work in stripe sequence (as given beginning on page 130) until collar measures 11 in (28 cm).

Bind off loosely.

See page 148 for finishing instructions, setting in sleeves using the straight bind-off method.

Earth Stripe Wrap

KAFFE FASSETT

YARN
Rowan Kidsilk Haze

A	Hurricane 632	1	x 25 g
B	Jacob 631 (or Putty 626)	1	x 25 g
C	Elegance 577 (or Ember 644)	1	x 25 g
D	Drab 588	2	x 25 g
E	Candy Girl 606	1	x 25 g
F	Meadow 581	2	x 25 g
G	Majestic 589	2	x 25 g
H	Trance 582	2	x 25 g
I	Jelly 597	1	x 25 g
J	Blushes 583	1	x 25 g

NEEDLES AND CROCHET HOOK
1 pair size 6 (4mm) needles
Size G-6 (4mm) crochet hook

GAUGE
24 sts and 28 rows to 4 in (10 cm) measured over St st using size 6 (4mm) needles and yarn DOUBLE.

FINISHED SIZE
Finished wrap measures approx 19¼ in (49 cm) wide by 58¾ in (149 cm) long, excluding fringe.

US CROCHET ABBREVIATIONS
ch = chain; **sc** = single crochet.

KNITTER'S TIP
The long fringe of this wrap is added afterward, and the colors of each knot of the fringe match the colors used for the stripes. However, if you find you're running a little short of one shade, don't worry—simply use what you have, remembering to mix the shades within each knot.

Pattern note: The crochet instructions in this pattern use US terminology. The US single crochet (sc) is equivalent to the UK double crochet (dc).

WRAP
Using size 6 (4mm) needles and yarns G and H held together, cast on 115 sts.
Beg with a K row and stripe row 1, work in St st in stripe sequence as given for Earth Stripe Tunic (see pages 130–131) until wrap measures 58¼ in (148 cm), ending with RS facing for next row.
Bind off.

FINISHING
Press as described on page 148.
Edging
With RS facing, using size G-6 (4mm) crochet hook and yarns D and H held together, join yarn to edge of wrap with a slip stitch, ch 1 (does NOT count as st), work 1 round of sc evenly around entire outer edge of wrap, working 3 sc in each corner point and ending by joining with a slip stitch to first sc.
Next round (RS): Ch 1 (does NOT count as st), 1 sc in each sc to end, working 3 sc in each corner point and ending by joining with a slip stitch to first sc.
Fasten off.
Fringe
Cut 19¾ in (50 cm) lengths of yarn and, using same color combinations as used for stripe sequence, knot groups of 8 of these lengths (4 of each color) through ends of wrap to form fringe—make approx 36–38 knots evenly spaced across each end.

Geneva Camisole

SARAH HATTON

SIZES AND YARN

	XS	S	M	L	XL	XXL	
To fit bust	32	34	36	38	40	42	in
	81	86	91	97	102	107	cm

Rowan Classic Pure Silk DK

Tranquil 156	7	7	8	8	9	9	x 50 g

Originally knitted and photographed (above) in Rowan 4-Ply
Soft in Rain Cloud 387

NEEDLES

1 pair size 2 (2.75mm) needles
1 pair size 3 (3.25mm) needles

BEADS—approx 750 [790: 820: 910: 950: 1,030] silver-lined
clear glass beads

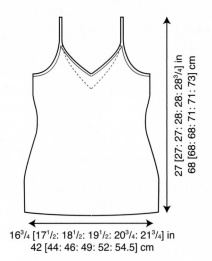

27 [27: 27: 28: 28: 28³/4] in
68 [68: 68: 71: 71: 73] cm

16³/4 [17¹/2: 18¹/2: 19¹/2: 20³/4: 21³/4] in
42 [44: 46: 49: 52: 54.5] cm

NEW YARN SUBSTITUTION

The original yarn used for this beaded camisole was a sleek and
smooth super-fine pure wool yarn. We could have chosen
Rowan Pure Wool 4-Ply as the substitute as it will knit to
exactly the same gauge, but we felt it might be a little too rough
against the skin and that this design needed a more extravagant
look. So we chose Rowan Classic Pure Silk DK (right) instead.
Although this yarn is thicker than the original, it is a very soft
and fluid yarn that knits up perfectly on smaller needles.
However, if you want to knit the camisole in Rowan Pure Wool
4-Ply, you need 6 [6: 6: 6: 7: 7] balls of this yarn. Or you could
try a summery version, knitted in pure cotton Rowan Classic
Siena. For this, you need 7 [7: 7: 8: 8: 8] balls.

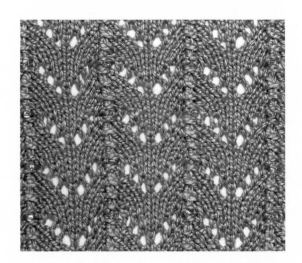

KNITTER'S TIP

The beads on this camisole can have a tendency to slip
through to the wrong side, where they won't show. Once
you've finished knitting, gently ease any beads that have
slipped through back onto the right side of the work.

GAUGE

28 sts and 36 rows to 4 in (10 cm) measured over St st using size 3 (3.25mm) needles.

SPECIAL ABBREVIATIONS

bead 1 = place a bead by bringing yarn to front (RS) of work and slipping bead up next to st just worked, slip next st purlwise from left needle to right needle and take yarn back to back (WS) of work, leaving bead sitting in front of slipped st on RS.

Beading note: Before starting to knit, thread beads onto yarn. To do this, thread a fine sewing needle (one that will easily pass through the beads) with sewing thread. Knot ends of thread and then pass end of yarn through this loop. Thread a bead onto sewing thread and then gently slide it along and onto knitting yarn. Continue in this way until required number of beads are on yarn. Do not place beads on edge sts of rows as this will interfere with seams.

BACK

Using size 3 (3.25mm) needles, cast on 125 [131: 137: 145: 153: 161] sts.
Row 1 (RS): K2 [2: 2: 3: 1: 2], bead 1, *K2, bead 1, rep from * to last 2 [2: 2: 3: 1: 2] sts, K2 [2: 2: 3: 1: 2].
Work in garter st for 3 rows, ending with RS facing for next row.
Now work in patt as foll:
Row 1 (RS): K3 [0: 3: 3: 1: 1], (K2tog, K3, yo, K1) 0 [1: 1: 0: 1: 0] times, *yo, K3, sl 1, K2tog, psso, K3, yo, K1, rep from * to last 2 [5: 8: 2: 6: 0] sts, (yo, K3, sl 1, K1, psso) 0 [1: 1: 0: 1: 0] times, K2 [0: 3: 2: 1: 0].
Row 2: Purl.
Row 3: K3 [0: 3: 3: 1: 1], (K2tog, K2, yo, K2) 0 [1: 1: 0: 1: 0] times, *K1, yo, K2, sl 1, K2tog, psso, K2, yo, K2, rep from * to last 2 [5: 8: 2: 6: 0] sts, (K1, yo, K2, sl 1, K1, psso) 0 [1: 1: 0: 1: 0] times, K2 [0: 3: 2: 1: 0].
Row 4: Purl.
Row 5: K3 [0: 3: 3: 1: 1], (K2tog, K1, yo, K3) 0 [1: 1: 0: 1: 0] times, *K2, yo, K1, sl 1, K2tog, psso, K1, yo, K3, rep from * to last 2 [5: 8: 2: 6: 0] sts, (K2, yo, K1, sl 1, K1, psso) 0 [1: 1: 0: 1: 0] times, K2 [0: 3: 2: 1: 0].
Row 6: Purl.
Row 7: K3 [0: 3: 3: 1: 1], (K2tog, yo, K4) 0 [1: 1: 0: 1: 0] times, *K3, yo, sl 1, K2tog, psso, yo, K4, rep from * to last 2 [5: 8: 2: 6: 0] sts, (K3, yo, sl 1, K1, psso) 0 [1: 1: 0: 1: 0] times, K2 [0: 3: 2: 1: 0].
Row 8: P2 [5: 3: 2: 1: 0], (bead 1, P4) 0 [0: 1: 0: 1: 0] times, *P5, bead 1, P4, rep from * to last 3 [6: 9: 3: 7: 1] sts, (P5, bead 1) 0 [0: 1: 0: 1: 0] times, P3 [6: 3: 3: 1: 1].
These 8 rows form patt.
Cont in patt for 32 rows more, ending with RS facing for next row.

Keeping patt correct, dec 1 st at each end of next and every foll 6th row until 105 [111: 117: 125: 133: 141] sts rem.
(**Note:** When working shaping through patt, place markers either side of edge patt reps. Work sts beyond markers in St st. When decreasing, move markers in to edge of next patt rep when required. When increasing, move markers out to edge of next patt rep when there are sufficient sts.)
Work 13 rows, ending with RS facing for next row.
Inc 1 st at each end of next and every foll 8th row until there are 117 [123: 129: 137: 145: 153] sts, taking inc sts into St st until there are sufficient to work in patt.
Work even until back measures 19 [19: 18¾: 19¾: 19¼: 20] in (48 [48: 47: 50: 49: 51] cm), ending with RS facing for next row.
Shape armholes
Keeping patt correct, bind off 7 [8: 8: 9: 9: 10] sts at beg of next 2 rows. 103 [107: 113: 119: 127: 133] sts.
Divide for neck
Next row (RS): (K1, P1) twice, patt 43 [45: 48: 51: 55: 58] sts, (P1, K1) twice and turn, leaving rem sts on a holder.
Work each side of neck separately.
Next row: (P1, K1) twice, patt to last 4 sts, (K1, P1) twice.
These 2 rows set the sts—first and last 4 sts of every row in rib with all other sts still in patt.
Keeping sts correct as now set, cont as foll:
Next row (RS): K1, P1, K1, P2tog, patt to last 5 sts, P2tog tbl, K1, P1, K1.
Next row: P1, K1, P1, sl 1, K1, psso, patt to last 5 sts, K2tog, P1, K1, P1. 47 [49: 52: 55: 59: 62] sts.
Working all decreases as set by last 2 rows, dec 1 st at armhole edge on next 9 [9: 11: 11: 13: 13] rows, then on foll 5 [6: 6: 7: 6: 7] alt rows **and at same time** dec 1 st at neck edge on next 9 [11: 11: 15: 19: 23] rows, then on every foll alt row. 19 [18: 18: 17: 18: 17] sts.
Dec 1 st at neck edge **only** on 2nd and every foll alt row until 8 sts rem.
Work 1 row, ending with RS facing for next row.
Next row (RS): K1, P1, K1, P2tog, K1, P1, K1. 7 sts.
Change to size 2 (2.75mm) needles.
Cont in rib as set on these 7 sts until armhole measures 8 [8: 8¼: 8¼: 8¾: 8¾] in (20 [20: 21: 21: 22: 22] cm), ending with RS facing for next row.
Shape shoulder
Bind off rem 7 sts.
With RS facing, rejoin yarn to rem sts, K2tog, P1, K1, P1, patt to last 4 sts, (P1, K1) twice.
Complete to match first side, reversing shapings.

FRONT

Work as given for back until 12 rows less have been worked than on back to beg of armhole shaping, ending with RS facing for next row.

Divide for neck

Next row (RS): Patt 54 [57: 60: 64: 68: 72] sts, (P1, K1) twice and turn, leaving rem sts on a holder.

Work each side of neck separately.

Next row: (P1, K1) twice, patt to end.

These 2 rows set the sts—neck edge 4 sts of every row in rib with all other sts still in patt.

Keeping sts correct as now set and working all decreases in same way as given for back, cont as foll:

Dec 1 st at neck edge of next 1 [1: 1: 3: 7: 10] rows, then on foll 4 [4: 4: 3: 1: 0] alt rows. 53 [56: 59: 62: 64: 66] sts.

Work 1 [1: 1: 1: 1: 0] row, ending with RS facing for next row.

Shape armhole

Keeping patt correct, bind off 7 [8: 8: 9: 9: 10] sts at beg and dec 1 st at end of next row. 45 [47: 50: 52: 54: 55] sts.

Work 1 row.

Next row (RS): (K1, P1) twice, patt to last 5 sts, P2tog tbl, K1, P1, K1.

Next row: (P1, K1) twice, patt to last 4 sts, (K1, P1) twice. 44 [46: 49: 51: 53: 54] sts.

These 2 rows set the sts—first and last 4 sts of every row in rib with all other sts still in patt.

Keeping sts correct as now set and working all decreases in same way as given for back, dec 1 st at armhole edge on next 11 [11:

13: 13: 15: 15] rows, then on foll 5 [6: 6: 7: 6: 7] alt rows **and at same time** dec 1 st at neck edge on next and every foll alt row. 17 [17: 17: 17: 18: 17] sts.

Dec 1 st at neck edge **only** on 2nd and every foll alt row until 8 sts rem.

Work 1 row, ending with RS facing for next row.

Next row (RS): K1, P1, K1, P2tog, K1, P1, K1. 7 sts.

Change to size 2 (2.75mm) needles.

Cont in rib as set on these 7 sts until armhole measures 8 [8: 8¼: 8¼: 8¾: 8¾] in (20 [20: 21: 21: 22: 22] cm), ending with RS facing for next row.

Shape shoulder

Bind off rem 7 sts.

With RS facing, rejoin yarn to rem sts, K2tog, P1, K1, P1, patt to end.

Complete to match first side, reversing shapings.

FINISHING

Press as described on page 148.

Sew both shoulder seams using backstitch, or mattress stitch if preferred.

See page 148 for finishing instructions.

About Sarah Hatton

Sarah Hatton was born in St. Albans and spent the early part of her life based in Hertfordshire. Having done an art foundation course close to home, she moved to Yorkshire to complete a degree in Fashion Design at Bretton Hall College, part of the University of Leeds. Sarah has been based at Green Lane Mill since 2004 and is part of Rowan's in-house design team.

Taught to knit at the age of five, Sarah has always had a love of textiles and had a passion for dressing up as a child. As a teenager she showed a flare for customizing her own clothes and was always up-to-the-minute with fashion in her own dress sense. Immediately after graduating, Sarah was offered her first job as a designer with a hand-knit company. It was here she got to develop her skills in knitting, pattern writing, and design. Sarah prides herself on the fact that since graduating she has always worked in the hand-knitting industry.

Sarah's inspiration is usually garment shape, and although she rarely works in more than one color, she produces amazingly wearable garments that explore and push the boundaries of shape and texture. Sarah has a keen eye for all the latest trends and through her work with Rowan Studio publications interprets these into popular commercial knitwear. These handy small brochures have been instant collectables, and Studio 1 patterns are still highly sought after.

The Studio shoots with quirky touches, such as a nautical theme or fun with balloons or feminine flowers, are a real reflection of Sarah's design eye and unique style. Who knows, in 30 years time we may be putting together an exhibition of these fashion forward magazines. Start collecting!

Geneva Cardigan

ERIKA KNIGHT

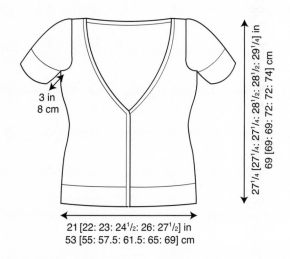

21 [22: 23: 24½: 26: 27½] in
53 [55: 57.5: 61.5: 65: 69] cm

3 in
8 cm

27¼ [27¼: 27¼: 28½: 28½: 29¼] in
69 [69: 69: 72: 72: 74] cm

SIZES AND YARN

	XS	S	M	L	XL	XXL	
To fit bust	32	34	36	38	40	42	in
	81	86	91	97	102	107	cm

Rowan Kidsilk Haze

	4	4	5	5	5	6	x 25 g

Photographed in Smoke 605

NEEDLES

1 pair size 2 (2.75mm) needles
1 pair size 3 (3.25mm) needles

BUTTONS—9

GAUGE

25 sts and 34 rows to 4 in (10 cm) measured over St st using size 3 (3.25mm) needles.

BACK

Using size 3 (3.25mm) needles, cast on 140 [146: 152: 162: 170: 180] sts.
Row 1 (RS): K0 [0: 1: 0: 0: 0], P1 [0: 2: 0: 0: 1], ★K2, P2, rep from ★ to last 3 [2: 1: 2: 2: 3] sts, K2 [2: 1: 2: 2: 2], P1 [0: 0: 0: 0: 1].
Row 2: P0 [0: 1: 0: 0: 0], K1 [0: 2: 0: 0: 1], ★P2, K2, rep from ★ to last 3 [2: 1: 2: 2: 3] sts, P2 [2: 1: 2: 2: 2], K1 [0: 0: 0: 0: 1].
These 2 rows form rib.
Work in rib for 26 rows more, ending with RS facing for next row.
Beg with a K row, work in St st for 2 rows, ending with RS facing for next row.
Next row (dec row) (RS): K2, sl 1, K1, psso, K to last 4 sts, K2tog, K2.
Working all side seam decreases as set by last row, dec 1 st at each end of 6th and every foll 6th row until 118 [124: 130: 140: 148: 158] sts rem.
Work 19 [19: 17: 21: 19: 23] rows, ending with RS facing for next row.

Next row (inc row) (RS): K2, M1, K to last 2 sts, M1, K2.
Working all side seam increases as set by last row, inc 1 st at each end of 6th and every foll 6th row until there are 132 [138: 144: 154: 162: 172] sts.
Work 19 [19: 19: 25: 23: 25] rows, ending with RS facing for next row. Back should measure 19¼ [19¼: 19: 20¼: 19¾: 20½] in (49 [49: 48: 51: 50: 52] cm).
Shape armholes
Bind off 6 [7: 7: 8: 8: 9] sts at beg of next 2 rows. 120 [124: 130: 138: 146: 154] sts.
Next row (RS): K2, sl 1, K1, psso, K to last 4 sts, K2tog, K2.
Next row: P2, P2tog, P to last 4 sts, P2tog tbl, P2.
Working all armhole decreases as set by last 2 rows, dec 1 st at each end of next 5 [5: 7: 7: 9: 9] rows, then on foll 4 [5: 4: 5: 5: 7] alt rows. 98 [100: 104: 110: 114: 118] sts.
Work even until armhole measures 8 [8: 8¼: 8¼: 8¾: 8¾] in (20 [20: 21: 21: 22: 22] cm), ending with RS facing for next row.
Shape shoulders and back neck
Next row (RS): Bind off 9 [9: 10: 12: 12: 13] sts, K until there are 12 [13: 14: 15: 16: 17] sts on right needle and turn, leaving rem sts on a holder.
Work each side of neck separately.
Bind off 3 sts at beg of next row.

Bind off rem 9 [10: 11: 12: 13: 14] sts.

With RS facing, rejoin yarn to rem sts, bind off center 56 [56: 56: 56: 58: 58] sts, K to end.

Complete to match first side, reversing shapings.

LEFT FRONT

Using size 3 (3.25mm) needles, cast on 73 [76: 79: 84: 88: 93] sts.

Row 1 (RS): K0 [0: 1: 0: 0: 0], P1 [0: 2: 0: 0: 1], ★K2, P2, rep from ★ to last 8 sts, K2, (P1, K1) 3 times.

Row 2: (P1, K1) 3 times, ★P2, K2, rep from ★ to last 3 [2: 1: 2: 2: 3] sts, P2 [2: 1: 2: 2: 2], K1 [0: 0: 0: 0: 1].

These 2 rows form rib.

Work in rib for 26 rows more, ending with RS facing for next row.

Next row (RS): K to last 6 sts, (P1, K1) 3 times.

Next row: (P1, K1) 3 times, P to end.

These 2 rows set the sts—front opening edge 6 sts still in rib with all other sts now in St st.

Keeping sts correct as set and working all shaping as given for back, cont as foll:

Dec 1 st at beg of next and every foll 6th row until 62 [65: 68: 73: 77: 82] sts rem.

Work 19 [19: 17: 21: 19: 23] rows, ending with RS facing for next row.

Inc 1 st at beg of next and every foll 6th row until there are 67 [70: 73: 79: 83: 88] sts.

Work 3 [3: 3: 3: 1: 3] rows, ending with RS facing for next row.

Shape front slope

Next row (RS): K to last 8 sts, K2tog, (P1, K1) 3 times.

Working all front slope shaping as set by last row, cont as foll:

Dec 1 st at front slope edge on 2nd and foll 12 alt rows **and at same time** inc 1 st at side seam edge on 2nd [2nd: 2nd: 2nd: 4th: 2nd] and 1 [1: 1: 0: 0: 0] foll 6th row. 55 [58: 61: 66: 70: 75] sts.

Work 1 row, ending with RS facing for next row.

Shape armhole

Bind off 6 [7: 7: 8: 8: 9] sts at beg and dec 1 st at end of next row. 48 [50: 53: 57: 61: 65] sts.

Work 1 row.

Working all armhole decreases as set by back, dec 1 st at armhole edge of next 7 [7: 9: 9: 11: 11] rows, then on foll 4 [5: 4: 5: 5: 7] alt rows **and at same time** dec 1 st at front slope edge of next and foll 7 [8: 8: 9: 10: 11] alt rows. 29 [29: 31: 33: 34: 35] sts.

Dec 1 st at front slope edge **only** on 2nd [2nd: 4th: 4th: 4th: 2nd] and foll 3 [2: 0: 0: 0: 0] alt rows, then on every foll 4th row until 18 [19: 21: 24: 25: 27] sts rem.

Work even until left front matches back to beg of shoulder shaping, ending with RS facing for next row.

Shape shoulder

Bind off 9 [9: 10: 12: 12: 13] sts at beg of next row.

Work 1 row.

Bind off rem 9 [10: 11: 12: 13: 14] sts.

Mark positions for 9 buttons along left front opening edge—first to come in row 5, last to come just below beg of front slope shaping, and rem 7 buttons evenly spaced between.

RIGHT FRONT

Using size 3 (3.25mm) needles, cast on 73 [76: 79: 84: 88: 93] sts.

Row 1 (RS): (K1, P1) 3 times, ★K2, P2, rep from ★ to last 3 [2: 1: 2: 2: 3] sts, K2 [2: 1: 2: 2: 2], P1 [0: 0: 0: 0: 1].

Row 2: P0 [0: 1: 0: 0: 0], K1 [0: 2: 0: 0: 1], ★P2, K2, rep from ★ to last 8 sts, P2, (K1, P1) 3 times.

These 2 rows form rib.

Work in rib for 2 rows more, ending with RS facing for next row.

Row 5 (buttonhole row) (RS): K1, P1, K1, yo, K2tog (to make a buttonhole), patt to end.

Working 8 buttonholes more in this way to correspond with positions marked for buttons on left front and noting that no further reference will be made to buttonholes, cont as foll:

Work in rib for 23 rows more, ending with RS facing for next row.

Next row (RS): (K1, P1) 3 times, K to end.

Next row: P to last 6 sts, (K1, P1) 3 times.

These 2 rows set the sts—front opening edge 6 sts still in rib with all other sts now in St st.

Keeping sts correct as set and working all shaping as given for back, cont as foll:

Dec 1 st at end of next and every foll 6th row until 62 [65: 68: 73: 77: 82] sts rem.

Work 19 [19: 17: 21: 19: 23] rows, ending with RS facing for next row.

Inc 1 st at end of next and every foll 6th row until there are 67 [70: 73: 79: 83: 88] sts.

Work 3 [3: 3: 3: 1: 3] rows, ending with RS facing for next row.

Shape front slope

Next row (RS): (K1, P1) 3 times, sl 1, K1, psso, K to end.

Working all front slope shaping as set by last row, complete to match left front, reversing shapings.

SLEEVES

Using size 3 (3.25mm) needles, cast on 68 [70: 72: 74: 76: 78] sts.

Row 1 (RS): K1 [0: 0: 0: 1: 0], P2 [0: 1: 2: 2: 0], ★K2, P2, rep from ★ to last 1 [2: 3: 0: 1: 2] sts, K1 [2: 2: 0: 1: 2], P0 [0: 1: 0: 0: 0].

Row 2: P1 [0: 0: 0: 1: 0], K2 [0: 1: 2: 2: 0], ★P2, K2, rep from ★ to last 1 [2: 3: 0: 1: 2] sts, P1 [2: 2: 0: 1: 2], K0 [0: 1: 0: 0: 0].

These 2 rows form rib.

Cont in rib, inc 1 st at each end of 3rd and foll 8 alt rows, taking inc sts into rib. 86 [88: 90: 92: 94: 96] sts.

Work in rib for 3 rows more, ending with RS facing for next row. (24 rows of rib completed.)

Beg with a K row, work in St st for 4 rows, ending with RS facing for next row.

Shape sleeve cap

Bind off 6 [7: 7: 8: 8: 9] sts at beg of next 2 rows. 74 [74: 76: 76: 78: 78] sts.

Working all decreases in same way as for armhole, dec 1 st at each end of next and foll 7 alt rows, then on 3 foll 4th rows, then on every foll alt row until 22 sts rem.

Work 1 row, ending with RS facing for next row.

Bind off rem 22 sts.

FINISHING

Press as described on page 148.

Sew both shoulder seams using backstitch, or mattress stitch if preferred.

Back neckband

With RS facing and using size 2 (2.75mm) needles, pick up and knit 62 [62: 62: 62: 64: 64] sts from back neck bound-off edge. Bind off knitwise (on **WS**).

See page 148 for finishing instructions, setting in sleeves using set-in method.

KNITTER'S TIP

Knitted in a gossamer light yarn on fine needles, this cardigan is the perfect "topping" for a night out, or a summer evening. But, as the cardigan itself is so light, be sure to choose buttons that don't weigh it down. Heavy buttons will distort the garment and pull it out of shape.

About Erika Knight

Erika's ethos has always been to inspire, innovate, and collaborate to make a difference. As a renowned design consultant to the fashion and yarn industry, Erika has worked with Rowan for over three decades contributing both to the Rowan magazines and also acting as a consultant. Originally from a fine arts background, she has worked in most areas of knit and fabric design from original concept, garment design, pattern, and print through to yarn design and production.

Erika's trend-forecasting skills revived her passion for the hand made, and her "Simple" philosophy has created a unique interpretation on craft through her highly acclaimed knitting and crochet books. She has lectured at the Victoria and Albert Museum in London, as well as leading art institutions and universities in the UK.

Erika is passionate in promoting and developing ecologically and ethically resourced product and raw materials, which she believes has had a profound effect on how she now lives her life.

Fontaine

MARION FOALE

SIZES AND YARN

XXS	XS	S	M	L	XL	XXL	XXXL	
To fit bust								
32	34	36	38	40	42	44	46	in
81	86	91	97	102	107	112	117	cm

Rowan Classic Cashsoft 4-Ply

Bark 432

| 11 | 11 | 11 | 12 | 13 | 14 | 14 | 15 | x 50 g |

Originally knitted and photographed (above) in Rowan 4-Ply Soft in Vine 402

NEEDLES

1 pair size 2 (2.75mm) needles

1 pair size 0 (2mm) needles

BUTTONS—8

NEW YARN SUBSTITUTION

We substituted a cashmere blend yarn for the pure wool used for the original of this jacket to give it a real feel of luxury. A blend of extra fine merino wool, acrylic microfiber, and cashmere, Rowan Classic Cashsoft 4-Ply (right) will knit to exactly the same gauge as the original yarn. Knitted on slightly thinner needles than would normally be used for a yarn of this thickness, the textured stitch pattern creates a firm fabric that gives the jacket a good structured feel.

KNITTER'S TIP

Take care when pressing this garment that you don't "squash" the texture! Pressing too vigorously will flatten the fabric, altering the gauge, and thereby making your jacket too big.

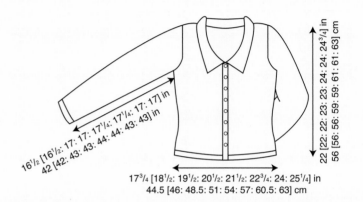

16½ [16½: 17: 17: 17¼: 17¼: 17: 17] in
42 [42: 43: 43: 43: 44: 44: 43: 43] cm

22 [22: 22: 23: 24: 24: 24: 24¾] in
56 [56: 56: 59: 61: 61: 63] cm

17¾ [18½: 19½: 20½: 21½: 22¾: 24: 25¼] in
44.5 [46: 48.5: 51: 54: 57: 60.5: 63] cm

GAUGE

35 sts and 44 rows to 4 in (10 cm) measured over patt using size 2 (2.75mm) needles.

BACK

Using size 2 (2.75mm) needles, cast on 165 [171: 179: 189: 199: 209: 221: 231] sts.

Work in garter st for 2 rows, ending with RS facing for next row.

Row 3 (RS): K0 [0: 2: 0: 2: 0: 3: 0], P0 [3: 5: 2: 5: 2: 5: 3], *K5, P5, rep from * to last 5 [8: 2: 7: 2: 7: 3: 8] sts, K5 [5: 2: 5: 2: 5: 3: 5], P0 [3: 0: 2: 0: 2: 0: 3].

Row 4: P0 [0: 2: 0: 2: 0: 3: 0], K0 [3: 5: 2: 5: 2: 5: 3], *P5, K5, rep from * to last 5 [8: 2: 7: 2: 7: 3: 8] sts, P5 [5: 2: 5: 2: 5: 3: 5], K0 [3: 0: 2: 0: 2: 0: 3].

Rows 5–14: (Rep rows 3 and 4) 5 times.

Now work in patt as foll:

Row 1 (RS): P0 [0: 2: 0: 2: 0: 3: 0], K0 [3: 5: 2: 5: 2: 5: 3], *P5, K5, rep from * to last 5 [8: 2: 7: 2: 7: 3: 8] sts, P5 [5: 2: 5: 2: 5: 3: 5], K0 [3: 0: 2: 0: 2: 0: 3].

Row 2: K0 [0: 2: 0: 2: 0: 3: 0], P0 [3: 5: 2: 5: 2: 5: 3], *K5, P5, rep from * to last 5 [8: 2: 7: 2: 7: 3: 8] sts, K5 [5: 2: 5: 2: 5: 3: 5], P0 [3: 0: 2: 0: 2: 0: 3].

Rows 3–6: (Rep rows 1 and 2) twice.

Row 7: Rep row 2.

Row 8: Rep row 1.

Rows 9–12: (Rep rows 7 and 8) twice.

Last 12 rows form patt.

Work in patt for 12 rows more, ending with RS facing for next row.

Shape back panel

Next row (RS): Patt 40 [43: 47: 52: 57: 62: 68: 73] sts and turn, leaving rem sts on a holder.

Work 5 rows on these sts, ending with RS facing for next row. Break off yarn and leave these sts on a 2nd holder.

With RS facing and using size 0 (2mm) needles, rejoin yarn to sts left on first holder, K3tog, K1, (K2tog, K1) 26 times, K3tog and turn, leaving rem 40 [43: 47: 52: 57: 62: 68: 73] sts on first holder.

Work in garter st on these 55 sts **only** for 11 rows, ending with RS facing for next row.

Break off yarn and leave these 55 sts on a 3rd holder.

With RS facing and using size 2 (2.75mm) needles, rejoin yarn to rem sts on first holder and work in patt for 6 rows, ending with RS facing for next row. Break off yarn.

Join sections

Next row (RS): Patt across 40 [43: 47: 52: 57: 62: 68: 73] sts on 2nd holder, place marker on needle, patt across 55 sts on 3rd holder, place marker on needle, patt across rem 40 [43: 47: 52: 57: 62: 68: 73] sts. 135 [141: 149: 159: 169: 179: 191: 201] sts.

Work 3 rows, ending with RS facing for next row.

Next row (dec row) (RS): *Patt to within 2 sts of marker, work 2 tog tbl, slip marker onto right needle, work 2 tog, rep

from * once more, patt to end.

Work 5 rows.

Keeping patt correct, rep last 6 rows twice more, then first of these rows (the dec row) again. 119 [125: 133: 143: 153: 163: 175: 185] sts.

Work 9 rows, ending with RS facing for next row.

Next row (inc row) (RS): *Patt to within 1 st of marker, inc in next st, slip marker onto right needle, inc in next st, rep from * once more, patt to end.

Rep last 10 rows 8 times more. 155 [161: 169: 179: 189: 199: 211: 221] sts.

Work even until back measures 15 [15: 14½: 15¾: 15¼: 16: 15¾: 16½] in (38 [38: 37: 40: 39: 41: 40: 42] cm), ending with RS facing for next row.

Shape armholes

Keeping patt correct, bind off 7 [8: 8: 9: 9: 10: 10: 11] sts at beg of next 2 rows. 141 [145: 153: 161: 171: 179: 191: 199] sts.

Dec 1 st at each end of next 1 [1: 3: 3: 5: 5: 7: 7] rows, then on foll 12 [12: 12: 14: 14: 15: 17: 18] alt rows. 115 [119: 123: 127: 133: 139: 143: 149] sts.

Work even until armhole measures 7 [7: 7½: 7½: 8: 8: 8¼: 8¼] in (18 [18: 19: 19: 20: 20: 21: 21] cm), ending with RS facing for next row.

Shape shoulders

Bind off 7 [8: 8: 9: 9: 10: 10: 11] sts at beg of next 6 rows, then 8 [7: 9: 8: 9: 9: 11: 11] sts at beg of foll 2 rows.

Bind off rem 57 [57: 57: 57: 61: 61: 61: 61] sts.

LEFT FRONT POCKET LINING

Using size 2 (2.75mm) needles, cast on 33 sts.

Row 1 (RS): (P5, K5) twice, P4, K4, P5.

Row 2: K5, P4, K4, (P5, K5) twice.

Rows 3 and 4: Rep rows 1 and 2.

Row 5: (K5, P5) twice, K4, P4, K5.

Row 6: P5, K4, P4, (K5, P5) twice.

Rows 7–10: (Rep rows 5 and 6) twice.

Row 11: (P5, K5) twice, P2, P2tog tbl, K2tog, K2, P5. 31 sts.

Row 12: K5, P3, K3, (P5, K5) twice.

Row 13: (P5, K5) twice, P3, K3, P5.

Rows 14 and 15: Rep rows 12 and 13.

Row 16: Rep row 12.

Row 17: (K5, P5) twice, K3, P3, K5.

Row 18: P5, K3, P3, (K5, P5) twice.

Rows 19 and 20: Rep rows 17 and 18.

Row 21: (K5, P5) twice, K1, K2tog tbl, P2tog, P1, K5. 29 sts.

Row 22: P5, K2, P2, (K5, P5) twice.

Break off yarn and leave rem 29 sts on a holder.

LEFT FRONT

Using size 2 (2.75mm) needles, cast on 75 [78: 82: 87: 92: 97: 103: 108] sts.

Work in garter st for 2 rows, ending with RS facing for next row.

Row 3 (RS): K0 [0: 2: 0: 2: 0: 3: 0], P0 [3: 5: 2: 5: 2: 5: 3], ★K5, P5, rep from ★ to last 5 sts, K5.

Row 4: ★P5, K5, rep from ★ to last 5 [8: 2: 7: 2: 7: 3: 8] sts, P5 [5: 2: 5: 2: 5: 3: 5], K0 [3: 0: 2: 0: 2: 0: 3].

Rows 5–14: (Rep rows 3 and 4) 5 times.

Now work in patt as foll:

Row 1 (RS): P0 [0: 2: 0: 2: 0: 3: 0], K0 [3: 5: 2: 5: 2: 5: 3], ★P5, K5, rep from ★ to last 5 sts, P5.

Row 2: ★K5, P5, rep from ★ to last 5 [8: 2: 7: 2: 7: 3: 8] sts, K5 [5: 2: 5: 2: 5: 3: 5], P0 [3: 0: 2: 0: 2: 0: 3].

These 2 rows set position of patt as given for back.

Counting in from beg of last row (front opening edge), place marker between 30th and 31st sts.

Keeping patt correct as now set, cont as foll:

Next row (dec row) (RS): Patt to within 2 sts of marker, work 2 tog tbl, slip marker onto right needle, work 2 tog, patt to end. Work 9 rows.

Keeping patt correct, rep last 10 rows once more, then first of these rows (the dec row) again. 69 [72: 76: 81: 86: 91: 97: 102] sts. Work 1 row, ending with RS facing for next row.

Place pocket

Next row (RS): Patt to last 49 sts, slip next 29 sts onto a holder and, in their place, patt across 29 sts of pocket lining, patt to end.

Reposition marker on last row between 27th and 28th sts in from front opening edge.

Work 7 rows, ending with RS facing for next row.

Rep dec row once more, then work 9 rows.

Rep last 10 rows twice more. 63 [66: 70: 75: 80: 85: 91: 96] sts.

Next row (inc row) (RS): Patt to within 1 st of marker, inc in next st, slip marker onto right needle, inc in next st, patt to end. Work 9 rows.

Rep last 10 rows 4 times more, then the first of these rows (the inc row) again. 75 [78: 82: 87: 92: 97: 103: 108] sts.

Work even until left front matches back to beg of armhole shaping, ending with RS facing for next row.

Shape armhole

Keeping patt correct, bind off 7 [8: 8: 9: 9: 10: 10: 11] sts at beg of next row. 68 [70: 74: 78: 83: 87: 93: 97] sts.

Work 1 row.

Dec 1 st at armhole edge of next 1 [1: 3: 3: 5: 5: 7: 7] rows, then on foll 5 [5: 6: 4: 5: 5: 4: 4] alt rows. 62 [64: 65: 71: 73: 77: 82: 86] sts.

Work 1 row, ending with RS facing for next row.

Shape neck

Next row (RS): Work 2 tog, patt to last 11 sts and turn, leaving rem 11 sts on a holder. 50 [52: 53: 59: 61: 65: 70: 74] sts.

Keeping patt correct, dec 1 st at each end of 2nd and foll 5 [5: 4: 8: 7: 8: 11: 12] alt rows. 38 [40: 43: 41: 45: 47: 46: 48] sts.

Dec 1 st at neck edge **only** on 2nd and every foll alt row until

29 [31: 33: 35: 36: 39: 41: 44] sts rem.

Work even until left front matches back to beg of shoulder shaping, ending with RS facing for next row.

Shape shoulder

Bind off 7 [8: 8: 9: 9: 10: 10: 11] sts at beg of next and foll 2 alt rows.

Work 1 row.

Bind off rem 8 [7: 9: 8: 9: 9: 11: 11] sts.

RIGHT FRONT POCKET LINING

Using size 2 (2.75mm) needles, cast on 33 sts.

Row 1 (RS): P5, K4, P4, (K5, P5) twice.

Row 2: (K5, P5) twice, K4, P4, K5.

Rows 3 and 4: Rep rows 1 and 2.

Row 5: K5, P4, K4, (P5, K5) twice.

Row 6: (P5, K5) twice, P4, K4, P5.

Rows 7–10: (Rep rows 5 and 6) twice.

Row 11: P5, K2, K2tog tbl, P2tog, P2, (K5, P5) twice. 31 sts.

Row 12: (K5, P5) twice, K3, P3, K5.

Row 13: P5, K3, P3, (K5, P5) twice.

Rows 14 and 15: Rep rows 12 and 13.

Row 16: Rep row 12.

Row 17: K5, P3, K3, (P5, K5) twice.

Row 18: (P5, K5) twice, P3, K3, P5.

Rows 19 and 20: Rep rows 17 and 18.

Row 21: K5, P1, P2tog tbl, K2tog, K1, (P5, K5) twice. 29 sts.

Row 22: (P5, K5) twice, P2, K2, P5.

Break off yarn and leave rem 29 sts on a holder.

RIGHT FRONT

Using size 2 (2.75mm) needles, cast on 75 [78: 82: 87: 92: 97: 103: 108] sts.

Work in garter st for 2 rows, ending with RS facing for next row.

Row 3 (RS): ★K5, P5, rep from ★ to last 5 [8: 2: 7: 2: 7: 3: 8] sts, K5 [5: 2: 5: 2: 5: 3: 5], P0 [3: 0: 2: 0: 2: 0: 3].

Row 4: P0 [0: 2: 0: 2: 0: 3: 0], K0 [3: 5: 2: 5: 2: 5: 3], ★P5, K5, rep from ★ to last 5 sts, P5.

Rows 5–14: (Rep rows 3 and 4) 5 times.

Now work in patt as foll:

Row 1 (RS): ★P5, K5, rep from ★ to last 5 [8: 2: 7: 2: 7: 3: 8] sts, P5 [5: 2: 5: 2: 5: 3: 5], K0 [3: 0: 2: 0: 2: 0: 3].

Row 2: K0 [0: 2: 0: 2: 0: 3: 0], P0 [3: 5: 2: 5: 2: 5: 3], ★K5, P5, rep from ★ to last 5 sts, K5.

These 2 rows set position of patt as given for back.

Counting in from end of last row (front opening edge), place marker between 30th and 31st sts.

Keeping patt correct as now set, cont as foll:

Next row (dec row) (RS): Patt to within 2 sts of marker, work 2 tog tbl, slip marker onto right needle, work 2 tog, patt to end. Work 9 rows.

Keeping patt correct, rep last 10 rows once more, then first of

these rows (the dec row) again. 69 [72: 76: 81: 86: 91: 97: 102] sts.
Work 1 row, ending with RS facing for next row.

Place pocket

Next row (RS): Patt 20 sts, slip next 29 sts onto a holder and, in their place, patt across 29 sts of pocket lining, patt to end.

Complete to match left front, reversing shapings.

SLEEVES

Using size 2 (2.75mm) needles, cast on 69 [69: 73: 73: 77: 77: 81: 81] sts.

Work in garter st for 2 rows, ending with RS facing for next row.

Row 3 (RS): K2 [2: 4: 4: 0: 0: 0: 0], P5 [5: 5: 5: 1: 1: 3: 3], *K5, P5, rep from * to last 2 [2: 4: 4: 6: 6: 8: 8] sts, K2 [2: 4: 4: 5: 5: 5: 5], P0 [0: 0: 0: 1: 1: 3: 3].

Row 4: P2 [2: 4: 4: 0: 0: 0: 0], K5 [5: 5: 5: 1: 1: 3: 3], *P5, K5, rep from * to last 2 [2: 4: 4: 6: 6: 8: 8] sts, P2 [2: 4: 4: 5: 5: 5: 5], K0 [0: 0: 0: 1: 1: 3: 3].

Rows 5–14: (Rep rows 3 and 4) 5 times.

Now work in patt as foll:

Row 1 (RS): P2 [2: 4: 4: 0: 0: 0: 0], K5 [5: 5: 5: 1: 1: 3: 3], *P5, K5, rep from * to last 2 [2: 4: 4: 6: 6: 8: 8] sts, P2 [2: 4: 4: 5: 5: 5: 5], K0 [0: 0: 0: 1: 1: 3: 3].

Row 2: K2 [2: 4: 4: 0: 0: 0: 0], P5 [5: 5: 5: 1: 1: 3: 3], *K5, P5, rep from * to last 2 [2: 4: 4: 6: 6: 8: 8] sts, K2 [2: 4: 4: 5: 5: 5: 5], P0 [0: 0: 0: 1: 1: 3: 3].

Rows 3–6: (Rep rows 1 and 2) twice.

Row 7: Rep row 2.

Row 8: Rep row 1.

Rows 9–12: (Rep rows 7 and 8) twice.

Last 12 rows form patt.

Cont in patt, shaping sides by inc 1 st at each end of next and every foll 6th row to 77 [85: 83: 91: 91: 99: 107: 115] sts, then on every foll 8th row until there are 107 [109: 113: 115: 119: 121: 125: 127] sts, taking inc sts into patt.

Work even until sleeve measures 16½ [16½: 17: 17: 17¼: 17¼: 17: 17] in (42 [42: 43: 43: 44: 44: 43: 43] cm), ending with RS facing for next row.

Shape sleeve cap

Keeping patt correct, bind off 7 [8: 8: 9: 9: 10: 10: 11] sts at beg of next 2 rows. 93 [93: 97: 97: 101: 101: 105: 105] sts.

Dec 1 st at each end of next and every foll alt row to 43 sts, then on foll 11 rows, ending with RS facing for next row.

Bind off rem 21 sts.

FINISHING

Press as described on page 148.

Sew both shoulder seams using backstitch, or mattress stitch if preferred.

Button band

With RS facing and using size 0 (2mm) needles, pick up and knit 134 [134: 134: 141: 141: 148: 148: 155] sts evenly down left front opening edge, from neck shaping to cast-on edge.

Work in garter st for 12 rows, ending with **WS** facing for next row.

Bind off knitwise (on **WS**).

Buttonhole band

With RS facing and using size 0 (2mm) needles, pick up and knit 134 [134: 134: 141: 141: 148: 148: 155] sts evenly up right front opening edge, from cast-on edge to neck shaping.

Work in garter st for 3 rows, ending with RS facing for next row.

Row 4 (buttonhole row) (RS): K24, yo, K2tog, (K13 [13: 13: 14: 14: 15: 15: 16], yo, K2tog) 7 times, K3.

Work in garter st for 8 rows more, ending with **WS** facing for next row.

Bind off knitwise (on **WS**).

Collar

With RS facing and using size 0 (2mm) needles, beg and ending halfway across top of bands, pick up and knit 3 sts from top of buttonhole band, K 11 sts from right front holder, pick up and knit 54 [54: 54: 58: 58: 58: 62: 62] sts up right side of neck, 57 [57: 57: 57: 61: 61: 61: 61] sts from back, and 54 [54: 54: 58: 58: 58: 62: 62] sts down left side of neck, K 11 sts from left front holder, then pick up and knit 3 sts from top of button band. 193 [193: 193: 201: 205: 205: 213: 213] sts.

Work in garter st for 2 rows, ending with RS of collar (WS of body) facing for next row.

Row 3 (RS of collar): K2, inc in next st, K to last 4 sts, inc in next st, K3.

Work 3 rows.

Rep last 4 rows 13 times more, ending with RS of collar facing for next row. 221 [221: 221: 229: 233: 233: 241: 241] sts.

Bind off in K1, P1 rib.

Pocket tops (both alike)

Slip 29 sts from pocket opening holder onto size 0 (2mm) needles and rejoin yarn with RS facing.

Work in garter st for 10 rows, ending with **WS** facing for next row.

Bind off in K1, P1 rib (on **WS**).

See page 148 for finishing instructions, setting in sleeves using the set-in method.

Donatello

MARIE WALLIN

SIZES AND YARN

	S	M	L	XL	
To fit bust					
	32–34	36–38	40–42	44–46	in
	81–86	91–97	102–107	112–117	cm

Rowan Wool Cotton and Kidsilk Aura

A Wool Cotton in Bilberry 969					
	2	3	3	3	x 50 g
B Wool Cotton in Mocha 965					
	2	2	2	3	x 50 g
C Kidsilk Aura in Walnut 764					
	2	2	3	3	x 25 g
D Wool Cotton in Deepest Olive 907					
	3	4	4	4	x 50 g
E Kidsilk Aura in Damson 762					
	2	2	3	3	x 25 g
F Wool Cotton in Coffee Rich 956					
	2	3	3	3	x 50 g
G Kidsilk Aura in Mallard 769					
	4	4	4	5	x 25 g
H Wool Cotton in Chestnut 966					
	2	2	3	3	x 50 g
I Kidsilk Aura in Terracotta 772					
	3	3	3	4	x 25 g

CROCHET HOOK

Size E-4 (3.5mm) crochet hook

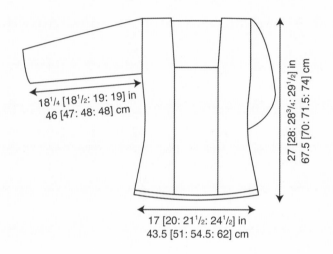

18¼ [18½: 19: 19] in
46 [47: 48: 48] cm

27 [28: 28¾: 29½] in
67.5 [70: 71.5: 74] cm

17 [20: 21½: 24½] in
43.5 [51: 54.5: 62] cm

KNITTER'S TIP

Make sure you don't make the foundation chains of the center panels too tight as this will distort the work. Try to work the chain loosely. If you find it difficult to work loose chains evenly, use a larger hook size for the chains, then change back to the normal hook size for the first row.

GAUGE

18 sts and 11 rows to 4 in (10 cm) measured over double crochet fabric using size E-4 (3.5mm) hook.

US CROCHET ABBREVIATIONS

ch = chain; **dc** = double crochet; **sc** = single crochet; **sl st** = slip stitch; **sp** = space.

Pattern note: The crochet instructions in this pattern use US terminology. The US single crochet (sc) is equivalent to the UK double crochet (dc), and the US double crochet (dc) is equivalent to the UK treble (tr).

BACK

Center panel

Using size E-4 (3.5mm) hook and yarn A, ch 45.
Row 1 (RS): Work (4 dc, ch 3, 1 dc) all in 7th ch from hook, *skip 4 ch, work (4 dc, ch 3, 1 dc) all in next ch, rep from * to last 3 ch, skip 2 ch, 1 dc in last ch, turn. 8 patt reps.
Row 2: Ch 3 (counts as first dc), skip last 2 dc of previous row,

*work (4 dc, ch 3, 1 dc) all in next ch sp**, skip 5 dc, rep from
* to end, ending last rep at **, skip 4 dc, 1 dc in top of 3-ch at
beg of previous row, turn.

Row 2 forms patt.

Keeping patt correct, now work in patt in stripes as foll:

Row 3: Using yarn B.

Rows 4 and 5: Using yarn C.

Row 6: Using yarn D.

Rows 7 and 8: Using yarn E.

Rows 9 and 10: Using yarn F.

Row 11: Using yarn G.

Row 12: Using yarn I.

Rows 13 and 14: Using yarn D.

Row 15: Using yarn H.

Rows 16 and 17: Using yarn A.

Rows 3 to 17 form stripe sequence.

Keeping patt and stripe sequence correct, work even until center
panel measures 25½ [26½: 27¼: 28] in (65 [67: 69: 71] cm).
Fasten off.

Right back side panel

With RS facing, using size E-4 (3.5mm) hook and yarn D, join
yarn with a sl st to right end of foundation-ch edge, ch 1 (does
NOT count as st), work 117 [121: 124: 128] sc evenly up row-
end edge of center panel, ch 4, turn. 121 [125: 128: 132] sts.

**Joining in and breaking off colors as required, cont in stripes
as foll:

Row 1: Using yarn E, ch 3 (counts as first dc), skip ch at base
of these 3-ch, 1 dc in each of next 3 ch, 1 dc in each sc to end,
turn. 121 [125: 128: 132] sts.

Row 2: Using yarn I, ch 3 (counts as first dc), skip dc at base of
3-ch, 1 dc in each dc to end, working last dc in top of 3-ch at
beg of previous row, turn.

Row 2 forms dc fabric.

Keeping dc fabric correct, now work in stripes as foll:

Row 3: Using yarn H.

Row 4: Using yarn B.

Row 5: Using yarn F.

Row 6: Using yarn A.

Row 7: Using yarn G.

Row 8: Using yarn D.

Last 8 rows form stripe sequence.

Cont in dc fabric and stripe sequence for 3 [7: 9: 13] rows more,
ending with RS facing for next row.

Shape side seam and armhole

Keeping stripes correct, cont as foll:

Next row (RS): Ch 3 (counts as first dc), skip dc at base of 3-ch,
1 dc in each of next 82 [84: 85: 87] dc, turn. 83 [85: 86: 88] sts.

Next row: Ch 3 (counts as first dc), skip dc at base of 3-ch,
1 dc in each of next 25 [26: 27: 28] dc, 1 sl st in each of next
18 dc, 1 dc in each dc to end, working last dc in top of 3-ch at
beg of previous row, turn.

Next row: Ch 3 (counts as first dc), skip dc at base of 3-ch,
1 dc in each of next 30 [31: 32: 32] dc, turn. 31 [32: 33: 33] sts.

Next row: 1 sl st in each of first 8 dc, 1 dc in each dc to end,
working last dc in top of 3-ch at beg of previous row, turn.

Next row: Ch 3 (counts as first dc), skip dc at base of 3-ch,
1 dc in each of next 14 [15: 15: 16] dc.

Fasten off.

Left back side panel

With **WS** facing, using size E-4 (3.5mm) hook and yarn D, join
yarn with a sl st to left end of foundation-ch edge, ch 1 (does
NOT count as st), work 117 [121: 124: 128] sc evenly up row-
end edge of center panel, ch 4, turn. 121 [125: 128: 132] sts.

Noting that RS of right back side panel is **WS** of this panel and
vice versa, complete to match right back side panel from **.

FRONT

Center panel

Work as given for center panel of back until this panel measures
20 [20¾: 21¾: 22½] in (51 [53: 55: 57] cm).

Fasten off.

Left front side panel

With RS facing, using size E-4 (3.5mm) hook and yarn D, join
yarn with a sl st to right end of foundation-ch edge, ch 1 (does
NOT count as st), work 92 [96: 99: 103] sc evenly up row-end
edge of center panel, ch 29, turn. 121 [125: 128: 132] sts.

**Joining in and breaking off colors as required, cont in stripes
as foll:

Row 1: Using yarn E, ch 3 (counts as first dc), skip ch at base
of these 3-ch, 1 dc in each of next 28 ch, 1 dc in each sc to
end, turn. 121 [125: 128: 132] sts.

Complete as given for right back side panel from row 2.

Right front side panel

With **WS** facing, using size E-4 (3.5mm) hook and yarn D, join
yarn with a sl st to left end of foundation-ch edge, ch 1 (does
NOT count as st), work 92 [96: 99: 103] sc evenly up row-end
edge of center panel, ch 29, turn. 121 [125: 128: 132] sts.

Noting that RS of left front side panel is **WS** of this panel and
vice versa, complete to match left front side panel from **.

SLEEVES

Using size E-4 (3.5mm) hook and yarn A, ch 75 [80: 75: 80].

Work row 1 as given for center panel of back. 14 [15: 14:
15] patt reps.

Now work rows 2–17 as given for center panel of back.

Rows 3–17 form stripe sequence.

Keeping patt and stripe sequence correct, cont as foll:

Row 18: Ch 3 (counts as first dc), 1 dc in dc at base of 3-ch,
skip next dc, *work (4 dc, ch 3, 1 dc) all in next ch sp**, skip
5 dc, rep from * to end, ending last rep at **, skip 4 dc, 2 dc in
top of 3-ch at beg of previous row, turn.

Row 19: Ch 3 (counts as first dc), 1 dc in dc at base of 3-ch,

1 dc in next dc, skip next dc, *work (4 dc, ch 3, 1 dc) all in next ch sp**, skip 5 dc, rep from * to end, ending last rep at **, skip 4 dc, 1 dc in next dc, 2 dc in top of 3-ch at beg of previous row, turn.

Row 20: Ch 3 (counts as first dc), 1 dc in dc at base of 3-ch, 1 dc in each of next 2 dc, skip next dc, *work (4 dc, ch 3, 1 dc) all in next ch sp**, skip 5 dc, rep from * to end, ending last rep at **, skip 4 dc, 1 dc in each of next 2 dc, 2 dc in top of 3-ch at beg of previous row, turn.

Row 21: Ch 3 (counts as first dc), work (4 dc, ch 3, 1 dc) all in dc at base of 3-ch, skip 4 dc, *work (4 dc, ch 3, 1 dc) all in next ch sp**, skip 5 dc, rep from * to end, ending last rep at **, skip 4 dc, work (4 dc, ch 3, 1 dc) all in next dc, skip 2 dc, 1 dc in top of 3-ch at beg of previous row, turn. 16 [17: 16: 17] patt reps.

Rep last 4 rows 0 [0: 1: 1] time more. 16 [17: 18: 19] patt reps.

Work even until sleeve measures 19¾ [20: 20½: 20½] in (50 [51: 52: 52] cm).

Fasten off.

FINISHING

Press as described on page 148.
Sew both shoulder seams using backstitch.

Neck edging
With RS facing, using size E-4 (3.5mm) hook and yarn D, join yarn with a sl st to neck edge of left shoulder seam, ch 1 (does NOT count as st), then work 1 round of sc evenly around entire neck edge, join with a sl st to first sc.
Fasten off.

See page 148 for finishing instructions, setting in sleeves using the square set-in method.

Hem edging
With RS facing, using size E-4 (3.5mm) hook and yarn D, join yarn with a sl st to base of left side seam, ch 1 (does NOT count as st), then work 1 round of sc evenly around entire lower edge (ensuring number of sc worked is divisible by 4), join with a sl st to first sc.

Next round: Ch 1 (does NOT count as st), 1 sc in first sc, *skip 1 sc, 5 dc in next sc, skip 1 sc, 1 sc in next sc, rep from * to end but omitting sc at end of last rep, join with a sl st to first sc.
Fasten off.

Sleeve edgings (both alike)
Work as given for hem edging, but start by joining yarn D to base of sleeve seam.

About Marie Wallin

Marie joined the Rowan creative design team in 2005 as their head designer, and Magazine 40 was her first magazine at the creative helm. She not only creates many designs but also art directs and organizes the photo shoots.

Marie was born in Bolton and after a science-based education went on to pursue her first love of art and design by taking a degree in Knitwear Design at De Montfort University. She was taught to knit at the age of 6 or 7 and learned to crochet when she was a little older.

After leaving college with a first-class honors degree, Marie went on to set up her own knitwear design label

which she sold throughout Japan and the US. Marie is a prolific and highly creative designer and her knitwear has been part of many collections in high-street retailers in the UK.

Recently, Marie has been heading Rowan's eco drive and the return to sourcing natural and sustainable yarns. The introduction of the Purelife brand in 2007 (yarns that are formed in an ethical and environmental way) has been a great success globally and is a subject close to Marie's heart.

Knitting Pattern Information

Sizing

Fashions have changed over the years and the amount of "ease" on knitted garments has changed, too, to reflect this. But you may prefer your garment to fit more tightly, or to have more "ease." If you want your garment to fit you the same way as the one in the photograph fits the model, then choose the size to knit by selecting the size that matches your bust measurement. If you'd like it tighter or looser, choose a smaller or larger size. You may find it helpful to measure a garment you have, and like the fit of, and then knit the size that will give you this finished measurement. Each pattern features an illustration of the size of the finished garment—use this to help you choose the size you want to knit.

Most of the patterns are given in more than one size. Where the figures vary for the different sizes, these are given in brackets or parentheses. Where only one figure is given, this relates to all sizes. You may find it helpful to circle all the figures for the size you are knitting before you begin.

Gauge

Obtaining the correct gauge is the key to knitting a successful garment. If your gauge does not match the gauge stated in the pattern, your garment will not fit like you want it to, it may not fit together when you come to sew it up, and you may find you run out of yarn or have some left over. It is therefore essential that you check your gauge before starting your garment.

To check your gauge, knit a gauge swatch at least 5 in (12 cm) square. Use the needle size and yarn specified in the instructions and work in the stitch pattern given in the gauge section of the pattern. Once your swatch is knitted, measure and mark 4 in (10 cm) across the work. If the number of stitches within this measurement matches the stated number, your gauge is correct. In the same way, measure your row gauge. If both these numbers match those stated in the gauge section, your garment will fit you, and fit together, in the way it should. If you have more stitches and rows than stated, your gauge is tight and you need to knit another gauge swatch using thicker needles. If you have less stitches and rows, your gauge is loose and you need to try again using thinner needles. Once you have achieved the correct gauge, make a note of the needle size you used and, if necessary, adjust the size of any other needles used for the garment in the same way.

(continued on page 148)

Abbreviations

alt	alternate
approx	approximately
beg	begin(ning)
cm	centimeter(s)
cn	cable needle
cont	continu(e)(ing)
dec	decreas(e)(ing)
foll	follow(s)(ing)
garter st	garter stitch (K every row)
in	inch(es)
inc	increas(e)(ing)
K	knit
m	meter(s)
M1	make one stitch by picking up loop between needles and knitting into back of this loop
M1P	make one stitch by picking up loop between needles and purling into back of this loop
mm	millimeter(s)
oz	ounce(s)
P	purl
p2sso	pass 2 slipped stitches over
patt	pattern; *or* work in pattern
psso	pass slipped stitch over
rem	remain(s)(ing)
rep	repeat(ing)
rev St st	reverse stockinette stitch (RS rows P, WS rows K)
RS	right side
sl 1	slip one stitch
St st	stockinette stitch (RS rows K, WS rows P)
st(s)	stitch(es)
tbl	through back of loop(s)
tog	together
WS	wrong side
yd	yard(s)
yo	yarn over; yarn over right-hand needle to make a new stitch
-	no stitches, times, or rows to be worked for this size
0	no stitches, times, or rows to be worked for this size

Yarn quantities

The quantities of yarn stated are approximate and based on average requirements. This is particularly relevant where we have substituted new yarns for those no longer available.

Charts

Several of the designs in this book are knitted from charts. Each square on the chart represents one knitted stitch, and each row of squares represents one row of knitting. Unless stated otherwise, work all odd-numbered rows as right-side rows, reading the chart from right to left, and work all even-numbered rows as wrong-side rows, reading the chart from left to right. Refer to the written instructions to find out which section of the chart should be repeated, if relevant.

The color of yarn or type of stitch to use will be shown on the key accompanying the chart. Where appropriate, make sure you read the special abbreviations section of the pattern to make sure you know exactly how to work any special stitch group, for example, cables.

Many designs will require you to start and end your rows at differing points across the chart, and this will be indicated on the chart. Make sure you begin and end your rows at the correct point for your chosen size.

Lace stitch patterns

When working a lace design from a chart, ensure you only work an increase if there are sufficient stitches to work the corresponding decrease, to ensure the number of stitches remains constant. You may find it helpful to place markers on your needle at the edge of the outer pattern repeat. Work the stitches beyond these markers in stockinette stitch, moving the markers out or in, by one full pattern repeat, as becomes appropriate when increases or decreases have been worked.

Knitting with more than one color

There are two main ways of knitting with more than one color in a row—the Fair Isle method and the intarsia method. Ensure you knit using the colorwork method stated in the pattern—using the incorrect method could mean you run out of yarn or have some left over. It will also affect the gauge.

Fair Isle

This style of knitting uses the same colors in a repeating pattern across each row, with the color not in use being stranded loosely across the wrong side of the work. These stranded lengths of yarn, or "floats", mean the knitted fabric is thicker than areas knitted in just one color. Take care not to pull the yarn not in use too tightly across the wrong side of the work as this will distort the knitting. Avoid long floats of yarn on the wrong side of the work that could get snagged in wear by weaving this yarn into the knitting every three or four stitches.

Intarsia

This type of colorwork features blocks of different colors across the knitting, and the resulting fabric is the same thickness as if knitted using just one color. Use a separate ball of yarn for each block of color and twist the two colors together where they meet on the wrong side to avoid holes forming along the line where the two colors meet.

Finishing instructions

Once you have spent many hours knitting your garment, it would be a shame to spoil it now! Take care when sewing seams and pressing your work so the completed garment has a truly professional-looking finish.

Pressing

Pin out each piece to the correct size and press following the instructions on the yarn label. If the yarn should NOT be pressed, cover it with a clean damp cloth and leave it to dry naturally. Do NOT press any ribbed areas, or sections in garter stitch.

Seams

Join all knitted sections using back stitch, or mattress stitch, taking care to match any textured or color pattern correctly.

Once all main knitted sections are complete, sew the relevant shoulder seam(s) as explained in the pattern. Complete any borders or bands as given in the "Finishing" section, sewing seams as stated.

Once the shoulder seams are joined, set in the sleeves following these guidelines:

Straight bind-off method: Matching the center of the sleeve bound-off edge to the shoulder seam, sew the sleeve to the back and front(s). Place the ends of bound-off edge at the markers if appropriate, or slightly stretch the bound-off edge when sewing it to the body.

Square set-in method: Matching the center of the sleeve to the shoulder seam, sew the bound-off edge of the sleeve to the row-end edges of the armholes. Then sew the row-end edges of the top section of the sleeve to the armhole bound-off stitches.

Shallow set-in method: Match the center of the final bound-off edge of the sleeve to the shoulder seam, and the shaped edges at the start of the sleeve cap to the shaped edges at the base of the armholes. Sew the sleeve to the body, easing in any slight fullness.

Set-in method: Match the center of the final bound-off edge of the sleeve to the shoulder seam, and the bound-off edges of the start of the sleeve cap to the bound-off edges at the base of the armhole. Sew the sleeve the to body, easing in any slight fullness.

Once the sleeves are sewn in place, sew the side and sleeve seams. Slip stitch any pocket linings in place on the inside, and neatly sew down the ends of pocket tops or borders. Carefully press the seams. Lastly, sew on buttons to correspond with the buttonholes.

Yarn information

YARN DESCRIPTIONS

The following list covers all of the Rowan yarns used in this book. The yarn descriptions will help you find a substitute yarn if necessary (see pages 54–55 for more about yarn substitution). Always refer to the yarn label for pressing and washing recommendations.

Rowan Classic Baby Alpaca DK

A lightweight alpaca yarn; 100 percent alpaca; 1¾ oz/50 g (approximately 109 yd/100 m) per ball; recommended gauge—22 sts and 30 rows to 4 in/10 cm measured over St st using size 6 (4mm) needles.

Rowan Classic Cashsoft Aran

A medium-weight wool-and-cashmere-mix yarn; 57 percent merino wool, 33 percent microfiber, 10 percent cashmere; 1¾ oz/50 g (approximately 95 yd/87 m) per ball; recommended gauge—19 sts and 25 rows to 4 in/10 cm measured over St st using size 7 (4.5mm) needles.

Rowan Classic Cashsoft 4-Ply

A super-fine-weight wool-and-cashmere-mix yarn; 57 percent merino wool, 33 percent microfiber, 10 percent cashmere; 1¾ oz/50 g (approximately 197 yd/180 m) per ball; recommended gauge—28 sts and 36 rows to 4 in/10 cm measured over St st using size 3 (3.25mm) needles.

Rowan Classic Pure Silk DK

A lightweight silk yarn; 100 percent silk; 1¾ oz/50 g (approximately 137 yd/125 m) per ball; recommended gauge—22 sts and 30 rows to 4 in/10 cm measured over St st using size 6 (4mm) needles.

Rowan Classic Siena

A super-fine-weight cotton yarn; 100 percent mercerized cotton; 1¾ oz/50 g (approximately 153 yd/140 m) per ball; recommended gauge—28 sts and 38 rows to 4 in/10 cm measured over St st using size 2–3 (2.75–3mm) needles.

Rowan Cotton Glace

A fine-weight cotton yarn; 100 percent cotton; 1¾ oz/50 g (approximately 126 yd/115 m) per ball; recommended gauge—23 sts and 32 rows to 4 in/10 cm measured over St st using size 3–5 (3.25–3.75mm) needles.

Rowan Denim

A lightweight cotton-mix yarn; 75 percent cotton, 25 percent acrylic/microfiber; 1¾ oz/50 g (approximately 175 yd/160 m) per ball; recommended gauge—20 sts and 28 rows (before washing) and 20 sts and 32 rows (after washing) to 4 in/10 cm measured over St st using size 6 (4mm) knitting needles.

Rowan Felted Tweed DK

A lightweight wool-alpaca-mix yarn; 50 percent merino wool, 25 percent alpaca, 25 percent viscose; 1¾ oz/50 g (approximately 189 yd/175 m) per ball; recommended gauge—22–24 sts and 30–32 rows to 4 in/10 cm measured over St st using size 5–6 (3.75–4mm) knitting needles.

Rowan Kid Classic

A medium-weight mohair-mix yarn; 70 percent lambswool, 26 percent kid mohair, 4 percent nylon; 1¾ oz/50 g (approximately 153 yd/140 m) per ball; recommended gauge—18–19 sts and 23–25 rows to 4 in/10 cm measured over St st using size 8–9 (5–5.5mm) needles.

Rowan Kidsilk Aura

A medium-weight mohair-mix yarn; 75 percent kid mohair, 25 percent silk; ⅞ oz/25 g (approximately 82 yd/75 m) per ball; recommended gauge—16–20 sts and 19–28 rows to 4 in/10 cm measured over St st using size 6–10 (4–6mm) needles.

Rowan Kidsilk Haze

A lightweight mohair-mix yarn; 70 percent super kid mohair, 30 percent silk; ⅞ oz/25 g (approximately 229 yd/210 m) per ball; recommended gauge—18–25 sts and 23–34 rows to 4 in/10 cm measured over St st using size 3–8 (3.25–5mm) needles.

Rowan Purelife Organic 4-Ply

A super-fine-weight cotton yarn; 100 percent organic cotton; 1¾ oz/50 g (approximately 180 yd/165 m) per ball; recommended gauge—28 sts and 38 rows to 4 in/10 cm measured over St st using size 3 (3.25mm) needles.

Rowan Pure Wool Aran

A medium-weight wool yarn; 100 percent super-wash wool; 3½ oz/100 g (approximately 186 yd/170 m) per ball; recommended gauge—17–19 sts and 23–25 rows to 4 in/10 cm measured over St st using size 7–8 (4.5–5mm) needles.

Rowan Pure Wool DK

A lightweight wool yarn; 100 percent super-wash wool; 1¾ oz/50 g (approximately 137 yd/125 m) per ball; recommended gauge—22 sts and 30 rows to 4 in/10 cm measured over St st using size 6 (4mm) needles.

Rowan Pure Wool 4-Ply

A super-fine-weight wool yarn; 100 percent super-wash wool; 1¾ oz/50 g (approximately 176 yd/160 m) per ball; recommended gauge—28 sts and 36 rows to 4 in/10 cm measured over St st using size 3 (3.25mm) needles.

Rowan Scottish Tweed DK

A lightweight wool yarn; 100 percent pure wool; 1¾ oz/50 g (approximately 123 yd/113 m) per ball; recommended gauge— 20–22 sts and 28–30 rows to 4 in/10 cm measured over St st using size 6 (4mm) needles.

Rowan Summer Tweed

A medium-weight silk-cotton-blend yarn; 70 percent silk, 30 percent cotton; 1¾ oz/50 g (approximately 118 yd/108 m) per hank; recommended gauge—16 sts and 23 rows to 4 in/10 cm measured over St st using size 8 (5mm) needles.

Rowan Wool Cotton

A lightweight wool-cotton-blend yarn; 50 percent merino wool, 50 percent cotton; 1¾ oz/50 g (approximately 123 yd/113 m) per ball; recommended gauge—22–24 sts and 30–32 rows to 4 in/10 cm measured over St st using size 5–6 (3.75–4mm) needles.

STANDARD YARN-WEIGHT SYSTEM

Categories of yarn, gauge ranges, and recommended knitting needle sizes from the Craft Yarn Council of America.
YarnStandards.com

Yarn-weight symbol and category names	0 LACE	1 SUPER FINE	2 FINE	3 LIGHT	4 MEDIUM	5 BULKY	6 SUPER BULKY
Types of yarns** in category	10-count crochet cotton, fingering	sock, fingering, baby, UK 4-ply	sport, baby	light worsted, DK	worsted, afghan, Aran	chunky, craft, rug	bulky, roving
Knit gauge ranges* in St st to 4 in (10 cm)	33–40*** sts	27–32 sts	23–26 sts	21–24 sts	16–20 sts	12–15 sts	6–11 sts
Recommended needle in metric size range	1.5–2.25 mm	2.25–3.25 mm	3.25–3.75 mm	3.7.5–4.5 mm	4.5–5.5 mm	6.5–8 mm	8mm and larger
Recommended needle in US size range	000 to 1	1 to 3	3 to 5	5 to 7	7 to 9	9 to 11	11 and larger

★ GUIDELINES ONLY The above reflect the most commonly used gauges and needle sizes for specific yarn categories.

★★ The generic yarn-weight names in the yarn categories include those commonly used in the US and UK.

★★★ Ultra-fine lace-weight yarns are difficult to put into gauge ranges; always follow the gauge given in your pattern for these yarns.

Rowan Yarn Addresses

Contact the distributors listed here to find a supplier of Rowan hand-knitting yarns near you. For countries not listed, contact the main office in the UK or the Rowan website:
www.knitrowan.com

UK
Rowan, Green Lane Mill, Holmfirth,
West Yorkshire HD9 2DX.
Tel: +44 (0) 1484 681881.
Fax: +44 (0) 1484 687920.
E-mail: mail@knitrowan.com

AUSTRALIA
Australian Country Spinners,
314 Albert Street, Brunswick, Victoria 3056.
Tel: (61) 3 9380 3888. Fax: (61) 3 9387 2674.
E-mail: sales@auspinners.com.au

AUSTRIA
Coats Harlander GmbH,
Autokaderstrasse 31, A-1210 Wien.
Tel: (01) 27716-0. Fax: (01) 27716-228.

BELGIUM
Coats Benelux, Ring Oost 14A,
Ninove, 9400.
Tel: 0346 35 37 00.
E-mail: sales.coatsninove@coats.com

CANADA
Same as USA.

CHINA
Coats Shanghai Ltd., No. 9 Building,
Boasheng Road, Songjiang Industrial Zone,
Shanghai, 201613.
Tel: (86-21) 5774 3733.
Fax: (86-21) 5774 3768.

DENMARK
Coats Danmark A/S, Nannagade 28,
2200 Kobenhavn N.
Tel: 35 86 90 50. Fax: 35 82 15 10.
E-mail: info@hpgruppen.dk
www.hpgruppen.dk

FINLAND
Coats Opti Oy, Ketjutie 3, 04220 Kerava.
Tel: (358) 9 274 871. Fax: (358) 9 2748 7330.
E-mail: coatsopti.sales@coats.com

FRANCE
Coats France/Steiner Fréres,
SAS 100 avenue du Général de Gaulle,
18 500 Mehun-Sur-Yèvre.
Tel: 02 48 23 12 30. Fax: 02 48 23 12 40.

GERMANY
Coats GMbH, Kaiserstrasse 1,
D-79341 Kenzingen.

Tel: 7644 8020. Fax: 7644 802399.
www.coatsgmbh.de

HOLLAND
Same as Belgium.

HONG KONG
Coats China Holding Ltd.,
19/F Millenium City 2, 378 Kwun Tong Road,
Kwun Tong, Kowloon.
Tel: (852) 2798 6886. Fax: (852) 2305 0311.

ICELAND
Storkurinn, Laugavegi 59, 101 Reykjavek.
Tel: (354) 551 8258.
E-mail: storkurinn@simnet.is

ITALY
Coats Cucirini srl, Via Sarca 223,
20126 Milano.
Tel: 800 992377.
Fax: 0266111701.
E-mail: servizio.clienti@coats.com

JAPAN
Puppy-Jardin Co. Ltd.,
3-8 11 Kudanminami, Chiyodaku,
Hiei Kudan Bldg. 5F, Tokyo.
Tel: (81) 3 3222-7076.
Fax: (81) 3 3222-7066.
E-mail: info@rowan-jaeger.com

KOREA
Coats Korea Co. Ltd., 5F Kuckdong B/D,
935-40 Bangbae-Dong, Seocho-Gu, Seoul.
Tel: (82) 2 521 6262. Fax: (82) 2 521 5181.

LEBANON
y.knot, Saifi Village,
Mkhalissiya Street 162, Beirut.
Tel: (961) 1 992211. Fax: (961) 1 315553.
E-mail: yknot@cyberia.net.lb

LUXEMBERG
Same as Belgium.

MEXICO
Estambres Crochet SA de CV,
Aaron Saenz 1891-7, Monterrey, NL 64650.
Tel: +52 (81) 8335-3870.

NEW ZEALAND
ACS New Zealand,
1 March Place, Belfast, Christchurch.
Tel: 64-3-323-6665. Fax: 64-3-323-6660.

NORWAY
Coats Knappehuset AS,
Pb 100 Ulset, 5873 Bergen.
Tel: (47) 55 53 93 00.
Fax: (47) 55 53 93 93.

SINGAPORE
Golden Dragon Store,
101 Upper Cross Street #02-51,
People's Park Centre, Singapore 058357.
Tel: (65) 6 5358454. Fax: (65) 6 2216278.
E-mail: gdscraft@hotmail.com

SOUTH AFRICA
Arthur Bales PTY, P.O. BOX 44644,
62 4th Avenue, Linden 2104.
Tel: (27) 11 888 2401. Fax: (27) 11 782 6137.

SPAIN
Oyambre, Pau Claris 145,
80009 Barcelona.
Tel: (34) 670 011957. Fax: (34) 93 4872672.
E-mail: oyambre@oyambreonline.com

Coats Fabra, Sant Adria 20,
08030 Barcelona.
Tel: 93 2908400. Fax: 93 2908409.
E-mail: atencion.clientes@coats.com

SWEDEN
Coats Expotex AB, Division Craft,
Box 297, 401 24 Göteborg.
Tel: (46) 33 720 79 00. Fax: (46) 31 47 16 50.

SWITZERLAND
Coats Stroppel AG, Stroppelstrasse 16,
CH-5300 Tungi (AG).
Tel: 056 298 12 20. Fax: 056 298 12 50.

TAIWAN
Cactus Quality Co. Ltd.,
P.O. Box 30 485, Taipei.
Office: 7Fl-2, No. 140, Roosevelt Road,
Sec 2, Taipei.
Tel: 886-2-23656527. Fax: 886-2-23656503.
E-mail: cqcl@m17.hinet.net

THAILAND
Global Wide Trading,
10 Lad Prao Soi 88, Bangkok 10310.
Tel: 00 662 933 9019. Fax: 00 662 933 9110.
E-mail: theneedleworld@yahoo.com

USA
Westminster Fibers Inc.,
165 Ledge Street, Nashua,
NH 03060.
Tel: 1-800-445-9276.
E-mail: rowan@westminsterfibers.com
www.westminsterfibers.com

Acknowledgments

We would like to thank the following:
The designers for their original designs and all those who worked on the various
Rowan magazines from which they have been drawn; Amanda Macmillan, Emma Wood
and Sharon Brant for their initial work on the book; Sally Harding for editorial work;
Nicky Downes for design; Sue Whiting for technical help and advice; Lisa Richardson
for checking patterns and drawing diagrams; John Heseltine for swatch photography;
and Lyndsay Kaye and David Macleod for support.

For photography, thanks also to:
Tony Boase pages 15 (left and top right), 24, 27; Tim Bret-Day page 13 (left); Peter
Christian Christiansen pages 50, 51; Danilo Giuliani page 47; Tim Evan Cook pages 14,
15 (bottom right); Eamonn J. McCabe pages 9, 12 (styling by Caroline Baker),
13 (right), 17 (bottom), 19 (bottom); Philip North-Coombes pages 19 (top), 37;
Kristin Perers pages 42, 45, 46; Sheila Rock page 4; Joey Toller pages 1, 2, 5, 16, 18,
22, 23, 25, 26, 28, 29, 30, 31 (bottom), 32, 33, 36, 38, 39, 40, 41, 43, 48.